Dr Naomi Fisher is a clinical psychologist and mother of two self-directed learners. She has a Doctorate in Clinical Psychology and a PhD in Developmental Cognitive Psychology, focusing on autism. She combines years of hands-on experience of self-directed education with an in-depth knowledge of the psychology of learning and wellbeing. Her work has been published in *The Green Parent*, *The Psychologist*, *SEN Magazine*, *Juno* and *Tipping Points*. She is a regular speaker on self-directed education, presenting at the Freedom to Learn Forum and the Homeschooling Summit, and is featured on podcasts including *The Emotional Curriculum*, *Off-Trail Learning* and *Lockdown Learning*. She lives in Hove, England, with her family.

© Justine Desmond Photography

T0271646

Naomi Fisher

CHANGING OUR MINDS

How children can take control of their own learning

Preface by Peter Gray

ROBINSON

ROBINSON

First published in Great Britain in 2021 by Robinson

A CIP catalogue record for this book is available from the British Library

ISBN: 978-1-47214-551-2

Typeset in Times by Initial Typesetting Services, Edinburgh
Printed and bound in Great Britain by Clays Ltd, Elcograf S.p.A.

Papers used by Robinson are from well-managed forests and other responsible sources

Robinson
An imprint of
Little, Brown Book Group
Carmelite House
50 Victoria Embankment
London EC4Y 0DZ

An Hachette UK Company
www.hachette.co.uk

www.littlebrown.co.uk

For Abel and Jessamy,
who show me what a self-directed education really means.

Contents

Acknowledgements

Thank you first to the editorial team at Robinson and particularly Andy McAleer who has been inspiring and encouraging all the way along.

I was inspired by all the children I met in Britain and France who refused to give up their autonomy in the name of education. Their spirit is the power behind this book.

So many people helped me develop my thinking during the writing of this book. Some made the time to talk with me formally, while others read my articles, chatted online or in person.

My interviewees were Blake Boles, Kevin Currie-Knight, Rebecca English, Pat Farenga, Peter Gray, Harriet Pattison, Gina Riley and Alan Thomas. They all pointed me in new directions and expanded my thinking, and their influence went far beyond the quotes you read in the book. Their generosity made it possible. Any errors are entirely my own.

Blake Boles also read an early draft of the book and was consistently encouraging, for which I thank him. Without him, it might never have got this far. Alexander Khost encouraged me to write.

Without Kezia Cantwell-Wright, Laura McAleer and Heidi Steel, this book would never have been more than a pipe dream. They all encouraged me in different ways, and were happy to keep discussing just how this type of education actually works, way beyond when others would have gone to bed.

I have been lucky to have met some inspirational and challenging educators along the way with whom I could debate ideas, even when we vehemently disagreed. I apologise if I have forgotten anyone and I thank you all for keeping me thinking: Jane Clossick, Emma Forde, Nicola Gallie, Lucy Green, Sally Hall, Geraldine Homewood, Ailbhe Hurley, Juliet Kemp, Carole Lovesey, Elizabeth Mills, Kari Müller,

Angie Mullin, Rebecca Pennington, Francesca Brooker-Rao, Sue Reid, Kate Robson, Parvine Shahid and Saskia Takens-Milne.

I'd also like to thank Katharine Thoday for many fruitful and animated discussions about how things could be different, and Rebekah Lattin-Rawstrone for encouraging me to take writing seriously.

I thank all the contributors to the final chapter; they are named there and further details are included if you would like to read more of their writing.

Lastly, I would like to thank my family. I am so lucky to have them. My parents, Jane and Simon, encouraged me never to assume that just because everyone else does something it is the right thing to do. My sisters, Susie and Abi, are a source of constant support and encouragement; and my brother, Jonah, works tirelessly to prevent us all from falling into an echo chamber.

My children, Abel and Jessamy, show me daily how much more I have to learn about self-directed education, and how schooled my thinking continues to be. Jonny's support has meant everything as we follow this unconventional path, even though it would have been so much easier to ignore the questioning and follow the system. Without you, none of it would have happened. Thank you.

Case Studies

This book contains case studies of children and families. These children are not real; I have created illustrative examples. While all the things I describe have happened, they have not all happened to a particular child who I have met. Any resemblance to a real person is purely accidental.

A Note on Language

In the UK, the term commonly used for children educated outside school is 'home education' and this term is enshrined in law. Many home educators in the UK feel very strongly about using this term rather than 'home schooling' as it makes it clear that they are not attempting to replicate school at home and that education is not the same as school. I have used this term throughout this book. In the USA and in other countries, the official term is 'home-schooling' and this is the term that Peter Gray has used in his Preface.

Preface

by Peter Gray,
Research Professor of Psychology and
Neuroscience at Boston College

There was a time when I was inclined to believed that parents have a lot of control over who their children become. I had studied psychology as an undergraduate and the consistent message was that people are shaped by their environment. Parents have a good deal of control over the environment of their children, so parents shape their children. Right? Well, no, not really.

When I was twenty-five, very shortly after my undergraduate days, my son entered the world and my old view was turned upside down. Here was this little guy, who clearly was already his own person. I could do things that helped him be happy, or unhappy, but I couldn't change who he was. I didn't catch on right away but, over time, he taught me that my job as a parent was not to shape him but to get to know him. Who is he? What does he need and want? How can I provide it? How must I change to get along with this individual? He clearly was shaping me more than I was shaping him. And now, after decades of research into child development, I'm more convinced than ever that the job of parents is to get to know their children, to learn from them what they need, to provide for those needs, and to help them find the places in the world where they can be the kind of person that they want and maybe need to be.

Naomi Fisher – perhaps from her experiences as a clinical psychologist who has worked with many children and families, and perhaps from her experiences as a parent – understands this very well. This book is about children's education outside of conventional schooling, so you might think it is about how children learn from parents. Well, it is a little bit about that, but it's much more about how parents learn from children. 'Changing our minds' means evolving from the belief that children are passive recipients of lessons and behavioural shaping to the understanding that children, from the moment they are born onward, are actively creating themselves. Learning, real learning, the kind that sticks and has an impact on a person's life, is always generated from within. The child (and later the adult) is, at every moment, trying to make sense of the world. That sense has to be generated from within, otherwise it is nonsense and is either quickly forgotten or remembered only as trivia. Nobody knows how another person makes sense of the world or what aspect of the world that person is ready to make sense of at any given time. That is why education, real education, is always self-directed. Or at least self-chosen. Sometimes, a self-directed learner will freely choose to have another person direct some aspect of their education. But even then, the learner is in charge. He or she chose to enlist the help of the teacher and he or she can quit at any time.

As Naomi points out, the system of schooling we call 'conventional' was not founded on a scientific understanding of how children learn. It was actually developed initially, quite explicitly, for the purpose of obedience training and indoctrination. It was invented at a time when people believed that children are naturally sinful and must be strictly trained to obey authority in order to overcome that sinfulness. It also maintained that there are certain truths (originally mostly from the Bible) that everyone must accept as doctrine, no questions asked. The basic format of schooling – with all children being 'taught' the same lessons at the same time, regularly tested, and rewarded for passing and punished for failing – was well designed for obedience training and indoctrination. That format has been passed down essentially unchanged from generation to generation. We have changed how we talk about school, not how we do it. Very few educators today would say that the primary purposes of education are indoctrination and obedience training. They are much more likely to talk about fostering critical thinking, creativity and a love of learning. Yet they labour under a system that was not designed for that and doesn't work for that.

Preface

Think about it. Really, almost the only way children can fail in school is not to do what they are told to do, and the only way they can pass is to do what they are told to do. Challenging authority almost always gets you into trouble in school. And what is it you must do? You must memorise and feed back what you were 'taught'. If you were to design a school for critical thinking, creativity and a love of learning, it would look nothing like our conventional schools. It would look like Sudbury Valley or any of the other schools now throughout the world that have been designed to support Self-Directed Education.

When my son, at age nine, finally convinced his mother and me that we must remove him from conventional schooling, we enrolled him at the Sudbury Valley School, designed for Self-Directed Education. You can find a full description of the school by googling it, so I'll just note here that the school enrols children from age four onwards through teenage years, does not segregate children by age, does not offer courses (unless asked for by children) or tests, is democratically run by the children and staff together, and is a place where children can explore, play, socialise and, in other ways, follow their own interests all day, day after day, with no adult interference. It operates on about half the per-student cost of the local public schools.

I, at that time, had many of the same questions that you probably have if you are thinking of Self-Directed Education for your child or children. Would he learn to discipline himself for hard work? Would he learn what he needs to know for a satisfying and meaningful adult life? Would he be able to go on to higher education if he chose to do so? I found that the answer to all of those questions was 'yes', not just for my son but generally for all the students. I conducted a study of the graduates of the school and found that they were doing very well in the world, and then I went on to conduct research aimed at finding out how children become educated when they are free to take charge of their own learning[1].

My research and that of others convinces me that children come into the world biologically designed to educate themselves[2]. The com-

---

1   Gray & Chanoff (1984); Gray (2013, 2017)
2   Gray (2016)

ponents of that design are no mystery. There are two primary aspects to education – learning what and learning how. Or, to put it differently, acquiring information and acquiring skills. Curiosity is the primary drive that motivates the acquisition of information. Children are constantly exploring the world in order to find out what is out there and what the properties of those things are. What can they do with them? Playfulness is the primary drive that motivates skill learning. Children all over the world play at the activities that are most important for them to learn. They play at physical skills, at language, at making things, at imagination and hypothetical thinking, at social skills, and in ways that help them learn to deal with fear and anger – emotion regulation skills.

A third crucial educative drive is sociability; children want to connect with other people and, as part of doing so, they want to know what others know and to share with others what they know. When children play and explore in groups, the discovery of one becomes the discovery of all. When not playing, children are observing others and learning by watching and listening. These drives can be effective only when children have time and freedom to exercise them. All three of these drives are pretty much shut off in school.

Schools quash curiosity by convincing children that their questions aren't important; it is the questions of the curriculum that matter, regardless of whether the children or even the teacher is interested in those questions. Play, if it exists at all in school, becomes breaktime – a break from learning rather than an essential vehicle of it. And sociability – helping one another – is cheating. So schools shut off children's natural ways of learning and then try to teach by reward and punishment. Some teachers might try to promote curiosity, play and sociability in the conventional school, but the school is just not set up for it. In a school where everyone is supposed to learn the same things at the same time in the same way and prove it through testing, then curiosity, play and sociability only get in the way.

In the United States and a few other countries, there are two main legal ways for families to avoid conventional schooling and choose Self-Directed Education for their children. One is to enrol their child in a school designed for Self-Directed Education, such as a

Sudbury model school; and the other, much more common, is through home-schooling. At present, nearly 4 per cent of American school-aged children are registered as home-schooled. In theory, as the name implies, home-schooling is school at home. But, in reality, it is not. Or, I should say, it very rarely is.

Parents might start off thinking they are going to run a little school at home for their children, giving lessons and testing and grading just like in school. But the children pretty quickly convince them otherwise. The children hate the lessons and rebel, and the parents themselves begin to see why the children hate them. At the same time, the parents notice that their children are constantly learning by following their own interests. And they see that what they are learning is at least as valuable as what they would be learning by following an imposed curriculum – and it is far more fun. Critical thinking, curiosity and a love of learning really do bloom in these conditions.

Parents may continue, to varying degrees, with lessons at home, but the lessons are strongly shaped by the children's interests. Many schools talk about child-centred lessons, but with twenty to thirty (or more) kids in a class and the requirement that they all take the same tests, it's not really possible. At home it is possible. In fact, at home it's pretty much unavoidable if there are going to be lessons at all and peace in the family.

Parents also quickly realise that they don't have to be experts at everything the children want to learn. Children move on in all kinds of directions that often go well beyond the knowledge, skills and interests of their parents. That's always been true, but now the Internet has made that far easier and even more true than it was in the past.

Some families go all the way with Self-Directed Education in the home-schooling context. They dispense with any pretext of an imposed curriculum. According to US government statistics, somewhere between 10 and 20 per cent of home-schooling families in the United States fall into this category. These are the families that commonly label themselves as 'unschoolers'. In these families, children are explicitly and entirely in charge of their own education. The parents help in ways that they can, according to the children's wishes, but they do not impose lessons.

Unschooling works best in families that have strong and healthy relationships both within and outside the family. Children, especially as they grow older, need to expand beyond the family, so families that are well connected with other families and the community as a whole are much better settings for unschooling – or any brand of home-schooling – than families that are more isolated. Children learn best when they can observe and interact with many people, who vary in age, interests, opinions and personality. At a school like Sudbury Valley in Massachusetts, that happens naturally within the school; but in home-schooling, the parents must make it possible.

In collaboration with Gina Riley, I have conducted follow-up research on a group of seventy-five grown unschoolers and found that they, just like graduates of democratic schools, were doing very well in life[3]. They were pursuing careers that, in many cases, were direct extensions of passionate interests they had developed in childhood play; and the responsibility they were granted in childhood for directing their own behaviour and learning seemed to pay dividends in the form of high levels of personal responsibility and self-direction in adulthood.

Changing minds and changing behaviour are two different things. I've met many parents who are convinced, by logic and evidence, that their children would be better off in Self-Directed Education than in the conventional school, but just can't get themselves to take the plunge. In a survey that Gina Riley and I conducted of 232 unschooling families, we asked, 'What, for your family, have been the biggest challenges or hurdles to surmount in unschooling?' Far and away the most frequent answer had to do with the feelings of social pressure and criticisms – from relatives, friends, neighbours and even strangers – that they experienced for doing something non-normative.

We are creatures of norms; it is hard to run against the social tide. Non-normal seems to imply abnormal, and abnormal is bad. It takes courage to do what you think or even know is right when most others don't understand. Gradually, however, as more people are taking the route of Self-Directed Education, the sense of it being non-normal is diminishing.

---

3   Gray & Riley (2015); Riley & Gray (2015)

I subscribe to the tipping point theory of social change; at first, just a few brave pioneers take the new route. They carve the way and it becomes easier for the next slightly bigger wave to follow. Eventually, enough have taken that route so that everyone knows someone who has. At that point, it no longer seems abnormal and, if it is a clearly better route than the old one, the floodgates open.

We're on that trajectory with Self-Directed Education, I'm pretty sure. I don't know when the gates will open, but I hope it's within my lifetime. This book will help.

References

Gray, P – *Free to Learn: Why Unleashing the Instinct to Play Will Make Our Children Happier, More Self-Reliant, and Better Students for Life*, New York: Basic Books (2013)

Gray, P – 'Children's Natural Ways of Learning Still Work – Even for the Three Rs', in DC Geary & DB Berch (Eds), *Evolutionary Perspectives on Child Development and Education* (pp 63–93), Springer (2016)

Gray, P – 'Self-Directed Education – Unschooling and Democratic Schooling', in G Noblit (Ed), *Oxford Research Encyclopaedia of Education*, Oxford University Press (2017)

Gray, P & Chanoff, D – 'Democratic Schooling: What Happens to Young People Who Have Charge of Their Own Education?', *American Journal of Education, 94,* 182–213 (1986)

Gray, P & Riley, G – 'Grown Unschoolers' Evaluations of Their Unschooling Experiences: Report I on a Survey of 75 Unschooled Adults', *Other Education, 4(#2),* 8–32 (2015)

Riley, G & Gray, P – 'Grown Unschoolers' Experiences with Higher Education and Employment: Report II on a Survey of 75 Unschooled Adults', *Other Education, 4(#2),* 33–53 (2015)

1

Getting an Education

It's September. My inbox fills with pictures of shining children, dressed up in their brand-new school uniforms and beaming for the camera. With their white socks, grey skirts or trousers, and their neatly brushed hair, the message couldn't be clearer. The free and easy pre-school years are over; it's time to get down to work.

The start of school is a time of excitement and anticipation. Children are filled with awe about the new world that is about to open up to them. Parents are holding their breath as their babies take this first step towards independence. We tell our four-year-olds that school will be wonderful, that they'll make new friends and learn things they couldn't do at home. They believe us.

And off they go.

For some, the promise is fulfilled. School is a chance to make new friends and be inspired. For others, it leads to disillusionment and disappointment. For all of them, the next twelve years will be a defining part of their lives. They will never forget their time at school.

Most of us cannot imagine how a child can become educated if they don't go to school. This means that when a child is not thriving at school, we don't really consider alternatives. We try different schools, or more support at school. We take the child to be assessed for disorders and pay for therapists, all in the hope that we can get the help they need to get them through school. Leaving the school system altogether is usually portrayed as a disaster; it's called 'dropping out', and nothing good comes of that.

But what really goes on at school that is so essential? Attending school is a time-consuming business. Children attend five days a week from the age of around four to sixteen or even eighteen. In this amount of time, an adult could complete four undergraduate degrees, or train as a doctor twice over. We insist that our children invest an enormous amount of their time and energy in school. Is it worth the effort?

When School Stops

I'm writing this in spring 2020. September now seems like a world away. Schools are closing around the world due to the COVID-19 outbreak. Children (and their parents) are facing months at home.

The papers are full of articles about how to 'keep up with their learning'. Teachers advise sticking to schedules and putting in the hours, just like you would at school. In one typical article in the *Guardian*, Amanda Grace, a primary school deputy head teacher, is uncompromisingly clear: 'Start every morning with a timetable and stick to your timings. Use language such as 'now' and 'next'. For younger children, you can build in very clear timings such as ten minutes reading followed by ten minutes of Lego, role-playing, chase games or exercises.'

In other words, she's advising you on how to control your child, at home. Just like at school.

Schools do things in a certain way because they have to. When you have thirty children in a small room who are all meant to learn the same things, you need a timetable and clear timings. You need a fixed playtime and bottoms on seats for much of the rest of the time. If you don't work out ways to control those children, mayhem will ensue. These methods aren't anything to do with education. They are to do with the logistics involved with managing large numbers of people. Somehow, the things which schools do in order to manage children have become part of what we think a 'good education' should include. So when school stops, many of us try to reproduce the same thing at home in the belief that this is the ideal.

It's a sign of how deep our schooling goes, the difficulty that we have in imagining any alternative. It just doesn't occur to us to wonder if this is actually the best way to learn. Even if we hated school, and our children in turn hate school, we carry on going through the motions.

When children are off school, most parents discover pretty quickly that what works at school doesn't work at home. While they try to organise the child's day into a routine with English and Maths every morning, they discover that out of school, there's not much you can do when the child says 'no'. And 'no' is what many of them do say when the novelty has worn off. Sticking to a timetable feels futile when the child puts their head down on the table or refuses to talk. Trying to reproduce school at home is often a fast track to failure.

It's a sobering moment for parents, when they realise that, given the choice, their children really don't want to do the things that they do at school. At school, children are powerless. They have no choice at all about what they do, or when they do it. When children have more power – as they often do at home – they choose something different.

This doesn't mean, however, that education outside conventional school is futile. On the contrary, education outside school can be exciting, rigorous and stimulating. It does mean that a different approach is needed, one that respects the child's views, and puts them in control of their learning; education that starts with empowerment rather than compliance.

In order to do this, we have to let go of principles that have been schooled into us. In particular, we have to let go of the idea that all children must learn the same things in the same order. We would never expect this of adults, and there is no reason to expect it of children. We need to let go of the idea that adults are the best people to plan children's learning, and the myth that learning can be effectively controlled through rewards and punishments.

This means that education becomes something very different. The aim of this type of education is for each child to find joy in learning and discover what interests them. Childhood can be a chance for each child to get to know themselves and what they care about. This is not only good for learning, it's good for their emotional wellbeing as well.

To start this process, we need to learn to distinguish between education and school. We need to stop thinking that education means teaching a standardised curriculum and micromanaging children's time. These are things which the *school* requires, not education. We need to stop telling children what they should know and, instead, give them opportunities to thrive.

These Aren't New Ideas

Oddly, these ideas about education aren't new or particularly radical. Educators have noticed for centuries that children learn better when they can choose what they do. In the 1860s, Leo Tolstoy set up a school for peasant children on his estate, Yasnaya Polyana. There, attendance was optional, and education started with the children's interests. Tolstoy wrote: 'The more convenient a method of instruction is for the teacher, the less convenient for the pupils. The only right way of teaching is that which is satisfactory for the pupils.'

Slightly more recently, 'free schools' came in and out of vogue for much of the twentieth century. In 1921, A.S. Neill started Summerhill, perhaps the best known of its type. Summerhill, in Suffolk, England, has a programme of teacher-led lessons, but they are optional. Many children choose not to attend, and they are not pressured to do so. Daniel and Hanna Greenberg founded Sudbury Valley School in Massachusetts, USA, in 1968. Sudbury Valley has no programme of lessons unless the students request it. Both schools are open and thriving in 2020.

You'd never know that these schools existed, though, if you go through the conventional school system. They simply don't figure in most people's mental maps.

Developmental psychologists have long sung the praises of social and play-based learning for children. Social psychologists have found that the more autonomy a person has, the better the quality of their motivation. These insights don't seem to have made it into the education system, except for the very youngest. For young children, it's accepted that best educational practice involves allowing them to choose what they do, probably because they are extremely good at resisting any efforts to do otherwise. As children grow older, 'learning' becomes something which they are obliged to do by others, often against their will. Their learning environment narrows, from the varied multi-sensory choices of a good nursery classroom to desks and textbooks. By the time children are teenagers, the only choice they get is between subjects and, therefore, which set of information they will be committing to memory. They can choose History or Geography, but the structure and underlying principles are the same. There's no way to choose to do something really different – to start a project, for example, where you don't know what the endpoint might be. To express your thoughts about what you are learning through sculpture or dance, rather than through an essay. To explore your interests in an open-ended way, following what intrigues you at the time, or to get a part-time job and learn as you earn.

How Did We Get Here?

It hasn't always been the case that we sent four-year-olds to school. In fact, for most of human history, school wasn't an option at all for most children. Compulsory education started in Prussia (now part of Germany) in 1763 but wasn't quickly adopted by other countries, perhaps due to worries that it would be expensive and might unsettle their social order. France made primary education compulsory in 1882, around the same time as England. American states passed laws between 1852 and 1918, when Mississippi became the last state to make school attendance compulsory.

Even now, differences exist between countries as to *what* exactly is compulsory. In Sweden and Germany, it is school. In most of Europe and the United States, it is education. Parents can provide education outside of school if they so desire, although they may be subject to checks by the state as to how they are choosing to educate their child.

Before school was universal, children learnt the skills they would need as adults in a variety of ways. In Europe, this was very different depending on your social status. Upper-class children had tutors or governesses or attended schools. Poorer children helped their parents, did apprenticeships or learnt a trade on the job. Outside Europe, children were educated in a variety of ways, many of them not based on written language. Native Americans tell of an education based on oral histories and storytelling, alongside practical skill acquisition through participating in the activities of the tribe. Historians in Southern Africa describe how village elders and traditional leaders would pass on knowledge and skills to children, equipping them to play a useful role in their society. Children were also expected to learn through participation in the life of their tribe, including activities based around religion, daily living and warfare. Other cultures had different ways of educating children, often with some formal instruction combined with informal learning, observation and play.

Our perspective on education has narrowed since then. The vast majority of people across the globe now consider school to be the best way to educate a child. School has been promoted as the best and the only way for children to learn. Even methods which were previously used by the most privileged (such as home tutoring) are viewed as less than ideal. We think that 'education' must mean 'school'.

In the 130 or so years since compulsory education spread across large areas of the globe, the world we live in has transformed. Just the relatively recent arrival of the smartphone has meant that many people own a device capable of linking to vast amounts of information. The jobs we do, the way we spend our leisure time, all of this would be unrecognisable to a visitor from the 1880s. But what about school?

By the canal in east London, there is a small museum which only opens for a few days every month. Inside is a slice of Victorian history, for this is where Dr Thomas Barnardo opened the Copperfield Road Free School in 1877. This 'Ragged School' provided an education to the poor children of the East End for thirty-one years. Now, you can go along to classroom re-enactments and experience what school was like in Victorian times. I took my two children along.

After several false starts, we finally managed to arrive on a day when it was open to the public. As we got there, we were invited to dress up, putting on pinafores and flat caps. We sat on benches behind desks, while the teacher at the front taught us spelling and the alphabet. We copied what she said on to our slates with scratchy pencils. She told us off when we got it wrong and told us to be quiet when we talked to each other. Someone was given the dunce cap and told to sit in the corner.

My son wasn't impressed with his time travelling experience. 'It's like a school,' he whispered, just a bit too loudly. 'Can we go?'

We shamefully sidled out. I had an intense feeling that I was about to be told to go back to my seat and stop messing about.

He was right. If a Victorian teacher travelled forwards in time, they'd have no problem recognising a classroom and they'd know exactly where their place was. It hasn't changed. Teacher at the front delivering a lesson, group of children listening and apparently learning. For the poor children of Victorian London, this might have been the only way they could learn how to read and write. For modern children, things are very different.

We left and went to the gift shop, where we could buy a replica slate for £3.50. My daughter was intrigued. 'Can we get the Victorian iPad?' she asked. I knew what she meant; the grey slate with its wooden surround does look like an early, extremely dull, tablet computer.

Access to information has been transformed since Victorian times. In the 1890s, you had to carry knowledge in your head, or on your slate. If you didn't know something, you had to find the library or someone well-informed to ask. Now, one might say our problem is quite the opposite: too much information, everywhere we go.

Surely Everyone Does It Like Us?

Recently, a French friend of mine got in touch. Her sons attend French school and she teaches them English at home. She wanted to do dictation.

In France, there is a plethora of books and manuals for *dictée*; a quick search on Amazon.fr will bring up lists of books with titles such as *The Big Book of Dictation; 101 Dictations, 2,500 Difficulties Explained* (in French, of course). There are dictation books for every level, from the earliest years at primary school to the last years of high school.

That's because in French schools, young children sit at their desks from age six, and they write down what the teacher reads out to them. As accurately as they can, because they will be penalised for every error. French schools are focused on errors, there are no ticks for the things you get right. Just the number of the words you got wrong.

French people are convinced that *dictée* is essential in learning how to read and write. So much so, that when French schools slipped down the international league tables for reading in 2017, the education minister Jean-Michel Blanquer announced that primary school children would now have to do dictation every day.

However, if you move virtually over the Channel to Amazon. co.uk, the picture is somewhat different. There, searching for 'dictation' brings up dictaphones and some music books. No big books of dictations, no pictures of studious-looking children sitting at desks, no graded manuals. I see my friend's problem – there are simply no dictation books for English-speaking children. The reason is straightforward – English schools don't use dictation.

In France, it is widely accepted that regular dictation is necessary in order to learn to read and write properly. It's accepted as common sense. In Britain, it hardly registers as an option. This made me wonder – what other things might we consider essential without which, in fact, children can learn just fine? How would we ever know, while we all continue to do what we've always done?

Do We Need School?

Here, I'm going to take a small sidestep into social science research. Bear with me.

One of the things which causes the most debate in social science is the question of causality. It's relatively easy to show that two things happen at the same time, but it's much harder to show that one of them causes the other. For example, we could do a research study which measures children's height, and their reading ability, and we would find that taller children are better readers. This is called a correlation. This could lead us to conclude that height causes better reading, or even perhaps that better reading helps children grow taller. However, we'd be wrong. As children grow up, they tend to get better at reading, and they also usually get taller. Age is a 'third factor' which links height and reading.

Another correlation we would expect would be that the number of years children spend in school also relates to their reading ability. In this case, most people would assume that those years in school cause children to be better at reading. But how would we know if that wasn't the case? How can we tell if being at school causes better reading, or if there's a third factor at play?

Two important questions to ask when trying to show that

something causes something else are whether something is necessary, or sufficient. Necessary means that without it, the second thing will not happen. If school is necessary for learning to read, then no one would learn to read without attending school.

Sufficient means that something is enough, in itself, to cause the second thing to happen. If school were sufficient, then everyone who went to school would learn to read, but it wouldn't rule out other ways of learning. Perhaps informal education or tutors at home might work, too.

It doesn't take more than a cursory glance around you to see that school doesn't fulfil either of those criteria. It's not necessary, because some children do learn to read (and become educated) without attending school. And it's not sufficient, because lots of children do attend school and yet leave without the basic skills necessary for an adult life, including reading. This doesn't stop most of us assuming that without going to school, you're not getting an education.

So how can we assess the impact of school on children? How could we find out what difference it will make to a particular child if they attend school for twelve years?

On an individual level, we will never know. We can't turn the clock back and see what might have been. Usually, in order to look at the effect of something, we would compare two randomised groups to see the difference. We might give some children extra help in Maths, for example, and then compare them to another group of children who didn't get help and see if the first group of children get better at Maths.

Designing studies to compare schooled with not-schooled children is not as easy as extra Maths. We can't assign children to randomised groups and send half of them to school while giving the rest an out-of-school education. Their parents might not agree. We can't just compare children whose parents choose to educate them outside of school with those who go to school, because they aren't equivalent groups. It takes a lot of courage (and a rebellious streak) not to school your child when everyone around you is telling you that that is the right thing to do, and parents who make this choice may be less conventional in other ways too.

Some parents choose other forms of education when it becomes clear that their children are not thriving at school. This means that the children are likely to be different to those who remain in schools, again making it hard to compare. We can't compare different countries because wealthier countries tend to school all their children while poorer countries don't. It's tempting to assume that universal schooling is the *reason* that some countries are wealthier than others, but there really is no evidence for this.

In addition, how do we measure an effective education? Schools measure their success by exam results, but we might have higher expectations for education than that. We might want to see children enthused by learning and by the opportunities in front of them. You can't assess that with a standardised test.

School was never an evidence-based intervention. The Prussians did not start with large studies comparing different educational methods and then conclude that classrooms of desks with teachers and textbooks was the way to go. A single teacher addressing a large group of children was practical and cost-efficient, and so that's what they did.

Everyone Should Do It Like Us!

This lack of evidence for the beneficial impact of school hasn't put off those who claim that spreading the Western schooling model is the way to cure the world's problems. Over the last hundred years, not only has the way we educate children in the West narrowed, but we are doing our best to make sure that this happens globally.

Campaigns for global education accept the school model uncritically. Check out UNESCO, the United Nations Educational, Scientific and Cultural Organization. On the day I looked at their website, their page on educational initiatives was illustrated with photos of beaming and attentive-looking children in various countries of the world. There are children in Senegal clutching their pencils, sitting on wooden benches and watching the teacher at the blackboard. Egyptian children smile, identically dressed in their checked school uniform. The group of Muslim girls in Lebanon all look forward with their hands in the air. Rows of Ugandan children sit in their neat blue shirts and dresses while the teacher patrols the classroom. If children are dressed in uniform and sitting in rows, they must be learning.

'Educational initiatives' is a euphemism – they mean 'school'. If I wasn't so used to what school looked like, I might think there was something sinister about these pictures of identically dressed children around the world. These initiatives export a particular model of education round the world, using aid money.

It must be pretty good then, right? You'd have thought that to have the confidence to build schools around the world, it must have worked really well in the countries which have had universal schooling for over a century.

Well, it depends what you mean by 'worked'. Almost everyone goes, that's one metric. But over their school career, children become less and less motivated to learn. In the USA, about one in ten teenagers drop out and don't get a high school diploma at all, while in the UK around 40 per cent of teenagers don't get five good grades in their GCSE exams – regarded as the minimum needed to carry on in education and to demonstrate basic literacy and numeracy. Those aren't great statistics in a school system where the most important outcome is passing those exams. There are a lot of young people finishing education with nothing to show for all those years.

Don't Schools Reduce Inequality?

Back to that UNESCO website, where Gordon Brown, UN Special Envoy for Global Education, tells us what he thinks the point of education is: 'Without universal education – or in other words, winning the war against illiteracy and ignorance – we cannot also win the war against disease, squalor and unemployment. Without universal and high-standard education we can only go so far – but not far enough in breaking the cycle of poverty.'

Stirring stuff. Who could disagree? Universal education around the world sounds like a no-brainer.

Except, of course, that really he means 'school', not 'education' in a wider sense, and unfortunately years of universal schooling in

Europe, North America and many other countries across the world hasn't resulted in winning any war against ignorance. Nor has it broken the cycle of poverty. We still have disease, squalor and unemployment. Inequality is on the rise in many European countries, because this is the result of government policy, rather than lack of education. Why is there any reason to think that it would work differently elsewhere?

Most of us know someone whose life was transformed by doing well at school, or by a teacher who took an interest. The inspirational teacher is a trope which comes up regularly in popular culture – think *To Sir with Love*, *Dead Poet's Society* and *Good Will Hunting*. For some children, doing well at school means that they can live a very different life to their parents. We think about those people and assume that this means that schools are 'breaking the cycle of poverty', as Gordon Brown puts it.

For those individuals, yes it does. Succeeding at school does help some individual children out of poverty. The catch is that school cannot ever end poverty for all. The problems are a result of how society is organised, not mass educational failure.

Schools, in fact, exacerbate the inequalities which are already present. This is because they constantly compare children against each other, and the children know this. Those who do best get access to more interesting opportunities and are given awards. They are told that they are gifted and talented. Those who don't do so well are doomed to spend their time repeating the material they didn't learn the first time round, becoming disengaged and miserable in the process. They are told they have learning difficulties or special educational needs. These groups are associated with socio-economic status. Richer children are more likely to do well, while poorer children do less well.

In some countries, such as France and the USA, children have to repeat a whole year's worth of schooling if they fail to do well enough at the end of the year. In others, such as Germany and the UK, children are divided up into different classes and schools where they are given differing opportunities. Both systems give children a clear message of success or failure.

The Slow Readers Group

Allan Ahlberg's poetry book for children, *Please Mrs Butler*, is a treasure chest of memories for anyone who attended a British primary school in the 1970s and '80s. Each poem reminds me of a different aspect of that experience, right down to the hymns we used to sing, sitting cross-legged on the floor of the draughty assembly hall.

'Slow Reader' is a poem from the perspective of a child placed in the 'Slow Readers' group. At first it invites us to laugh, with its slowed down speed echoing the tedium of listening to a child read something that they can't quite yet manage. But then at the end there's a kick, a moment of honesty. We hear how the child feels – and they hate it.

Nowadays, the 'slow readers' are more likely to be called the Squirrels, or Red Group. We live in an era which is coy about names as blunt as the 'Slow Readers'. It doesn't make any difference. Research shows that even young children know whether they are considered to be 'clever' or not. Many schools help them with this by dividing them into ability groups from age four or five. Children are quickly aware of which group is at the top, middle or bottom, even if they are called the Kangaroos. And, unfortunately, on average it's the poorer children or those who are disadvantaged in other ways who end up in the lowest groups. They won't ever 'catch up' and they know it.

Those early labels form part of how children think about themselves for years afterwards. We know that from very young, children are sensitive to how capable they are perceived to be at school. We even know that how children perceive their abilities affects their success later, *independently of their actual abilities*. If children think they are good at Maths, then they perform better at Maths later in life – even if they weren't actually that capable to begin with.

Test, Test and Test Again

Every year in England, all ten-year-olds take a test in Spelling, Punctuation and Grammar. In recent years, this involved (among other things) them ticking boxes to indicate whether the word 'theirs' in a particular sentence was a co-ordinating conjunction, a subordinating conjunction, a possessive pronoun or a relative pronoun. This isn't something I've ever had to know, despite a successful school career, one bachelor and two doctoral degrees. Yet it's something that these children will have painstakingly been taught, probably several times. For some of them, this will have been really difficult. Some of them don't speak English as a first language or can't yet read well. No matter, this is what they must know and be tested on, because they are ten. This is learning which is completely detached from what is important to the learner.

Tests are a strange thing. People sit down in a room, with paper and pen and write answers to a set of questions. They can't talk to other people or look anything up and they only have a few hours. There really isn't much else in life that is like a test.

Yet the results of tests are used in ways which profoundly affect the life chances of the people who take them. This is increasing in education systems around the world, a phenomenon known as 'high-stakes testing'.

High-stakes tests aren't just used to assess children; they are used to rate a teacher's job performance, to compare schools with each other and sometimes to determine funding. These tests are promoted as a way to improve the education system and to improve account-ability. One thing is certain – test results are used to limit children's opportunities, because they are inherently competitive. The whole point of a test is to compare and contrast. If everyone does well in a test, then it's not a useful test. Someone has to be the loser.

In Singapore, children take an exam at the end of primary school (age twelve) which determines their entire life opportunities. It decides which school they can go to, which then decides which exams they can take, which decides what jobs they will be able to do. In France, if you don't do well enough in your end of year exams, you'll be back there again the next year, doing the whole thing again. In the UK, there are baseline tests for four-year-olds, and phonics tests for six-year-olds. At seven and ten, children take SATs – Reading, Science and Maths tests. Thousands of children take a test at age eleven which determines which school they will go to. Germany divides all of its children into different schools, with only 30 per cent of children going to the most academic (and prestigious) schools. Our addiction to testing and ranking children just won't go away.

Something strange happens when we start testing children. We lose faith in other methods of assessment. When baseline tests for four-year-olds are introduced, we're told that they're necessary, for how else will we know how they are doing?

I've never tested my children on anything, but I have a very good understanding of their abilities. I know how to pitch what I say at their level, and how to give just the right amount of detail in an answer. I know, when leafing through a book, whether it will be too complex or too simple for them. I know what sort of things will interest them.

This doesn't make me exceptional; most parents have this level of understanding of their child. We know their strengths and weaknesses and we adjust accordingly. People interact with younger and older children differently, and it's not something they have to do consciously. Research shows that other adults (and even older children) do this naturally when they interact with children. We have lost faith in this sort of relational and intuitive assessment, instead choosing to believe that the way our children answer a list of questions on a certain day is a truer reflection of their ability.

Standardising Children

Along with this push towards using standardised tests is an expectation that all children will meet the same educational goals.

Children are highly variable. Evolutionary psychologists see this as a strength for the human race. Diversity is necessary for optimal adaptation to new and challenging situations. But while we measure all children by the same yardstick, we turn that variability into a problem rather than an advantage.

There's a cartoon I particularly like which depicts an exam. The examiner sits behind his desk, staring at the examinees. He says, 'For a fair selection, everyone has to take the same exam: Please climb that tree.' The examinees look at him. They include a monkey, an elephant, a penguin, a bird and a goldfish in a bowl.

No prizes for guessing the winner.

The way the school system deals with human variation is to diagnose those who are just too different with 'special educational needs'. This is essentially a way of saying that the standard system doesn't fit this child – except that the way it is phrased suggests that it is the child who is the problem and who has 'additional needs', rather than the system failing to accommodate difference and diversity.

These children are present in every school system. The way in which different systems manage them differs from country to country, partly depending on cultural differences. The French system is particularly inflexible, and children who do not fit in with the school system are sometimes placed in psychiatric day hospital and their parents told that they are ineducable. In the USA, the approach leans towards diagnosis and drugs, with 10 per cent of children being diagnosed with attention deficit/hyperactivity disorder (ADHD) alone. These children will typically be told that their brains work differently to other people, and that they need extra support – often drugs – in order to do well at school. We don't actually know if there is a difference in their brains, since discernible differences cannot be seen on a brain scan and there is no medical test for ADHD. What we really know is that they don't fit in well with the requirements of the school system.

There's much talk about why the number of children diagnosed with special educational needs is going up year on year. My hypothesis is that it's because, as school requirements become more rigid, they require more standardised children. There's less wriggle room, no space to let a child have a year or two to mature before they learn to read or even before they start school, when you know they are going to fail their test at the end of term and people will want to know why.

When School Doesn't Work

Some children need something really different to school. They tell us this through their behaviour, their distress and the way in which they become increasingly less engaged with learning as they grow up. There are alternative ways to become educated. However, governments and schools continue to behave as if these are untested and dangerous, and to tell parents that school is the only place that their children will get an education.

There is substantial evidence that this is not the case. We can see from young children that it is not necessary to force children to learn. Humans are born curious and with a desire to learn from their environment. We can see from experiments and observational studies that children are motivated to learn complex skills without instruction. And we can see from studies of schools where children are not made to follow a curriculum that these children do become educated to the point where many of them attend college or university.

Once we understand that, then this puts attending school in a different light. For when we believe that school is essential, many of us ignore significant misgivings about how school affects our children. We believe that getting an education is so important that it's worth making other sacrifices for. If, however, school is just one way to get an education, then factors such as unhappiness, loss of joy in learning, anxiety or bullying become prices which may be too high to pay.

In this book, I'll discuss why many children don't thrive at school, including some of those who are academically successful. I'll look at how many common school practices have nothing to do with learning and are detrimental to children's wellbeing.

The second part of the book is practical and will help you think about the steps involved in facilitating a very different type of education. I'll cover the process of leaving school, the problems many families encounter when they take their child out of conventional education, and offer some ideas for how to deal with them. I'll discuss what children need to be able to direct their own education, and how the adults around them can put that in place.

I hope that, by the end, you'll have a good understanding of what education looks like when it doesn't involve school, and perhaps be ready to apply this to the lives and education of the children around you. For in order to allow children to learn without school, the adults around them need to change their minds.

Further Reading

Ahlberg, Allan – *Please Mrs Butler*, Puffin Books (1984)

Kohn, A – *What Does it Mean to Be Well-Educated?*, Beacon Press (2004)

Richardson, Will – *Why School? How Education Must Change when Learning and Information Are Everywhere*, TED Conferences (2012)

2

Learning – Scientists, Processors and Rats

Let's start with thinking about how people learn. Not just children, people of all ages. What magic needs to occur for someone to go from ignorance to knowledge? We often assume that this happens by a process of instruction. We assume that if a person listens attentively enough to someone who is teaching, they will learn. If that doesn't work, then you repeat the information, perhaps in a different format. And so on, until they get it.

However, even when you repeat the information again (and again), this process doesn't always work. Some things are just hard to learn, and some people just don't retain what they are told. To complicate things further, sometimes people can retain information and repeat it back, but with no understanding of what they have learnt. Why? What is actually happening in this process called 'learning'?

How we understand learning gets to the heart of what we think education should be. In fact, it gets to the heart of how we understand children and child development. For if learning really does happen best by instruction, then it makes sense for schools to maximise instruction time and minimise distractions. 'Bottoms on seats and fingers on lips', as my primary school teacher used to say. But what if learning doesn't actually work best like this? What if you can't reliably make learning to happen in another person by telling them what they should learn? In that case, we might need to reconsider the whole way schools are organised. Perhaps, rather than assuming children are not trying hard enough, maybe schools aren't designed well enough to enable young humans to learn.

In this chapter, I'm going to introduce some psychological models of learning. These fall into three broad groups: behaviourist, cognitive and constructionist. I'll discuss how these relate to what goes on in schools, and what it means when claims are made that an educational approach is 'based on science'.

A note before we start. Schools weren't based on learning theory. No one designed them to maximise learning, and governments didn't do research to find out how children learnt before rolling out universal schooling. Teacher-led instruction from textbooks was efficient, easy to standardise and relatively inexpensive. It became the norm due to convenience.

Theories of Learning

As an undergraduate psychology student, I was fascinated by learning. I hoped that my degree would finally explain to me how we learn, how this mysterious process actually worked. In particular, I was intrigued by the question of how a baby can come into the world knowing so little and yet, by the age of five, they have learnt to walk, talk, express their opinions and even sometimes to read and write. What could be going on? I signed up for courses called things like Learning, Memory and Cognition, and prepared to be enlightened.

What I got were rats and pigeons. Pigeons, it turns out, are very intelligent birds. They can be trained to peck at a particular button in order to get food, or to avoid another button to avoid punishment. They can make their way home over hundreds of miles, and no one knows exactly how they do it. Rats are even more intelligent, in their own way. They can be persuaded to run mazes for the right rewards, and to push on levers for food. Actually, it turned out to be a lot more interesting than I had thought, but I was no closer to the question of how humans actually learnt. Or even understanding exactly what learning is. Learning how to run around a maze seemed a very long way from the complex human behaviour I saw around me.

I was being introduced to behaviourism.

Bear with me now, as I take you on a whistle-stop tour of psychological theories of learning. How we understand learning has a huge impact on how we educate our children. Are we most interested in how they behave, or what they think? Do we think being able to transfer any learning to new situations is important, or are we focused on how they will perform in tests? Is it important that children are active participants in the learning process, or is it more a question of teachers passing on information in the most efficient manner?

Behaviourism

Early theories of learning started with animals. Specifically, early psychologists studied animal behaviour, and how it could be changed. To them, learning was a change in behaviour.

Ivan Pavlov, a Russian working at the turn of the twentieth century, is one of the most famous names in psychology, despite actually being a physiologist. He discovered by accident that he could train a dog to salivate when a bell was rung, because the bell had been previously rung when it was fed. The dog learnt that the bell meant food and salivated even when no food was available. This wasn't something the dog did intentionally; salivation is an automatic response to particular circumstances. That's known as 'classical conditioning'.

B.F. Skinner, working in Harvard in the 1930s and '40s, tried something different. He trained rats to push levers in order to get rewards. Unlike Pavlov's dogs, they had to demonstrate their learning by doing something, and therefore choice entered into the equation. If they pushed the lever, they could get sugar water. For some of them, Skinner trained them to push a lever to avoid a negative consequence like an electric shock. Learning that you can do something which causes something else to happen is known as 'operant conditioning'.

This is the basis of behaviourism. The most fundamental principle is that you can change behaviour through the deliberate manipulation of external events. Skinner's rats learnt to push a lever or, alternatively, to avoid pushing a lever, because of the consequences which the experimenter could control. Pavlov's dog started to salivate, because Pavlov had rung a bell when he provided food, and thus formed an association. In both cases, the experimenters, rather than the animals, controlled what learning should take place.

Psychologists were quick to see how this could be applied to children. In 1920, John B. Watson demonstrated classical conditioning on Little Albert, a nine-month-old baby. He did this by clanging an iron pipe and showing him a rat at the same time. Little Albert learnt to cry when he saw rats.

It wouldn't get through a modern ethics committee, particularly since they didn't decondition him afterwards. No one knows what happened to Little Albert but, by 1928, Watson was writing manuals on using behavioural principles to bring up children. He considered that there were only three unconditioned emotions: fear, rage and love. Everything else was learnt by behaviourist principles and therefore parents needed to be careful to condition their child in the right way.

Watson's advice hasn't dated well; in particular, his recommendation to interact with your children in a detached, business-like fashion. He did, however, start off a fashion for routine and habit-forming parenting which still continues today. Get the parent's behaviour right, was his message. The child will learn the correct behavioural associations, and all will be well.

Behaviourism in Real Life

All the schools I have visited have used behaviourist principles. They use rewards and punishments to control children's behaviour. Typical school rewards are grades, teacher approval, school prizes and good school reports. School punishments include bad grades, disapproval, being put on report, detentions and suspensions.

This works, on its own terms, for many children. Success is when there is a change in a child's behavioural: perhaps they remember to hand in their homework after being given a detention for forgetting. The result of this apparent success is that many schools and teachers forget that it misses something out.

That something is the experience of the child themselves.

It doesn't matter, from a behaviourist perspective, what the child thinks. A child might be complying with school requirements and yet feeling furious and resentful. When they are younger, many of them put up with it; as they get older, more of them start to show us how they feel.

The other problem is the child who doesn't respond to behavioural strategies. There's an assumption that the child *can* change, and if we just apply enough pressure, they will. So, if a child doesn't respond to lunchtime detention, they are given an after-school detention. If they don't respond to that, they are suspended for a day. If a day doesn't work, let's try a week. The onus is on the child to change, and the punishment increases until they do, or until they are permanently excluded from school.

Imagine you are learning how to juggle; perhaps how to juggle with five balls. You try and try, but you just keep dropping the balls. You can't even manage three; you are a novice juggler. Along comes a behaviourist teacher who says, 'If you don't drop a ball, I'll give you a prize.'

You try your very best, but you can't keep those balls up. The teacher changes tack. Now she says, 'If you drop a ball in the next ten seconds, I'm going to make you write a hundred lines.'

All to no avail. In fact, you seem to get even worse. Now you can't even spend your time practising juggling any more because you're mostly writing lines. The teacher ups the ante. 'Come on, try harder. Keep those balls up or you have to stay in this room for an extra hour.'

Filled with despair, you try your absolute hardest, but the balls just keep dropping.

'Right, that's it,' says the teacher. 'You're suspended. Go home for the rest of the week.'

Does it help you learn to juggle? Are you likely to keep trying?

Behaviourism assumes that the child can do the task . . . if only they would try hard enough. It's of no help at all for a child who isn't able to do a task. A small child being punished for wriggling in their seat, or an older child being punished for freezing due to anxiety during class and being unable to answer questions – both are in a similar situation. They can't comply, but it's not necessarily for lack of trying.

Beyond Behaviourism

By the 1960s, many psychologists were frustrated with the limits of behaviourism. It seemed like an overly simplistic way to understand complex human beings. Along came people like Jean Piaget and Lev Vygotsky, who were interested in how people thought, not just how they behaved. Behaviourism argues that humans learn in response to environmental stimuli; cognitive psychologists acknowledged that, in between the environment and behaviour, there was a thinking human being. The question was, how could you measure their learning?

Studying thoughts is tricky. Unlike with behavioural change, which can be seen, you can't ask a rat how its thinking has changed. Measuring a change in someone's thoughts usually involves having to ask them or test them.

Psychologists solved this problem in two ways. The first way was through close observations of children learning naturally. Piaget watched his nephew and daughter as they grew and developed an understanding of the world. The other approach was experimental, devising paradigms to look at how well people learnt in controlled situations, or tests to work out what children knew.

Both of these methods are still used today. Psychologists around the world design experiments in order to work out how people learn, with some methodologies not unlike those used for the rats and the pigeons. These types of experiments frequently involve people learning useless information. It's common for studies on memory, for example, to study people memorising lists, or abstract patterns. This is to avoid the thorny problem of people already knowing the information they are meant to be learning. However, it means that learning is taken out of context and is often devoid of any meaning for the learner. The assumption is that the same factors will come into play when remembering meaningful information.

In order to do experiments on the processes of learning, psychologists had to ignore many of the things which made learning interesting, and also ignore a lot of what people were learning. As an undergraduate, I participated in several different experiments on learning and memory. We were paid a small amount for doing so, and it was a different way to spend a couple of hours.

Thinking back now, I remember nothing of the actual content of the experiments. They were mostly dull and involved things like watching checkerboards on a screen and trying to remember which one was the same as the one I had seen earlier, or pressing a button whenever I saw a face that matched another face. I may have memorised some lists of words. What I remember best is the experimental room, small and dark, and the sign-up sheet that I had to write my name on in order to be paid £10 for my participation. And the joy at being paid at a time when I didn't have much spare money. That is what is stored in my long-term memory.

No one ever tested me to see if I could remember any of that, of course. They were only interested in whether I could remember the face or checkerboard.

Cognitive experiments on learning and memory are designed to focus on a particular question and, in order to do that, they simplify the situation down to the absolute basics. They strip learning of context, in order to understand the underlying processes. Which is useful if that's your aim. But just as with behaviourism, when these theories are applied in education, there's a tendency to ignore just how simplified the experiments were. Children can't be stripped down to underlying processes.

Memory and Cognition

Recently, a particular type of cognitive theory of learning has had a resurgence in education. Educationalists and cognitive scientists such as E.D. Hirsch and Daniel Willingham argue that we should directly apply cognitive models of memory to education and schools. They have the ear of government, and so these theories have led to widespread curriculum change in the UK and the USA.

It's easy to see why they have had such success. The model of learning they promote sounds so simple and adapts so well to the school model. Willingham sees learning as information committed to long-term memory. This model suggests that we have two forms of memory. Working memory is short-term, is limited in capacity and cannot be greatly expanded by training. We use our working memory when we repeat a phone number to ourselves, punch it into the phone and then immediately forget it.

Our long-term memories, by contrast, can hold vast stores of information, but we can only bring small amounts up to our working memory at a time. Training does not significantly expand our working memory. What is possible is expanding what an 'item' in our working memory might be. Here's an example to illustrate what this means:

Here's a set of letters; give yourself a few moments to look at them, then turn the page and see how many you can write down:
F I E N P D K M W P A Q B J O I

Typically, you'll have remembered between five and eight. That's a normal span for working memory.

Now try this one:
The enormous turnip jumped over the hedge.

How many letters did you remember here? If you got the whole sentence, it was 35.

And now try this one:
Jfd dscxdwers njeyy aqwqew ecxs ggnn okjko

Also 35 letters, but I'd be surprised if you got all of them. Why the difference?

In the 'enormous turnip' example, our brain combines the letters into words, and so we only need to remember the words rather than the individual letters. The meaning makes it easier to remember as well. Our expertise in reading changes how much information we can hold in our working memories. Words act as chunks of letters. In the final example, we don't have any meaningful combinations and so we are back to the individual letters being the basic piece of information – and we're stuck with our limited working memory.

There's good evidence that people who have more information stored in their long-term memory are more expert than those who have less. Advocates of applying this model to education are fond of talking about experts – in particular, chess experts. Studies of chess players have found that expert chess players can remember the positions of pieces on a chessboard far better than novices — but only when the pieces are in meaningful positions (i.e., positions that might arise during a game). If the pieces are randomly arranged, the novices and experts both have similar trouble remembering the positions. In a real chess game, background knowledge and expertise mean that experts have an advantage over novices, because they can clump what they see into meaningful chunks – just like you did with those words on the previous page. This enables them to manipulate large quantities of information, unlike the unfortunate novice who has to remember the position of each individual chess piece.

The difference between experts and novices isn't their working memory. In this model, the difference is simply the amount of information stored in their long-term memory.

Perhaps you can guess where this is going.

Creating Experts

In schools, those who advocate for this model suggest that the purpose of education should be to get as much information as possible into the long-term memory of children. The evidence, after all, shows that the difference between experts and novices is their long-term memory stores. They argue that, just like the chess players, having large stores of background information will enable children to manipulate more information in their working memory and to think like experts. Once the knowledge is there, so the theory goes, then creativity and higher-level thinking is possible.

These theories underpin the philosophy of several schools which have recently opened in the USA and UK. In the UK, Michaela Community School in west London is an example. Children at schools like Michaela are drilled in every lesson. They repeat material again and again, and are rigorously tested on it every day. For homework, they self-quiz. They follow along with what the teacher says in their books, are compelled to read over 10,000 words a day, and can be called on at any time to keep them focused on the lesson and to avoid the temptation to drift off into a daydream. Every moment of their day is controlled. It's a lot like a memory laboratory, no distractions allowed.

It all makes perfect sense if you see education as an extended memory experiment. We know that information is forgotten over time and, in order to keep it in memory, it has to be repeated. At schools like these, that's how the system works. It's built on cognitive science, as they are fond of saying.

There are a few quibbles with this approach, which even those of us who lack the massive amount of background knowledge necessary to be designated an 'expert' might have noticed.

Remember the chess players? They are highly expert and have enormous amounts of background knowledge about chess. The theory says that this is why they are expert, and if we could teach children lots of background knowledge, they would become experts, too.

Except that the way to learn to play chess is to do it. It's a process of playing, testing strategies, learning from others, perhaps reading books or websites. It's never a question of sitting in a classroom learning lots of chess facts and strategies and waiting for the day in the future when you will be deemed expert enough to actually start to play chess. The endpoint for those expert chess players might be lots of chess configurations in their long-term memory, but most of those they will have worked out as they played. They will make sense to them because they deeply understand the structure of the game of chess. The information might not even be available to them verbally, but be coded in a different part of their memory (this is called implicit learning, and we use it when we learn how to do things like ride a bicycle, or swim, which we may not be able to explain verbally even when we can do it).

In addition, very few people are obliged to play chess. It's not on the school curriculum. Those who become experts in playing chess are those who have chosen to put in the years of practice required. They are experts because they love playing chess and because people around them played chess with them. Their chess-playing has a purpose and context.

Proponents of the knowledge-based approach to education say

that children cannot be experts and think creatively until they have the necessary background knowledge. As the music teacher from Michaela Community School says, 'I don't let my Key Stage 3 pupils compose – they don't yet have the knowledge to do so meaningfully.' So, instead, she drills them on reading music and tonal triads. They separate learning and doing. Outside the memory lab, there is no evidence that this is the best way to learn.

The Strange Case of The Beatles

It's lucky The Beatles didn't go to Michaela. None of them ever learnt to read or write music. Paul McCartney, composer of some of the world's most famous songs, says, 'I don't see music as dots on a page. It's something in my head that goes on.' He uses software to convert his music into notation. He knows no formal music theory at all.

Would their music have been better if they had been drilled on music theory for years before being allowed to start to compose? How about if they had been told that they had to become expert before they could be creative? We'll never know. I sort of doubt it, though. The way they learnt music was by doing it, not by being drilled in it.

Like behaviourism, this sort of cognitivism is one level of explanation. It's about how information storage might work in the brain – but that's it. It doesn't tell us anything about the context of learning, about how culture interacts with learning, or how people learn from each other.

In fact, cross-cultural studies have found that one of the things which schooled children do better than those who do not attend school is remembering lists of unrelated information. Schooled children learn how to remember things, even when they don't make sense. It's a skill that is only useful in a school context, where children are tested on information which they may not understand and didn't choose to learn.

Where Are the People?

These theories of learning can't tell us why one person is fascinated by algebra, while another loves history. They can't even tell us why one person finds something easy while another works terribly hard and never gets above a 'C'. They can't tell us why Paul McCartney has music in his head.

To these cognitive scientists and educationalists, people are basically information processing units. Input goes in, they encode it, and then they can output it at a later date. Schools designed on this model focus on making the encoding as effective as possible, in the belief that that is what really matters. So, yes, approaches like this are based on cognitive science, but what their advocates don't say is that the cognitive science they are referring to is based on experiments, which strip the context from real life. And what is learning, without context?

It's memorising a list of random words.

There is something a bit odd about both behavioural and these particular cognitive theories, and it bothers me. They don't actually seem to be about humans. It's as if people's learning is detached from their personalities and lives, and their memory store exists as a separate hard drive into which we can plug information through drills and repetition.

Constructionism

Luckily, not all cognitive scientists focus on pigeons and memorising lists. Some observe children learning with wonder at their capabilities and capacity for reflection. One of these is Alison Gopnik, an American developmental psychologist and philosopher. Rather than trying to teach children information and testing them on their retention, Gopnik designs experiments to show what young children already know, and how this knowledge interacts with their experiences.

For example, it turns out that, faced with two adults giving them contradictory information, children as young as three or four make logical choices about who to believe. They tend to believe their parent over a stranger, but they also take account of how confidently things are said. They're more likely to believe someone who expresses their ideas with conviction than someone who sounds tentative.

And here's where this research starts to get really interesting. Because it turns out that instructing young children can actually stop them learning. Elizabeth Bonawitz (a research psychologist who collaborated with Alison Gopnik) and her research group looked head on at the difference between exploratory learning and instruction. They used a toy which did several different things. Adults offered the toy to a child, and for half the children they told them explicitly how one part of the toy worked. For the other half, they 'accidently on purpose' showed the child how one part worked but gave no instruction. The children who weren't instructed explored the toy and discovered all the other things it could do. The children who were instructed played with that toy in the way they were shown. The instruction seemed to stop them from looking for other possibilities. Other studies have found the same thing. When children are told how something works, they imitate. When they aren't told, they explore. And in the second case, they learn more.

Of course, if you see the point of education as the acquisition of a particular body of knowledge, this doesn't matter. Imitation is useful. Exploration and discovery aren't on the cards until the children become 'experts'. But if you're concerned about children losing their joy in learning as they go through school, perhaps this offers one clue as to how that might be happening.

Child-As-Scientist

Gopnik's writings are full of the children themselves. For her, children are never passive recipients; they bring their own prior knowledge and experience to every situation. From very early on, children actively try to understand what others are doing and why they are doing it, and adjust their behaviour accordingly. They are always active participants in their learning.

To Gopnik, schooling represents only one type of learning, and it's not one that is superior to other forms. She suggests that other forms of social learning are both deeper evolutionarily and more sophisticated. From her perspective, Western middle-class parents are immersed in a parenting culture which focuses on moulding children to create a particular outcome (a mindset which Gopnik characterises as the 'carpentry' approach to parenting). This fits well with school culture, which has similar aims. This isn't the only way to approach parenting, just as schooling isn't the only way to approach learning. Young children are not schooled, and yet they learn. For most of human history, children were not schooled, and yet they became functioning adults and learnt how to live in their society.

Gopnik's theory of learning and child development is sometimes called the 'theory-theory' because she argues that children construct their own theories about the world and use probabilistic reasoning to deduct likely answers. Fundamental to the approach is the idea that the child's own perspective interacts with what they are experiencing, and that learning is always an active process. Studies show how young children learn through observation and listening, make predictions and test hypotheses. This science of learning bears a lot of resemblance to what we see in self-directed children. It's not any less scientific because the children aren't being asked to memorise lists.

When we see learning as an interaction between the child themselves, their pre-existing knowledge and their environment, then it becomes clear why each child's learning trajectory can be so different, and how two children can learn such different things from the same experience.

Alert Awareness

In Western societies, this period of exploratory social learning is short-lived. Children are quickly channelled into school and formal learning, which is perceived to be more advanced and more important than informal learning. They are actively prevented from continuing to learn through exploratory play, as the focus in schools and parents shifts to literacy and numeracy. However, in some other countries, children do not all attend school and thus we can get some idea as to how children learn when they are not channelled in this way.

Studies in Guatemala by Barbara Rogoff and colleagues have shown that children who aren't formally educated remain in a state of 'alert awareness' for longer than children who go to school. They learnt through observation and imitation more effectively than a control group of schooled American children, who waited to be shown how to do something before paying attention.

Many cross-cultural psychologists argue that we should view school as a cultural phenomenon. Schools teach culturally specific skills, which are then tested in culturally specific tests. People's thinking and learning is always closely related to their cultural experience. We could see cognition and learning as something which develops as people learn how to live in their culture, rather than as something separate which can be abstracted and tested.

It's about as far from the information processing model of cognitive science as it is possible to get.

Learning Out of Context

Schools are carefully constructed learning environments which aim to deliver a particular type of learning. As such they take learning out of the context of life. Schooling involves an adult delivering specific actions towards a group of children with the aim of the children learning a particular set of knowledge or skills. This knowledge can in theory be used later but, right now, it's being learnt because the school chooses to teach it, rather than because a child needs to know it now in order to live their lives. The school, not the child, decides what is important.

Take the example of reading. Schools decide that children need to learn to read around the age of five. They teach reading as a technical skill. The child learns to read words such as 'cat' and 'hat' so that, in the future, they will be able to read books. Most of them don't learn to read through reading books of their choice, and they don't learn to read because they want to understand the books. The skill of reading is separated from its purpose.

This separation of learning from purpose is not based on science. Nowhere do the studies show that people learn best when what they are learning is not meaningful for them.

Communities of Practice

Harriet Pattison, Senior Lecturer in Early Childhood Studies at Liverpool Hope University, has done extensive research on how children learn to read informally. She introduced me to a way of seeing learning to read as a cultural process rather than a cognitive one: 'So you'd think of it more like learning to cook, because you're helping your mum in the kitchen. You're learning to read because you're doing it as a family practice rather than because you're making cognitive connections between sounds and symbols and so on, the way it's thought about in mainstream phonics practice.'

This is the idea of communities of practice, first proposed by cognitive anthropologist Jean Lave and educational theorist Etienne Wenger in 1991. Communities of practice are where people come together with a collective purpose, or to do something together. Through their interactions with each other, they learn, and they share information and experiences. The learning is embedded in the practice, so literacy is embedded in the family reading together for various purposes.

We are all in communities of practice when we do things with other people, perhaps at work, or if we join a book group, or a running club. Many communities of practice now exist online, where people discuss ideas and share their knowledge and skills. Pinterest is an example of community learning, with no instruction.

Much of the learning that goes on outside school can be seen through the lens of a community of practice. Children learn through doing, and their learning is enmeshed with its purpose. The two are never separated.

In the institution of school, the child's culture and internal world hardly matter unless they interfere with the instructional process. In fact, many early schools, particularly in America and Australia, were deliberately developed in order to wipe out indigenous cultures. School introduces a specific set of culturally specific standardised outcomes and prioritises them above all else.

Immersive Learning

In May 2018, we moved to Paris, France. Up to this point, my children had lived in England and spoke English. My daughter, aged almost seven, spoke nothing except English. She described herself on her first day at school as someone who couldn't speak French. She went into an entirely French self-directed school – a school with no lessons, curriculum or teachers, but where the everyday language was French.

For the first two months, she spoke English and almost only English. She sometimes said '*oui*' or '*non*'. Some staff members at the school spoke English, and they responded to her in English sometimes. No one insisted, and no one worried about her 'lack of progress' either (except me, quietly to myself). The other children spoke only French.

It was a hard few months for her. She loves to play, and her lack of French held her back. Over the summer, we returned to England and she hardly heard a word of French. One day, sitting in the car coming home from the supermarket, she said to me, 'Did you know that in French, the word comes after and in English it comes before?'

I wasn't sure what she meant.

She said, 'Like in French, it's "*une voiture rouge*", but in English, it's "a red car". The word comes after. Except with "*petit*", that comes before. It's "*une petite voiture rouge*" not "*une voiture petite rouge*" but in English it never comes after.' We hadn't been talking about adjectives, or French, or even cars.

In September, we returned to France, and she returned to school. I don't know exactly when she started but, by the third week, it was clear she was speaking French in sentences. Full, grammatical sentences.

Her story is fairly typical. She was clearly constructing her own understanding of French from watching and listening to others around her. She will have been committing words to long-term memory, as she heard them repeatedly. She'll also have been reinforced by others who reacted to her with approval when she tried to speak French. All of it was led by her desire to be able to communicate. None of it was due to a curriculum delivered by a teacher. She learnt to talk because she was in a community of people who spoke French, and she wanted to join them.

Learning by immersion is messy. You can't really tell how it's going for quite a long time; no one brings out lists of vocabulary; there's no logical order. You might learn how to say, 'Where can I find the Wi-Fi password?' before you can say, 'What's your name?' You learn what is around you. If you go to a park, you learn how to say 'slide' and 'playground' right there. You use whatever you learn as soon as you can, because you need it. If you wait to be an expert before you start speaking the new language, the odds are that you will never speak.

Language learning is a fantastic way to gain insight into how we learn in the real world, because speaking French in France is a real-life assessment. It's useful, flexible and meaningful. It's not so easy to see if someone truly understands Maths, or History, or English Literature. Instead, we take test results to be a marker of someone's ability. But passing standardised tests in French indicates very little about your actual ability to communicate in France. My daughter would definitely fail a French exam. She can't read or write in French. She can play in French. She can visit a French friend and tell them that she doesn't eat meat. Her French is suited to her environment and her needs. Even if she never becomes able to pass a French exam, her French is useful and meaningful.

Learning like this isn't neat or predictable, just like young human beings. When French is learnt in order to pass an exam, then it is no longer primarily a way to communicate. Instead, it is reduced to a set of tasks necessary for the exam – such as writing a postcard home from a holiday you didn't go on, for example, as I had to in my GCSE exam (and something which has always bothered me . . . wouldn't I be writing postcards home in English? Why would I write in French to my English parents?).

Why Do We Learn?

As theories of learning become more sophisticated, the question of *why* keeps coming up. Why do we do what we do, and why do we choose to learn, or not? Traditionally, human cultures have answered this question through communities of practice. We do what we do, because it is how we live our lives. We learn through doing, because those are the skills we need in order to live well.

Schools answer this question by creating a set of circumstances which they hope will give children reasons to learn. They need to do this because the social learning environment – a community – is sapped by dissociating learning from context. In Chapter 3, I'll look at the psychological theories behind why we do what we do.

The question of why we do things (or don't do things) is fundamental to what it means to be human. That's why education is not as simple as designing the right curriculum and watching the children learn. That might work for the rats running through their mazes, but human learning is far more complex. For humans, meaning and context are an integral part of why and what they learn. We ignore this at our peril.

Further Reading

Birbalsingh, Katharine (editor) – *Battle Hymn of the Tiger Teachers, The Michaela Way*, John Catt Publishers (2017)

Gopnik, Alison – *The Gardener and the Carpenter – What the New Science of Child Development Tells Us about the Relationship between Parents and Children*, Vintage (2017)

Pattison, Harriet – *Rethinking Learning to Read*, Educational Heretics Press (2016)

Rogoff, Barbara – *The Cultural Nature of Human Development*, OUP USA (2003)

Wenger, Etienne – *Communities of Practice: Learning, Meaning and Identity*, Cambridge University Press (2000)

Willingham, Daniel – *Why Students Don't Like School: A Cognitive Scientist Answers Questions about How the Mind Works and What It Means for the Classroom*, Jossey-Bass (2010)

3

Motivation – Stars, Stickers and Smiley Faces

When he was four, my son loved treasure hunts. He'd follow a series of clues around the house and would involve anyone who came to the house to visit. 'Treasure hunt' was, in fact, a misnomer. No treasure was necessary; for him, the process of following the clues was enough. Sometimes we hid a toy he already owned, sometimes the end was just the end. He'd get to the last clue, and sure enough we'd hear, 'Let's start again!' and he'd be ready for a whole new hunt. If only we could keep up the pace.

When other adults played this game with him, they were sure that we needed a 'real' reward, and would bring bags of sweets, stickers or new toys. Soon, he would ask at the beginning of a new treasure hunt whether there was 'real treasure' and, if not, he wouldn't do the hunt. What had been an enjoyable process had now become a means to an end. If the end wasn't there, he wasn't able to enjoy the process in the same way. I mourned the loss of our treasure-free hunts.

At around the same time, a friend sent us a code for a free trial of an educational computer programme. My son loved solving problems with numbers; he talked about numbers all the time. I thought he might like doing them on a computer. At first, he enjoyed the programme; it was easy for him and made pleasing noises when you got a sum right. Then he realised that he would only get the maximum number of stars if he got the answer to every problem correct the first time.

He came running to me. 'Mummy,' he said, 'I need you to do it.' He refused to try a single other problem, for fear of making a mistake and therefore not getting the full complement of stars. In vain I told him that the stars didn't matter, because it was clear that within the context of the programme they did matter. They were added up and, at the end of each level, the child was given a certificate with the number of stars on it. He wasn't prepared to risk being less than perfect, and therefore he needed me to do the maths for him.

We didn't subscribe to that programme.

In both cases, he was rewarded for doing an activity he enjoyed with the best of motives. The adults who came with 'treasure' thought they were making it more fun. The computer programme assumed that children needed to be rewarded in order to do maths. The result, however, was that he lost the original joy. He didn't want to carry on. This seems like it doesn't make sense. From a behavioural perspective, surely rewards are encouraging?

The Downside of Rewards

It turns out my son is just like other four-year-olds. As far back as 1973, psychologists showed that when they rewarded children for doing an activity (drawing with felt-tip pens) which they already enjoyed, they were subsequently less motivated to do the same activity when compared with children who were never rewarded. This is only one out of many studies showing that rewards can undermine motivation. It's been shown that rewards can reduce helpful behaviour in toddlers and reduce puzzle-playing in college students. In fact, it seems that a really good way to stop people from enjoying something is to reward them for doing it.

So, you're four years old, and you really like drawing pictures, and someone comes along and says, 'I'll give you a sticker for drawing a picture.' So you draw a picture. But then the next time you don't get a sticker, and you find you are less interested in drawing pictures. Some of your intrinsic motivation has gone. (I can't help but feel sorry for those children, stripped of some of their joy of drawing in order to prove a point about rewards. I hope they got it back.)

Intrinsic Motivation

When scientists talk about working memory, and retention of information, and forgetting curves, they often forget that, in the real world, *why* you do something matters. In the memory lab, the participants are motivated enough by the £10 reward to stay attentive. But if you're going to translate that to a classroom of unpaid children, you can't afford to ignore motivation.

Schools tend to manage motivation with behavioural techniques. They often assume that children must first be extrinsically motivated and then, as time goes on, they will develop intrinsic motivation. They reward children for doing what they want, and punish them when they don't comply. However, the finding that rewards can damage motivation means that this approach is doomed to failure over the long term. The more you try to motivate children with rewards, the less intrinsically motivated they will be. Which isn't really what you want to achieve with education.

Intrinsic motivation is doing something because you really enjoy it. Not all rewards undermine intrinsic motivation. Verbal rewards don't have the same effect as tangible rewards, so saying 'Thank you' isn't damaging in the same way as giving children sweets for good behaviour. And unexpected rewards are less damaging than expected rewards. It seems that rewards which people experience as 'controlling' are those which affect intrinsic motivation. And that, of course, will depend on the child. One child may feel controlled while another simply feels encouraged.

Motivated Monkeys

The studies on this date back to 1949, when Harry Harlow, a professor of psychology at the University of Wisconsin, set up a lab for studying learning in primates. As part of a study, they placed a mechanical puzzle in the cages of rhesus monkeys. Then, before they had had a chance to start implementing their planned rewards programme, the monkeys started playing with the puzzle by themselves. They kept playing and got better at solving the puzzles.

The way that animal behaviour was understood at the time didn't allow for this. This suggested that the main drives that powered behaviour were biological drives (such as hunger) or extrinsic motivations such as rewards or punishments. The monkeys were not being rewarded in any way for solving the puzzles – and yet they did, and continued to do so. Harlow's great insight was to propose that solving the puzzles was its own reward for the monkeys – they enjoyed it, and so they did it more. He proposed a third drive influencing behaviour: intrinsic motivation.

Harlow then added in an extrinsic reward – the monkeys got raisins for completing the puzzles. He predicted that this would lead to them performing better and completing more puzzles. To his surprise, that wasn't what he found. In fact, the monkeys who were rewarded made more errors, and solved the puzzles less frequently. It seemed like intrinsic motivation was vulnerable to external circumstances.

Puzzling Students

It took until 1969 for Edward Deci, a social psychologist, to investigate these ideas in humans. Using a task which most people find enjoyable for itself – a wooden puzzle cube – he found that when people were paid for completing the puzzle, it had an effect on their later motivation to play with it. Those who were paid stopped playing when they were no longer paid – whereas those who were never paid, kept going.

I'd recommend those puzzle cubes if you want to try out something intrinsically motivating. They are easy to find online. They are indeed lots of fun. If I leave them out on our coffee table, anyone who comes into our house starts fiddling and making shapes. My children have been known to fight over who gets to play with it next. I haven't experimented with rewarding them to do so, although sometimes it is tempting to see if it might reduce the number of arguments.

How Do We Facilitate Motivation?

Their research on intrinsic motivation led Deci and Ryan, a clinical and research psychologist, to come up with Self-Determination

Theory, which they describe as being 'concerned with the social conditions that facilitate or hinder human flourishing'. Self-determination theory is not just about intrinsic motivation, it's about how to facilitate higher-quality motivation and wellbeing.

It was Gina Riley who introduced me to self-determination theory. Riley is a professor in special education at Hunter College and she home-educated her son, who is now an adult and graduated from college last year. When we talked, she described to me the moment that changed her life.

'This goes back twenty or so years . . . I was a student writing my Master's thesis and I saw an article in the *New York Times* about intrinsic motivation. I had a three-year-old at the time; I was a young mum. I saw this article about Deci and Ryan and I thought, This is how I want to live my life! This is so amazing. If I were to shape a life, this is what it would be. I knew I was on an alternative path with my toddler, just following his interests. When he was five, I made the decision to home-school because I could see his natural intrinsic motivation and curiosity about the world. I didn't want to ruin it.'

Riley explained to me how she understands self-determination theory. 'Deci and Ryan define intrinsic motivation as something that comes out of curiosity, that comes out of interest, that comes from within. This is the opposite of extrinsic motivation which comes from somewhere else. One of the most interesting parts of self-determination theory is their sub-theory which is "cognitive evaluation theory". Cognitive evaluation theory describes the environmental tenets in which someone can facilitate intrinsic motivation in others. You can't force it; you can only facilitate it.'

Intrinsic motivation cannot be manipulated using behavioural strategies. In fact, these are likely to damage it.

This has serious implications for the way in which most schools currently work. Schools reward children for their academic performance. If Deci and Ryan are right, in the process they may be destroying their intrinsic motivation for academic pursuits. A reliance on external rewards traps schools in an eternal loop. The more they use external rewards, the less people enjoy learning. And the less people enjoy learning, the more schools have to rely on external motivation.

Just like with that maths programme, once you're doing it for stars or grades, the learning becomes secondary. You might as well get your mother to do it. Or copy your friend's answers in the break. Whereas, if you're learning for your own purposes, it would make no sense at all to get someone else to do it for you. In a very real sense, you would be cheating yourself. If you don't want to do it, you can just stop.

Parents and schools are so immersed in behaviourism that some-times it can be hard to think of alternatives – if you don't give stickers and praise, then what do you do? Cognitive evaluation theory suggests what needs to be in place in order to facilitate intrinsic motivation. Riley told me how she brings this into her classroom, where she trains teachers who will work in the public school system.

'The way you can facilitate it [intrinsic motivation] according to cognitive self-evaluation theory is by using the realm of competence, the realm of autonomy and the realm of relatedness. I talk to my students about competence; how to increase or facilitate competence in your students. We talk about things like making sure that our students really know their intrinsic strengths; what they are good at. Not rewarding or saying, "Good job . . ." but saying, "Oh my gosh, you are really a good writer . . ." not as a compliment but as genuine.

'We talk about competence also as having students see small suc-cesses, that all helps. And those small successes are becoming bigger successes, and then success you are really able to see . . . "Hey, I'm good at this, I'm competent in what I'm doing and I'm good at it." And you have to be careful because you can't get too extrinsic about it, it's about helping children or teens really see their authentic strengths.'

A word about autonomy: 'autonomy' is a person's ability to choose their actions, based on their own values and interest. An autonomous child has (age-appropriate) governance over their own lives. Psychologists sometimes talk about agency, which is a related but slightly different idea. Agency is the knowledge that you can make decisions with consequences. Young children experiment with agency when they drop their plate and see it fall, or hit a pot and make a noise, but they are only autonomous when their environment provides them with the space freely to explore and to use their agency to learn.

Autonomy is therefore both about the person (who needs to feel that they have the power to change things) and their environment (which needs to give them the opportunity to do so).

This means that parents and educators can either nurture or stifle autonomy, sometimes in unexpected ways. When a person's preferences align with the opportunities in their environment, they will feel more autonomous. A very structured and apparently controlling environment may feel freeing for someone who does not want to be making day-to-day decisions, and who knows they can choose to leave if they want to. Hours of unstructured play in the forest can be wonderfully freeing for a child who loves making dens and dams. Another child will find the forest frustratingly limited in scope because they would prefer to be reading books, painting, or taking part in organised activities. For them, being in the forest is a very different experience and they will not feel autonomous unless they are able to leave when they choose.

Attempts to manipulate behaviour will inevitably affect autonomy. Under this, I include both rewards and punishments, since these are attempts to change behaviour in line with someone else's values and interests. Emotional pressure will also harm a child's abilities to make autonomous choices. Using shame to control children's behaviour is so widespread that we may not even notice it. Techniques such as writing a child's name on a board or making them sit outside the classroom use the gaze of others to create shame – and therefore to push the children to make choices based on trying to avoid that shameful feeling.

Riley sees these three realms as fundamental to self-directed education for both home-educated children and those in self-directed schools. Autonomy, which Deci is careful to distinguish from independence or individualism, can be facilitated by a parent making 'autonomy-supportive' responses; competence can be fostered by helping children recognise their strengths; and relatedness – well, Riley clearly feels that this is at the heart of self-directed education.

'The last one, which I love because I come from attachment theory, is a sense of relatedness – and that's really having someone who has your back, no matter what. That, of course, facilitates intrinsic motivation, because if you feel someone has your back, no matter what, then you can make all these choices without fearing mistakes. It's unconditional autonomy support. That freedom of being unconditionally accepted, unconditionally related to – it doesn't have to be a parent, it could be a teacher or someone else.'

If learning is intrinsically rewarding, then adding external motivators will make it less likely that people will want to continue once there are no more rewards. For example, when they finish school and can decide for themselves whether to go on reading books or not.

The Spectrum of Motivation

It's not as simple as extrinsic motivators being detrimental while intrinsic motivation is good. Deci and Ryan have suggested that there is a spectrum of quality of motivation. The highest-quality motivation comes when we are intrinsically motivated, and the lowest when we are not motivated at all, which they call 'amotivation'. In the middle, however, there are different types of regulation. The more a person feels controlled from outside themselves, the lower the quality of their motivation (and therefore engagement).

Alongside amotivation is 'external regulation' – this is when someone is made to do something by the threat of punishment or disaster. Motivating statements such as 'If you don't do, this then I'll punish you' fall into this category. The person feels they are being forced to do something. Next along the scale is 'introjected regulation'. This involves doing something so that others don't think badly of you; for example, thinking you need to perform well at school because everyone expects it. We then start to move along to less damaging forms of regulation: 'identified regulation' where a person values an activity because they feel the goals are worthwhile; and 'integrated regulation', where someone is doing something because it fits with their sense of themselves and the person they feel they are.

	Not at all self-determined		Quality of Motivation			Totally self-determined
Type of Regulation	**Amotivation**	**External**	**Introjected**	**Identified**	**Integrated**	**Intrinsic motivation**
Adult attitudes	You're never going to amount to anything in life.	If you don't do this, I'll put you in detention.	If you don't do this then I'll be disappointed in you.	If you do this then you can learn to do this better.	That's something you are getting really good at.	What do you enjoy doing?
Child's internal responses	I won't do it.	I do it because I'm forced.	I do it because I feel guilty otherwise.	I do it because the goal is important to me.	I do it because it makes me feel good about myself.	I do it because I love it.

Figure 3.1 – Different types of regulation and their effect on motivation

Figure 3.1 is my interpretation of Deci and Ryan's theory in the context of parenting and education. The attitude of the adults around children makes a huge difference to how they feel about what they do. And the quality of their motivation affects how engaged they are, which then affects their learning.

Of course, regulation can be mixed. Lucky people might do something they enjoy, but which is also aligned with their values. Unlucky people might be doing something they feel forced to do, and they feel guilty about it when they don't do it.

The important thing about this theory is that it's not enough to make children do something and to assume that they will learn. Children can be made to go through the motions, absolutely, but the quality of their motivation (and therefore their learning) will be affected by how they feel about what they are doing.

The Legacy of Compulsion

Recently, I found myself in the middle of a conversation:

'Oh my goodness, do you remember Triple Physics on a Thursday afternoon? I almost died of boredom!'

'A Wizard of Earthsea, that's what I remember. I didn't bother to finish it and the teacher never noticed. My essays were based on the first half only!'

The women talking were my old school mates, from a highly selective and competitive girls' grammar school. We were all 'bright girls' who have become professional women. Among our number are lawyers, architects, doctors and dentists. When we discuss our memories of school, it's never about how interesting the lessons were.

I'm assuming that the person who planned lessons for us didn't anticipate that our memory of them twenty-five years later would be of tedium. They might have hoped that we would be inspired by them, even that we would enjoy them.

I personally should have loved school, particularly English. I read all the time as a teenager, often a book a day, flying through the pages. I carried a book with me at all times and a spare in case I finished the first. I read historical novels, non-fiction, classics and modern literature.

Except if I was compelled to read the book for school. When a book was assigned to us, suddenly it became a chore. This was the only time that I counted the pages, monitoring how many I had to read before I could legitimately take a break . . . and read something that I wanted to read instead. I found my thoughts drifting away, again and again. It's lasted, too. I have never been able to bring myself to reread any of the books I was made to read at school. Yet I'm pretty sure that if I had picked them up for myself, I'd have whizzed through them.

The joy often disappears when we have no choice. It's the same with walks in the forest, cooking a meal or learning a foreign language. When it's chosen, it is rewarding; when it's compulsory, it is tedious and time-consuming.

If the aim of our school was for us to get good grades in our exams, then they succeeded. For us, at least, the boredom did not result in our giving up. We were all sufficiently motivated by the idea of going to university and getting professional jobs and we weren't going to let *A Wizard of Earthsea* get in our way. But if the aim was for us to enjoy exploring the ideas and to leave enthused about learning, then the whole thing was a waste of everyone's time.

Remember those chess players, beloved of cognitive scientists? They became expert because they loved chess. The Beatles wrote music because they felt it in their heads. It's not the same thing at all as being drilled on scientific definitions, or musical notation. Experts have an internal drive to learn. At my school, we were made to learn, and we complied. But they couldn't make us enjoy it.

Motivating Through Grades

When I was thirteen, I attended an international American junior high school. We were graded relentlessly, tested regularly, and four times a year the 'Honor Roll' was posted around the building for all to see. Results above 90 per cent in everything was High Honors; no more than two marks between 80–90 per cent and everything else above 90 per cent was Honors; and if any of your grades dipped below 80 per cent, then you didn't make the list at all.

I was one of the lucky ones; the type of learning they valued came easily to me, and I made the High Honors list in my first term. I was intrinsically motivated to perform well, I enjoyed the work, but I also enjoyed the praise that came with doing well and felt that it was part of who I was. My teachers liked me, and I liked them. So I worked hard, and the quality of my motivation was high. Getting on the High Honors roll was just icing on the cake. I was internally driven, no one had to push or bribe me.

Then a new physical education (PE) teacher arrived – Ms Ponzio. She was a dance teacher, with a bouncy blonde ponytail and a shiny blue leotard (this was the 1980s). She announced that we would be doing dance every term from now on, and that this would make up a significant proportion of every grade.

Disaster. She couldn't have chosen anything worse. Dancing made me feel clumsy, arrhythmic and stupid. And we would have to perform our dances to the rest of the class and be graded on it. Also, it annoyed me because we were split up to do PE and the boys were not doing dance at all; they were running around playing basketball and baseball.

Anyway, to cut a long and painful story short, our dance was terrible. My group was made up of all the dance-phobics, and this was not some inspirational high school movie where we surprised everyone and gave the performance of the year. We bumped into each other . . . we tripped over . . . we lumbered around the stage and prayed for it to be over. We were given low grades and that was it for my chance of making the Honor Roll that term. It didn't matter how well I did in everything else, my mark for PE would prevent me from getting high marks across the board.

My motivation dived. I had been someone who enjoyed PE before and usually did well; the previous grading system for PE wasn't particularly onerous. Now, I couldn't see the point. This would happen every term and I would never make the Honor Roll again. So it didn't just affect how I felt about PE; it affected how I felt about everything else too. I was resentful, too, because I didn't see why I should have to do dance every term, just because there was a new teacher and I was female.

I moved quickly to feeling like there was no point in even trying any more. And it was due to an intervention which the school probably thought was to motivate us towards excellence, the Honor Roll. If it hadn't been for the Honor Roll system, it wouldn't have mattered if I did badly in PE, since my performance in everything else would be unrelated. By tying it all together, they created a system where, at least from my perspective at the time, once you'd done badly in one thing, you might as well do badly in the whole lot.

In terms of self-determination theory, I moved from being intrinsically motivated to feeling amotivated, overnight.

Unexpected consequences abound in the field of motivation. When we try to change other people's behaviour, it frequently doesn't work out in the way we anticipate. The more people feel controlled, the less engaged they are likely to be.

Autonomy and Video Games

This is something that Kevin Currie-Knight is acutely aware of. He's an ex-secondary school teacher, who now trains teachers at East Carolina College of Education. When thinking about how to plan his classes for his trainees, he was chewing on the puzzle of motivation. He was thinking particularly of video games. Video games are difficult, often repetitive and it can take hours and hours to get good at a particular game. And yet video games are an area where motivation is not a problem. In fact, for many people, the problem is that children are *too* motivated to play video games. If only, they say, they could put that motivation into school.

'So what researchers noticed,' observed Kevin Currie-Knight, 'is that video game manufacturers seem to have cracked the code that educators have been trying to crack for hundreds of years, which is how do you get kids to stay so motivated to learn this thing that they will repeatedly and voluntarily have failure after failure. *We're* trying to do this . . . how do *you* do this?'

For Currie-Knight, it boiled down to three things – video games combined learning, practice and evaluation in rapid succession, whereas schools separate out those things. Children can freely choose to play or not play video games, whereas at school they have no choice. And finally, children only play video games if they are interested. When they are no longer interested, they stop. They are autonomous.

He decided to experiment with his college students, to see if he could change their experience of his course by changing those parameters. The course is a compulsory one, and students have to pass it in order to become teachers, which put him at an immediate disadvantage as compared to video games. However, he decided to do what he could.

'So, I started dipping my toe very gradually in my own teaching. Instead of assigning tests and a teacher-assigned project with parameters, why don't I give them choices for a project? So, I started with six different ways you can do your project, and that worked well but, at some point, I was like, "Why am I limiting them to six? Why don't I just tell them – the only parameter for this project is to demonstrate to me somehow that you have got the main points of this unit . . . that's it!"

'And it just got better. I wasn't expecting that; I thought at some point it would go really badly. I imagined that students would low-ball their projects, just pick whatever the easiest thing is. What I found was almost the opposite . . . I mean, there's not an objective way for me to measure this, but my experience was they turned in projects that were bigger, longer. One student who is an art education major decided that she was going to do a painting that represents all of the themes in a particular relationship, and then she wrote about a page-long description about what each of the elements is and why it's there, and how that reflects what we did in the course. I don't think that anyone would ever have put in that amount of time.'

Motivation soared, and so did performance, even within the restrictions of a compulsory course.

Currie-Knight's experiments have raised some concerns from his colleagues that his students might have gaps in their knowledge. After all, he's letting them choose what they do. Surely it would be better just to teach them the curriculum?

'My concern with that question is that I think it's a very jaundiced view of how learning works,' Currie-Knight says. 'The idea is just like with K-12 [the publically supported education system from Kindergarten to twelfth grade in the States] that you fill kids with all the knowledge that you think they're going to need once they go out because, once they go out, if they have gaps in their knowledge, they're not going to be able to remedy those gaps.

'So, there are several problems with that. The first is that it's just not the world we live in any more. In 1935, if I missed something and I went out into the world and I couldn't find the resource somewhere, like in the library or from a friend, I would be in trouble. But nowadays, that's not as much of a concern.

'The second problem is that there seems to be an assumption within that question that suggests: if you teach it, students will come out knowing it. It's assumed that if we teach the same syllabus, people will come out knowing the same things. There's a fair amount of research that shows that students do an astonishing amount of forgetting. So when people say, "Your students are going to have gaps in their knowledge," my response is, "So are all the others."

Educational Experiments and Free iPods

Currie-Knight isn't the first person to be surprised by the behaviour of his students. Cathy N. Davidson, who was then Vice-Provost for Interdisciplinary Studies at Duke University, described in her book what she called a huge 'educational experiment' with the first-year students at Duke in 2003. Every student was given a free iPod, with no conditions. They asked students to think of ideas for learning applications and pitch their ideas to staff. That was it. At the time, there were no educational apps at all for the iPod and, of course, no iPhones or iPads. Later, they said that any student in any year could have a free iPod if they could convince their professor to use a learning app in their class.

The press coverage was scathing. iPods were seen as frivolous entertainment, not as learning devices. And then the ideas from the students started coming. The first podcasts were broadcast, iPods were used to share ideas between students and to give and receive feedback; iPods were used to aid medical diagnosis, and to practise musical performance. It was beyond anything that anyone had expected.

It was more than an exciting educational project for students, however. This had implications for how iPods and similar devices were seen. What had previously been perceived as a sophisticated entertainment device suddenly became something with the potential to open up access to learning for people across the world.

Motivation was not a problem here. These students were given more autonomy than in any other course, and they came alive with ideas and learning. There was no curriculum, and everyone could join in, not just the computer scientists and engineers. There was no reward for those first-year students at all – they already had their iPods.

We all know how this story ended. Thousands of educational apps are used every day on iPad and iPhones all over the world.

No assessments, no assignments, no tests, nothing keeping them on task. From a behavioural perspective, they shouldn't have bothered – what was the point? And yet they did. They came up with ideas and applications which transformed education and technology.

Further Reading

Davidson, Cathy – *Now You See it: How Technology and Brain Science Will Transform Schools and Business for the 21st Century*, Penguin Books (2011)

Deci, Edward – *Why We Do What We Do: Understanding Self-Motivation*, Penguin Books (1996)

Kohn, A – *Punished by Rewards: The Trouble with Gold Stars, Incentive Plans, 'A's, Praise and Other Bribes*, Houghton Mifflin (1999)

Pink, Daniel – *Drive: The Surprising Trust about What Motivates Us*, Canongate Books (2018)

Ryan, Richard & Deci, Edward – *Self-Determination Theory: Basic Psychological Needs in Motivation, Development and Wellness*, Guilford Press (2017)

4

Self-Directed Learning – What Happens When We Don't Make Children Learn?

The door is unobtrusive, I almost miss it. I ring the bell and the door is answered by a girl, aged about eight. She and her friends are chatting by the door while they drink orange juice. To their left is the computer room, where four boys are deeply involved in a computer game, and another small child is doing a somersault on the sofa. Straight ahead, in the common room, a girl is cooking herself spaghetti while three others play a board game around the table. Next is the quiet room, where someone appears to be asleep and someone else is taking notes from a book.

Downstairs, a child is running down the corridor to land on a huge mattress in the soft-play room. Next to them is the cinema room and an angry girl is coming out to tell off the corridor-runner – he's making too much noise and they can't hear *Harry Potter and the Prisoner of Azkaban*. In the art room, a group of girls are making bead necklaces and a small boy is painting. The music room is a site of intense activity, but all silent, since both the drum kit and keyboard are electronic and have headphones attached.

It doesn't look anything like a school.

But it is; it's a democratic, self-directed school – the forty-five children here can choose what they do and how they learn. And their choices don't look anything like a conventional education.

How Will They Learn If They Don't Go to School?

As a society, we aren't very good at envisioning how children learn if their time isn't controlled by adults. We talk about how they would 'run amok', or have images of children running riot, as in *Lord of the Flies*. Many people simply can't imagine what children would actually do if their day wasn't structured by an adult. Our collective experience is so dominated by schooling that a childhood without it is essentially invisible. The very idea of an alternative brings up worries about neglect and not fulfilling potential.

For those of us who grew up in a country with universal schooling, school and childhood are inextricably intertwined. We can't think of one without the other. It's usual for children over the age of five to be referred to as 'schoolchildren' even when they aren't actually at school. When a child goes to have swimming lessons, or joins a group like the Scouts, the first question asked after their name is usually their school year group. Out-of-school activities are divided up by school year, thus ensuring that it feels inevitable to children that they will only make friends with those in the same year as them.

Just how arbitrary these specific groupings are becomes clear when you move country. Suddenly being in Year 4 or 5 (as they are in the UK) is meaningless, because everyone else is in Standard 2 or 3 (South Africa), or 'CP' or 'CM' (as in France). The divisions are different, the class names are different – but the principle remains the same. 'Year group' seems stamped into children's experience, like the words running through a stick of Brighton rock.

This all makes it hard for many of us to imagine what a child would be like without these identifiers. How would they learn if not in a classroom? We think of children who do not have the opportunity to learn or be educated, and we think that they would be better off in school. We think of the millions of illiterate children across the world, and this seems like proof that school is necessary.

Self-directed education is not the same as just not going to school. Children need an environment of opportunities; they cannot learn if they don't have those chances. They need available adults who have time to spend with them – not teaching them, but talking and helping them follow their interests. If the adults around them do not have particular skills (like literacy and numeracy), the children will not be able to acquire them. They will learn the languages which surround them, and skills which they need in their community, but they need access to new experiences if they are to learn more than that.

Luckily, a few researchers have looked closely into how children learn when they are not taught. They identify patterns which are repeated as children make discoveries and share their learning with others. They all describe the intensely social nature of learning, how children are driven by curiosity to learn, and that by providing the right environment for this curiosity, learning can flow.

Unschooling, Life Learning or Self-Directed Education?

First, a word about language.

'Self-directed education', by my definition, is an education where the learner retains control of what they are learning. They are free to choose what they learn, and they are free to stop when they have learnt enough. They retain their control over what they do. Autonomy makes for efficient learning and high-quality motivation, which is why it is a crucial part of self-directed education,

In self-directed education, it is *who* holds the control that matters, not the content or style of what the learner is doing. If the learner chooses what to do, then it's self-directed. If a teacher chooses, and the learner can't say 'no', then it won't be self-directed. If an adult and child choose together, then it could be self-directed, depending on whether the child is able to express their preferences freely or not – and whether the adult is able to listen.

This means that you can't necessarily tell from the outside whether learning is self-directed. A self-directed learner can choose to follow a formal class and can stop when they have had enough. If they are being made to take the same class because someone else thinks they should, and they are pressured to continue when they want to stop, then it won't be self-directed.

Self-directed education is therefore somewhat of an umbrella term which encompasses a wide range of educational options. Home-educating families often describe themselves as 'unschoolers', a term coined by the educator and author John Holt, writing in the 1960s. 'Unschooling' means home education without following an imposed curriculum. Unschooling families will follow their child's interests, and parents are usually closely involved in their children's education, seeing themselves as facilitators. A few families call themselves 'life learners', which is essentially the same thing, but without the reference to 'school'. Unschooling is often something of a family identity, as it usually involves having a parent available full-time, at least until the children are teenagers.

Some educators talk about 'natural learning', by which they mean learning from the environment around you without instruction. This is about pedagogy rather than autonomy. It is possible for what adults perceive as natural learning to be forced and restrictive. This happens when adults deliberately limit their environment and do not allow children access to tools of the culture that they would enjoy and could learn from. The most common form of this is when families or schools ban all technology use by children and, instead, prioritise outside play or interaction with nature, saying that this is more natural. This type of education cannot be truly self-directed if children are not able fully to explore their interests and only some interests are valued. The person in control is still the adult.

Another distinction which is sometimes made is between 'formal' and 'informal' education. Formal education is typically used to describe what happens at school – teacher-led lessons which follow a structured curriculum. Informal education is often used to talk about learning which goes on outside the school environment; it is more spontaneous and is usually more child-centred, but can include things like trips to museums, activity camps or workshops. Again, this distinction is not always important in self-directed education, because a child may choose to follow a formal course in order to learn something specific, and some children may, in fact, prefer more structured learning.

Schools and learning communities can also foster self-directed education, and they take a variety of approaches. Most self-directed schools also have some form of self-governance, and so they go by the name 'democratic schools'. Sudbury-model democratic schools typically avoid all adult-led activities, preferring instead to create a free-flowing space within which children can generate ideas. Schools such as Summerhill and Sands School in Devon offer lessons which are optional. The Hadera-model schools in Israel are the largest democratic schools in the world and they often have various streams which offer varying degrees of structure.

In the rest of this chapter, I will focus on the process of self-directed learning. All the researchers discussed here have looked at learning when the child, not an adult, is in the driving seat.

The Hole in the Wall

Sugata Mitra, living and working in India in the 1990s, had no trouble imagining what happens when children don't go to school. He could see it all around him. Millions of children in India were not going to school and, of those who did go, many of them received a low-quality education. They were lacking in opportunities. Mitra wanted to harness technology to enable children to learn, even when they were far from a school.

So he sunk a computer into a wall near his office in New Delhi, India. The computer had online access and was designed to be accessible to children rather than adults (they put the computers low down the wall so adults would have to stoop to use them). Within a few moments, the children came. Within hours, with no instruction at all, they were surfing the Internet. Within six months, hundreds of local children had learnt how to use the computers, including sending and receiving emails, using programmes and games, and simple troubleshooting. They had also developed a language of their own to describe what they saw on screen.

This was the start of a series of experiments by Mitra and colleagues, termed 'Hole in a Wall', due to the ATM-like nature of the computers. They installed their computer kiosks in locations all over India. Thousands of children became computer literate, and similar kiosks were installed in Cambodia, South Africa and Egypt. Mitra found that children could learn how to use a computer independently of their educational level, literacy, socioeconomic status, intelligence, or any of the other factors which usually affect educational performance.

Mitra termed this 'minimally invasive education' (MIE), and over many experiments observed the learning process. This started with a discovery, usually accidental, which was observed by other children. These observers would repeat the discovery themselves and, in that process, they would make more discoveries. They would start to create a vocabulary to describe what was going on, and this would help them to generalise. They would discuss their findings with each other and share knowledge. At some point, no further discoveries would be made, and the children would repeat what they already knew. Then, another discovery would occur, either by accident or through new information introduced by a passing adult or child. This would start off a new cycle of learning. And round they would go again.

The research group identified that in order for this process to happen, certain conditions had to be met. The computer had to be outside, in a safe and public location. Many of the computers were in school playgrounds and were specially designed to survive life outside in India, all year round. Perhaps counterintuitively, sharing the computer was also crucial. The group of children was the medium within which exploration and discovery happened. The social context meant that each child did not have to discover everything by themselves, and the discussions between children led to new learning. Mitra also says that the computer use should not be supervised by an adult, and the kiosks were made clearly for children and not adults. Lastly, the computers and the Internet connection had to be reliable.

Mitra has showed that children can learn other subjects using technology, without teachers. He has found that Tamil-speaking children from a remote village could learn biotechnology from an outdoor computer, even when all the information was in English. Their scores on a test of biotechnology rose from 0 at the start to 30 per cent, comparable to scores at a local state school where the children were taught biotechnology. They added in a friendly and encouraging adult who knew nothing about biotechnology and found that the children's test scores rose to 50 per cent —equivalent to a control group who were fluent English speakers in a private school in Delhi. Other studies have found that children can improve their own pronunciation of English when given voice recognition software to play with. The software doesn't recognise their heavily accented English and so they adjust their speech to become more comprehensible.

Mitra moved to the UK and started testing his theories on children there. He went to Gateshead and worked with teachers to set up Self-Organised Learning Environments (SOLE) in primary schools. The basic idea was that several groups of children each shared a computer with an Internet connection. They were given GCSE-level questions to answer together (these were much harder than they would normally be attempting, as they were still at primary school). They were allowed to move around, to chat and to look at other groups. They were able to answer most of the questions. Two months later, they were tested in a typical exam situation, alone and without a computer. They still knew the answers. Some of them even did better than they had the first time round.

The connections between the children were a crucial part of the learning process that Mitra describes. The self-organisation he observed wasn't in each individual child, it was between children. Learning was shared. There was no competition and no expectation that they worked on their own. No instruction, no expert teacher and no curriculum. The Hole in the Wall experiments were so far away from what happens in a typical school as to be almost unrecognisable as education. And yet the children learnt, and retained what they learnt.

Learning without Teaching

This wouldn't surprise Harriet Pattison. Now a lecturer in Early Childhood Studies at Liverpool Hope University, she started off her career in education by home-educating her own children. Intrigued by what she observed, she decided to do an Open University course, hoping for insights into how they were learning about the world. When we talked, she explained how disappointed she was.

'There were so many things that stood out to me about the way my children behaved and the kind of things that they did. Things like their creativity, their imagination, their resourcefulness – the absorption that they had in the things that they did, the kinds of associations they made. And those things, they just didn't come up in the theories at all. I was thinking, where are they, what happened to them?'

Luckily for Pattison, the tutor on her OU course was Alan Thomas. Thomas is a developmental psychologist, currently a visiting lecturer at UCL Institute of Education, and with a strong interest in informal learning. As he explained to me, his interest started with wondering what went on when children were learning one-to-one.

'Everyone seemed to go into the magical ground between the teacher and the learner – the one-to-one if you like. And you don't get one-to-one at school. The only way you can get that is in home education. So that's what took me towards home education, to look at the one-to-one teaching to learning as I thought. [And then] I had my epiphany moment and discovered that lots of children weren't being taught at all. So, I thought, wow, this is amazing, and that's how I started my research.'

The Informal Curriculum

Thomas started to look at informal learning in home-educated children. He carried out in-depth interviews with a hundred families, half in Australia and half in the UK. Thomas's own preconceptions were challenged as he listened to these families.

'Lots of parents would start off quite formally. They'd take the children out of school, they'd think, "We have to start," and then the children would educate them. They would resist teaching. So, what I thought was magical was that these parents who were beginning to question mainstream education, they were like their own scientists, they were going with what worked. And what worked for them was nothing like what worked in schools.'

Thomas called what he observed 'the informal curriculum'. 'The informal curriculum is the world around you. And you just pick it up. I've reflected since then, it's not magical picking up. I often wonder if there's more teaching in informal education than there is in formal education, but it's more at the direction of the child. Parents have things around; they have books, so in a sense there's a lot of subtle passing on of knowledge and information and if a child isn't interested, you stop. There's absolutely no point [in continuing]. In a classroom, you have to continue but, at home, if someone is not listening to you and their eyes are glazed, there's no point.'

It's an important difference between informal learning and formal learning at school. Teachers have to carry on with their plan, doing what they can to keep the class engaged. Outside the classroom, when the child stops being interested, they move on.

I wonder whether this will mean that a child only has a fragmented and incomplete knowledge of the world, because their learning is often in small snippets, rather than in structured lessons. Thomas doesn't think so.

'What's formal is in the child's head. They construct it in their own way. I think I wrote once that curriculum logic and psychological logic do not equate. A curriculum is constructed by adults, thinking about children, but the children construct the knowledge in their own way.'

An analogy might be a puzzle. Children collect pieces of a puzzle and put them together, forming their own view of the world. A structured curriculum presents a puzzle which is already completed, and the teacher tries to communicate this to the child. In informal learning, the children make their own puzzle and often find their own pieces. So each completed puzzle will be different, and it can be taken apart and redone if a new piece arrives that doesn't fit.

The Messiness of Real Life

This doesn't make for neatly done puzzles, as Thomas told me.

'Informal education is messy. Like early childhood is messy, but they all come through it. By the time they are five, they are talking, they have picked up knowledge without being directly taught by schoolteachers. But [for schooled children] that comes to an end when you're five.'

Thomas tells me that he thinks the idea that we can transmit a fully formed understanding of a subject to children via teaching is far from proven. The teaching is just hot air unless a change takes place in the mind of the child.

In this way, we could think of all learning as self-directed, because we can never control what another person actually learns. Even children in school, being taught a standardised curriculum, will all emerge with a different understanding of the subject and different skill levels. Figure 4.1 below illustrates this. Jo, Poppy and Isaac are classmates, all apparently learning how to add fractions. Their teacher is delivering a carefully prepared lesson. Each child's experience of that lesson is very different.

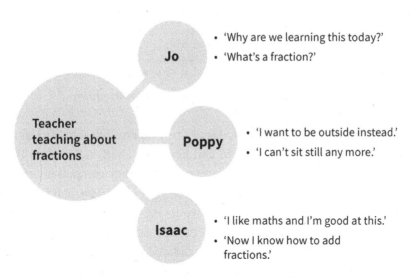

Figure 4.1 – Formal learning of fractions

From this perspective, control over children's learning is largely an illusion. You simply can't control what is going on in someone else's head, no matter how hard you try.

Figure 4.2 – Informal learning about fractions

Informal learning, by contrast, doesn't rely on an adult reliably transmitting information to multiple children. The child, rather than the teacher, is at the centre of the process and thus they can pull in information from wherever it comes. As my daughter learnt about fractions, she started by dividing cakes into two to share with her brother, and then into four to share with me and her dad as well. She would work out how boxes of ice lollies could be divided up fairly – six ice lollies between four of us means one and a half each, a tricky number when it came to ice lollies. One day she came and showed me a picture she'd drawn of different shapes divided into various fractions, and I showed her how to write a fraction. She played a bit with a maths app and did some exercises in a workbook. She understands fractions, but no one except her has ever planned her learning. Figure 4.2 shows this process.

Of course, the implications of this are frightening for many adults. If we can't control what a child learns, then how will they learn things we think are vital, like reading?

What If They Never Learn to Read?

After finishing her OU courses, Harriet Pattison decided to investigate this question, looking at how informally educated children learnt to read. She explained to me what she discovered.

'The main finding was that there were no hard and fast rules about learning to read. There is no essential core to this thing. There is no one thing, or two things, or three things that have to happen for reading to be accomplished . . . it's an incredibly diverse, plastic kind of process.'

Pattison asked 311 home-educating families to tell her how their children learnt to read. She described the responses as like opening the floodgates. Parents wrote pages and pages. What they wrote was challenging to mainstream ideas about reading acquisition.

'One of the most interesting things was that people who did clearly live in a highly literate environment read to their children and did lots of things which would probably count as literacy activities with their children; their children might not learn to read until they were in their early teens. So just exactly what this environment does, I didn't think was clear. It's very much pushed into the mainstream thinking that you've got to read to your children every night, and you've got to have this very concerted cultivation, and there were families that were doing that, and yet their children didn't start reading early and some started a lot later.'

She found that many of the children started reading much later than age seven, and this did not seem to indicate any underlying difficulty, because when they did start, they quickly caught up. But here, too, she emphasised how even when parents decided to intervene, this was unlikely to be a systematic, long-term intervention – and that this didn't seem to matter. The children still learnt to read.

'There were lots of incidences of parents saying, "I wanted them to learn informally but nothing was happening, and they were eight or nine, so I thought we've got to intervene now." Typically, what would happen would be that they'd made some kind of intervention, they'd say to the child, "We're going to do this thing." They'd get materials together, get some resources and say, "This is how we're going to tackle it." And then they'd say [to me], "We gave it up, because we were arguing, we weren't enjoying it." They'd give it up, and then maybe a varied time period later, maybe a couple of years later, the child would start reading. And that was quite a typical story.'

Another interesting group were the children who were specifically taken out of school because they had not learnt to read, and this was causing them difficulties with their progress at school.

'There was one girl who came out of school aged eight and her parents were told she was in the bottom 3 per cent of the country. She'd been labelled with all sorts of dyslexia and ADHD. Her parents said she was so paranoid about reading they couldn't go anywhere near it, they couldn't sit and read with her.

'So they did other things with her, followed her education in other ways, and she started reading by herself aged fourteen. She is highly dyslexic, she counts herself as highly dyslexic, but she went on to college and reads novels for pleasure. I was very, very struck by this. There were three stories in the research like that and I was very struck by them because, in our education system, if you're in the bottom 3 per cent of reading aged eight, you don't go on to college, you don't go on to read novels for pleasure.'

Pattison's research is striking. Not only did she find that many assumptions about learning to read did not hold outside of school, but she also found that perhaps school practices create problems where none need to exist. A late-reading child at school will generally be diagnosed with a learning disability. A late-reading child outside school might simply learn a bit later with no lasting effects, rather in the way that learning to walk at age eight months or eighteen months makes no difference at all to later walking ability. School learning relies on reading, but self-directed education does not. The wider scope of learning methods means that non-reading children can learn from audiobooks, videos, conversations, games and day-to-day experiences, without missing out because they can't yet read.

Play, Curiosity and Sociability

On the other side of the Atlantic, another psychologist was puzzling over how children learnt without being taught. Like Alan Thomas,

Peter Gray, Research Professor in Psychology at Boston College, hadn't planned to spend his career researching alternatives to school. He explained to me how it happened.

'I was brought into it when my own son was rebelling at school. I was doing a very different type of research at the time. He clearly wasn't going to adapt to school. He was refusing to follow the rules in school, and it was clear he needed something else. He made that very clear.'

The something else that Gray found was Sudbury Valley School (SVS) in Massachusetts, a democratic self-directed school.

As mentioned in Chapter 1, SVS has no scheduled lessons; children are free to do what they like, as long as it doesn't intrude upon the freedom of others or break the school rules, which are made and enforced by the students and staff together.

Gray, a successful product of the traditional school system himself, was concerned about his son's future. In order to reassure himself, as he told me when we talked, he carried out a survey of graduates.

'That convinced me that I didn't have to worry, that they were doing fine out there in the world. But it also intrigued me, because here they are, they're not doing much that looks like school and yet they are going on to live successful lives. They are going on to higher education if they choose to do so. How is it that they are becoming educated? What's actually happening with them? Looks like they are just playing and goofing around and doing what you would expect kids to do and yet they are becoming educated.'

Whereas the children that Thomas and Pattison studied were home-educated, and thus had an adult close at hand most of the time, the children at SVS were in a group environment. Therefore, they might be said to be even more 'untaught' than the home-educated children, who were frequently in conversation with their parents and often on the receiving end of a lot of informal teaching.

Perhaps because of this, Gray's research focused less on the process between children and adults, and more on what it is in the children which enables them to educate themselves. Gray suggests that children have biological drives which enable them to educate themselves when in an adequately equipped environment. He traces this back to human evolution, arguing that children in hunter-gatherer societies were able to educate themselves through unstructured play and that the innate nature of human children is unchanged from this time.

The observations that Gray did at Sudbury Valley School led him to develop a particular interest in play. In his view, the dramatic decline in the amount of time children have available for free play, combined with increasingly high pressure at school, accounts for the high increases in childhood anxiety and depression which we are seeing in Western cultures.

Innate Drives to Learn

Peter Gray explained to me the innate drives with which he felt children become educated.

'Curiosity – that's a no-brainer. You can't look at little children without realising how curious they are. Right from newborn on, they are exploring the world around them. Before they can move, they are exploring the world with their eyes, looking at new things more than old things. As soon as they can move, they are getting into everything because they want to see what they can do with it, what happens. Squeeze it or drop it, that's curiosity. They come into the world biologically designed to explore the world around them.'

This then interacts with the playfulness of children, and the way in which children use play to practise the skills of their culture.

'Once you start to look seriously at play, you realise that in every culture, children play at the skills that are important to their culture. So, hunter-gatherer kids play with bows and arrows, they play with digging sticks and fire and building dug-out canoes, and music. In our culture, of course, there are so many different things that we do that children play in many different ways but almost all children want to play with computers today. No surprise, right? You cannot exist in this culture without realising that that is the most important tool we've got. So children are just drawn in play to whatever they see. I think they are biologically predisposed to look around [and ask themselves], what is that people do in this culture? What is it that everybody does? What is it that I'm going to have to learn?'

He sees play as the way in which children can also develop emotion-regulation skills, through putting themselves at risk and developing their confidence. And the two things – curiosity and play – work together in tandem, as Gray sees it.

'Curiosity is how you learn answers to the questions that you have about the world, and play is how you develop skills.'

Then, crucially, he adds sociability, by which he also means the desire to learn from other people and to understand what is in their minds. Figure 4.3 shows this theory in schematic form. He sees sociability as a magnifier of learning – because the child no longer has to rely on their own curiosity and playfulness, they can also learn from the learning of others. As he says, this means that when one child discovers something, the other children in the group can all learn that, too, without having to make the discovery separately for themselves. This is what moves human learning beyond trial and error.

'This is what makes culture possible; the accumulation of culture. Every generation is paying attention to what the previous generation is doing ... They also naturally share knowledge with their friends, so one child's discovery becomes the discovery of the whole cohort.'

Figure 4.3 – Peter Gray's theory of the innate drives which enable self-directed education

Alongside play, curiosity and sociability, Gray also considers the ability to plan things, which he calls 'planfulness', as innate and important. There's something else, too, a quality which has not traditionally been valued by educationalists – 'wilfulness'.

'So, wilfulness, that's the early understanding of the child – not cognitive understanding but a gut-level understanding – that I have to be independent. I have to practise being my own person. I am dependent on all these people, I need to learn from all these people, I need to make connections with all these people. But, ultimately, I have to make my own decisions.'

Gray's central argument is that we can best harness these innate drives that all children possess through providing an environment within which they can educate themselves. This is in contrast to the approach of traditional school, which works to control and sometimes to squash these impulses. Think of how some schools limit interactions between students as they walk from class to class. There's a chance right there for a child to explain something to another child and for new learning to occur. It doesn't happen because, at these schools, learning is what happens when you listen to the teacher.

He makes the point that a child is always their own person, with their own interests. 'Because the truth of the matter, and evolutionary psychologists are very aware of this, is that even the parents' interests are not the same as the child's interests. There are often conflicts. So the child who would just obey is not going to be the child who is going to be successful.'

So what is needed for self-directed education to work? These sets of research come from different countries and cultures, and from very different starting points. They all observed children learning without formal teaching – street children in India, home-educated children in Australia and the UK, and democratically schooled children in the USA. Yet there are similarities in the process that they observe.

Connections and Space

For all of them, connections with other people are vital. Children cannot learn in isolation. This connection may be with other children, as in Mitra's and Gray's work, or mostly with a parent, as in Thomas's and Pattison's work. But a close relationship with other people who can immediately give feedback and add in new information is crucial.

The other essential element is space for the child to explore. Whether that is created by placing a computer outside, away from adult eyes, or by a self-directed learning community, a child needs to have opportunities to try out new things, to discover and ask questions without fear of judgement. The environment needs opportunities. For the Indian children, access to a computer meant that they did not need teachers; for the home-educated children, access to a parent ready to answer questions and discuss things with them provided a similar opportunity to explore.

Motivation is not a problem in this type of learning, because the child is free to start and stop when they want to. These researchers tell a story of children who are fully equipped from birth with the drives that they need to educate themselves, but who need the right opportunities and environment to do so. This sort of learning starts with discovery and multiplies when children can observe the discoveries of others.

An Environment of Opportunities

This research also makes clear why self-directed education is not the same thing as simply leaving children alone. Peter Gray expanded on this.

'In self-directed learning, children are going to learn what's in their environment. So, if people aren't reading, if they aren't talking about intellectual ideas, if people aren't speaking standard English, they're not going to learn those skills. And you could argue that those skills aren't so important but, if you believe that it's important to rise up within the culture, then you do need to acquire the skills that allow you to do so. It helps to speak standard English; you need to be able to read and write and work with numbers, and so on. And if you're growing up in a family where there's not much of that going on, and there's not much of that going on in your neighbourhood, then you're not going to acquire those skills.'

Adults Who Have the Children's Interests at Heart

Alan Thomas puts it differently. What he sees as vital is the relationship between parents and children, for parents will then create a learning environment for their children.

'[You need] . . . just a love for your children. That sounds clichéd almost but, if you've got love, it means you've got their interests at heart. You want them to read, you want them to be articulate, to be confident, to relate well to other people. You want all those things. You've set their lives apart. There's lots of teaching involved, without the children realising, and without the parents realising – setting up things, saying, "Do you think they might be interested?"'

Questions to Explore

Sugata Mitra suggests that schools need to shift their emphasis away from instruction towards enquiry to enable self-organised learning. He writes: 'They [children] need a learning environment and a source of rich, big questions. Computers can give out answers, but they cannot, as yet, make questions.'

Mitra thinks that teachers need to pose the questions but, in my experience, children themselves are a wonderful source of questions, particularly when they have never been told that it's time to focus on listening to a teacher instead of formulating their own thoughts. Their curiosity equips them with the ability to investigate the world through questions. When they can ask questions of each other, we would expect to see the social multiplying effect, resulting in them learning to ask better and more sophisticated questions.

Control Over Their Own Lives

When schools focus on following an academic programme of learning, they prevent children from learning in all the rich and varied ways available to them. They, in fact, deliberately attempt to limit children to only one form of learning. By doing this, we have no idea what other things those children are missing out on. The more controlling adults are over a child's environment, the more we risk them not learning the skills they may need in adult life.

As Peter Gray explains, what makes children convenient for adults may not serve them well in later life. We're not used to thinking about behaviour in terms of convenience; more typically we talk about 'good' or 'bad' behaviour. When we start to see all behaviour as communication, this makes no sense. 'Bad behaviour' is usually an expression of distress, while 'good behaviour' means compliance with adult expectations, which is generally far more convenient for the adults around the child. However, in the longer term, being focused on meeting the expectations of adults will not lead to that child developing an understanding of their own motivations and values.

Wilfulness, on the other hand, Gray considers to be an unexpected asset. 'That wilfulness, if we think about it on the positive side, is a drive to take charge of my own life. That drive for me to be in charge of my own life is part of the key to self-directed education. I need to figure out what I need to learn . . . I need to work out what I want to do in this world . . . I need to figure out how to make my way in this world . . . Although I can listen to other people, I can't depend on any other person, even my mother and father, to know better than me.'

From the outside, it can appear as if self-directed education requires little or no input from the adults around a child. This is because we are used to thinking that unless adults are controlling a child, we are doing nothing. We look for instruction, for teaching and work done, and when we don't see it, we assume that there is nothing else happening. In fact, self-directed education takes place in the interaction between a child and their environment, and the role of the adult is to create or choose that environment. Much of the work involved in doing this is invisible and, if it goes well, the child themselves will have no idea how much work has gone into their education. Unlike at school, where the work of educating is clearly arduous 'work', the work of a self-directed facilitator could involve being available to play games, making sure there are interesting books available in the library, looking out for local events and arranging meet-ups with friends. All of these will contribute to a child living in an interesting environment, full of opportunities for learning.

Further Reading

Gray, Peter – *Free to Learn*, Basic Books (2015)

Mitra, Sugata – *The School in the Cloud: The Emerging Future of Learning*, Corwin (2019)

Pattison, Harriet – *Rethinking Learning to Read*, Educational Heretics Press (2016)

Thomas, A & Pattison, H – *How Children Learn at Home*, Continuum (2008).

5

From Toddlers to Teens –
How Does Learning Change as
Children Grow?

Shula stood out as different, right from the start. When all the other children started pretending, rocking their dolls or making their cars go 'vroom', Shula was only interested in how things worked. She would spend hours watching the washing machine. As they walked along the street, Shula stood fascinated at the sight of cranes, rubbish trucks and road cleaners. At home, she would reconstruct them with cardboard boxes, plasticine and Duplo. She resisted all attempts to engage her in pretend tea parties, instead using the plates as wheels for the vehicles which she made but never played with. Her parents were concerned; other parents were muttering 'autism' under their breath to each other with raised eyebrows.

Then, one day when Shula was five, she climbed into a cardboard box. 'Vroom ... vroom ... we're off to the seaside!' she said. Her mother nearly fell over backwards in surprise. It was the first time Shula had pretended she was doing something. From that moment on, Shula started imaginative play. She made elaborate maps for her vehicles, but now she also took the vehicles on trips and told stories about what happened there. She set up shops to sell the things she made to her parents.

But Shula was five; she was at school. Most of the other children had been doing imaginative play since they were two or younger, and the messages they were getting was that the time for it to be their main focus was drawing to an end. Play was to be for playtime.

Shula's parents decided to keep her at home from school for a year so that she could focus on what she wanted to do right then. They felt that she needed the space to carry out the imaginative playing which, for some reason, she had not done when younger. So they gave her the space for unlimited play. They didn't tell her she was too big now and needed to focus on learning to read; they trusted her instincts and followed her lead.

In that year, Shula played with younger children who weren't yet at school and who loved pretend play. She played trains in the playground, and shops in the bushes. She told elaborate stories and drew pictures to illustrate them. Shula's social skills developed in leaps and bounds. At the end of the year, Shula's parents decided to keep on educating her at home, because they could see that Shula's instincts as to what she needed were spot on, but were often not in line with what school would expect of her.

Self-directed learning is well accepted for one section of our society – the youngest. Most of us have no problem with letting small children direct their own learning through play. This could be because trying to get them to do anything else is such a thankless task but, for whatever reason, young children are generally allowed to learn about the things that they are interested in. They explore their passions to the full. The intensity of these passions often surprises their parents, who find themselves with an extensive digger collection and making regular special trips to the building site at the other side of the park without knowing quite how it happened.

The result of this is that young children learn about quite different things. One learns about dinosaurs, another about the properties of mud and sand. One is fascinated by My Little Pony, while another can't get enough of Pokémon. These differences don't worry most parents, because they can see that the skills children are learning are higher-order skills – how to interact with other people, logical reasoning, how different concepts can fit together, how to plan a story or play a character. We don't expect young children to be learning useful information, and so we allow them to explore their interests, and acquire skills through doing so.

At some point between the ages of three and eight (depending on the country you live in and whether your parents pay for private school or not), these days of individualised learning come to an abrupt end. It's no longer acceptable to spend all your days pretending to be a dinosaur. This doesn't happen by accident. When a child starts school, the adults around them deliberately impose a new sort of learning. They start gently with little groups on phonics and reading diaries sent home. Within a couple of years, they have moved children on to spending most of the day seated at a table, completing tasks set by adults. Learning becomes something which is done because an adult says so, rather than because the child wants to know.

As this happens, learning becomes separated from its purpose. Maths starts to be about getting the right answers, rather than being a way to understand quantities and patterns we see around us. Reading is about putting together the right sounds to decode a word, rather than communication.

It's a big change. Before school, all skills are learnt because they are meaningful and useful for the child right now. But at school, the skills learnt are for the future – for the child, an unimaginably distant future where things like grammar and decimals will be all-important in some unspecified way. They aren't learnt because the child needs and wants to know them for their life right now, or even for their own future goals.

Adults do this for the child's benefit. They don't believe that children will learn necessary life skills without being made to do so by an adult.

In this chapter, I'll talk about how humans learn at different ages. I'll discuss the different ways in which learning is approached at different life stages. I'll also talk about how school interacts with children's developmental trajectories and what effect this has on their lives.

The Discovery Approach Just Isn't Going to Work

David Geary, Curators' Professor in the Department of Psychological Sciences at the University of Missouri, explained one perspective on the different ways that children learn in the *Times Educational*

Supplement in April 2020: 'Once you get to real academic learning, the child discovery approach is just not going to work.'

Geary makes a distinction between primary and secondary knowledge. Primary knowledge includes things we can pick up from the world around us – our native language, relating to other people, using tools which we see other people using around us. He suggests that children are innately predisposed to learning the things which are most important in their environment and typically need no explicit instruction to do this – in a similar way to Peter Gray's description of learning. However, Geary sees this type of learning as time-limited, and only appropriate when learning certain types of skills.

He defines academic skills as 'secondary knowledge'. These are skills which humans did not need to survive in pre-history and which, therefore, our brains have not evolved to learn. Reading, writing, algebra, essay writing – none of these were useful to our ancestors. He argues, 'Once you get to the non-evolved skills, the brain is not easily structured to learn those, so the structured environment has to provide that organisation to the child's experiences. The teacher is providing the structure that the brain is not providing. So one of the important distinctions is that the things that are sufficient for learning primary knowledge are not going to be sufficient in learning in secondary domains. There have been educational theories that have not made that distinction – whole word, whole maths and so on.'

It's an appealing theory and it seems to make intuitive sense. Plenty of educators who consider themselves progressive take this approach: let the children play up to a certain point, and then it's time to (gently) make them knuckle down for their own good.

Like many attractive theories, there are some nuggets of truth and then some huge leaps of logic. It's true that there is a lot which children won't just pick up from the world around them, and that this knowledge may be important for their futures. Learning how to take an exam, for example, is likely to be something that needs to be intentionally learnt –this is something I'll come back to in Chapter 6.

However, part of the story is missing.

There is another group of people for whom the majority of their education is led by their own interests. Like young children, they choose what they want to learn and how they want to learn it and, when they have had enough, they stop. Unlike young children, these people often engage in structured learning courses, which they may or may not complete. Apart from formal studying, they use a wide range of methods to learn, including YouTube videos, games, conversations, TV programmes, tutoring sessions and books. And who are these people?

Adults.

Adults acquire 'secondary knowledge' all the time. They learn because they want to, or they see a need for it in their career or life. Not only do adults not need to be obliged to learn, they will pay thousands of pounds for it. Adults don't just learn in order to get qualifications; many of us enjoy learning, particularly about things which interest us and in which we find purpose. Currently, I'm paying a French teacher to tell me where my worst language errors are. I anticipate paying her for a long time and I'm grateful for the opportunity to do so.

Our school system makes the assumption that between the ages of five and sixteen, young people must be made to learn. It isn't just structured learning that they are thought to need, it is *compulsory* structured learning. The link between compulsory learning and structured learning is so strong in our minds that many of us don't question the assumption that, in order for children to learn in a structured way, they must be compelled to do so.

Yet young children learn without compulsion, and so do adults. Why do we believe that compulsion is necessary for those aged between five and sixteen?

School or Disaster

One reason which is often given for compulsory learning is that the skills children need to acquire are just too important to risk the disaster of not acquiring them. Parents think that if they don't force their children to do maths, they are leaving it 'up to chance'. Reading is another area where the perceived alternative to compulsion – not learning to read – is seen as just too high-risk. We all know that there are many people in the world who do not learn to read, and so therefore that it is possible.

Some psychologists would agree. Geary thinks that children's brains cannot construct their own internal structure when learning academic information and that teachers need to do this for them. Traditional educationalists would agree, advocating a curriculum packed with information chosen by adults for children they don't know. This is often called the 'knowledge-rich' curriculum.

Other experts on learning disagree. Developmental psychologists noticed early on that children's learning is always an interaction between what they already understand and their experiences. Children bring their own beliefs and understanding to every situation and, rather than taking on someone else's structure wholesale, they construct their own 'mental models'. This is one reason why learning gets easier the more we know. As our mental models get more sophisticated, we can add new information into our existing framework, rather than having to start from the beginning each time. This means that learning is always individualised. Even a standardised environment such as school does not result in the same learning for every child.

The environment a child is in plays a crucial part in their education. If a child is surrounded with people who cannot or do not read, with no opportunities to learn, they cannot learn to read. This isn't the only alternative to formal schooling, however.

Discussions on education outside school are plagued by false dichotomies. As with Geary, traditional educationalists talk as if the only two options are a compulsory structured curriculum, or child-led discovery learning. As they would put it, formal school, or leaving education up to chance. They can get away with this because, after twelve years of schooling, most of us believe that if we hadn't been forced, we would never have chosen to challenge ourselves or to learn anything difficult. This isn't really surprising. Schools often explicitly tell us that we must be made to learn and that learning we choose for ourselves is less valuable. We distrust our ability to manage our own learning and so, in turn, we teach our children to distrust themselves.

It's true that if your priority is ensuring that all children learn the same things, you can't allow the children much choice about this. It's a contradiction in terms. When genuine choice enters education, we have to allow for the possibility that children's learning will become more individualised. It's not a genuine choice to say you can learn whatever you want, as long as you cover the contents of the Key Stage 2 History textbook. Whether or not you think that individual differences in learning is a problem depends on how you see education. Should it be a standardised process of all children learning the same things, or should it be about the child learning how to manage their own learning, with this process being more important than any specific content?

Adults are highly idiosyncratic, and their learning is equally non-standardised. You can see this if you get any group of adults together and ask them for their views on how a range of world problems should be solved – climate change, for example, or poverty. Reading a Facebook thread on any vaguely controversial issue also illustrates this point. Adults have very different concepts of the world; this affects what they learn from any new information they come across. Learning is a process of adding new information to our world view and making sense of what we see in the context of what we know already. It's never an objective process.

Again, it seems that the rules are different for those aged between five and sixteen. Individuality and diversity are important for adults. It's how they develop specialist skills. But for school-aged children, the curriculum doesn't allow for the development of strong preferences or interests until you get beyond the compulsory years, by which time many have already lost their joy in learning.

Just Learn It!

Another reason given for controlling children's learning is that it is the most efficient way for them to learn. It feels more efficient to tell children what we want them to know, and it seems quicker than giving them the opportunities to work things out for themselves. If all children could quickly learn essential information and skills from teachers, then it might be much more effective for them to do this. That would free them up to spend more time doing the things they love.

Unfortunately, anyone who has spent time in a school knows that children do not all quickly learn the information which is taught to them. Even when they do learn it, they often don't retain it. There is a fair amount of research which shows that children forget some of what they learn in school over the long summer holidays. This has led some to call for summer schools and shorter holidays. The effect is particularly strong for children from deprived backgrounds, perhaps because they are spending their summer doing fewer 'school-like' activities than their wealthier peers. Of course, there is the obvious point that children may be learning other things over the summer holidays which are not measured by school tests, and which are valuable. Practical skills such as cycling, swimming and cooking come to mind, as well as more abstract skills such as problem solving and time management.

However, if we accept that children are forgetting some of what they learn in school over the summer, then it begs the question: just how are children meant to be able to use their learning in the future, if they can't even keep hold of it over the few weeks of the summer holidays? Schools are all about learning now, so that you'll be able to use it later. How can it be justified to teach children things which they don't need now but will need in the future, when it's clear that they are rapidly forgetting what is taught to them?

One reason why this forgetting happens is that for lasting learning to occur, each child has to build their own internal understanding of the world. At school, there often isn't the time and space for this to happen. All but the quickest have to move on before they have really grasped each topic. Others can help, but they can't do the learning for the child. We retain information better when it makes sense to us and we have understood it for ourselves.

Imagine two children learning about decimals for the first time. They are both confused; they don't understand why the decimal point goes where it goes, nor how a decimal relates to a fraction. Why is the fraction $1/2$ but the decimal 0.5? The teacher patiently explains and illustrates. Suddenly, one child's eyes light up, they understand, and they are off, able to work out the decimals for $1/3$ and $1/4$ by themselves. But the child sitting next to them can't see what the fuss is about. They just don't get it, even after hearing the same teacher explain. They laboriously go through the steps in the workbook, but they don't understand why they are doing so. They may not have their 'Aha!'

moment for another year or two. In the meantime, they will be confused and frustrated and they will quickly forget any information they have apparently learnt, because it doesn't make sense to them.

That first child has just made a connection. They've had a flash of insight, a moment of discovery. Even if others have discovered decimals before, this child has worked it out anew, right now.

This process of making connections creates structure. Think of a time when you've had to learn something new in a short space of time. Perhaps starting a new job in a new area. Typically, for the first few weeks you'll feel at sea. Nothing will really make sense and you will feel incompetent and deskilled. If you keep going and are able to tolerate this time of uncertainty, after a few weeks things will start to fall into place. You'll construct a mental model of the area, and you'll be able to add new information to your existing model. In order to learn effectively, we need to be able to be able to tolerate a time where nothing quite makes sense. We need to learn how to be uncertain and to remain open to different possibilities.

Unfortunately, schools can't allow time for each child to come to their own understanding, because they need to be hurried on to the next stage of the curriculum. Instead of constructing mental models, children have to fall back on memorisation and rote learning. What they are learning just doesn't make sense to them and they haven't got time to work it out in their own way.

Outside school, however, what happens? Do children continue to make mud pies for ever, never acquiring difficult information or paying attention beyond the point where their initial interest wanes? Do they remain in the moment, like toddlers, always at the whim of their next distraction?

What Happens as Children Develop?

The most fundamental principle in developmental psychology is this: children of different ages are different. They think differently, they experience the world differently, and no matter how much a four-year-old learns, they will never think like a fourteen-year-old; they will just be an extraordinarily well-informed four-year-old.

This sounds obvious, but it wasn't always widely accepted. The concept of childhood as a period of life where children are understood to have different needs and responsibilities to adults is a relatively recent one.

This difference is not just due to learning. Brains develop over time. The way in which they develop is down to the experience of the person, but it's also due to biology. The brain of a small child is qualitatively different to that of an older child, which is different again to that of a teenager. This development is important, because it's my argument that the shift in how we learn, which is assumed to be due to schooling, is, in fact, largely due to brain development, and *it would happen anyway*. Adults are more sophisticated and think differently to children, no matter how much formal education they have had.

Cross-cultural studies bear this out. There are differences between people who have been to school and those who haven't – children who have been to school are better at memorising lists, for example, and remembering information which doesn't makes sense to them. They do better at things that they have been taught to do and which do not occur in life outside school, like taking tests. Adults who do not go to school may (or may not) lack academic skills but their thinking is still qualitatively different to that of children. The idea that some adults are like children has, in fact, been used as justification in the past for oppression and control of entire cultural groups. English and French colonialists in the nineteenth and twentieth centuries saw African and Asian people as more like children than adults. They used this to justify their authoritarian and brutal regimes, casting themselves in a parental role. Needless to say, there is absolutely no evidence that adults who have not received a formal education continue to need parenting.

Those who haven't been to school are better at learning through observation and often demonstrate knowledge in their lives which they can't show in tests. They remain in a state of 'alert awareness' for longer, learning from their environment rather than waiting for instruction. Children who sell things for a living demonstrate sophis-ticated mathematical knowledge in the course of their work but can't necessarily pass tests of the same concepts. Schooled children can show the same pattern in reverse – they can pass tests but not apply their learning to practical situations.

Becoming an Expert Learner

Developmental psychologist Alison Gopnik closely observes how children learn. She describes the shift which happens from the early years of discovery to later 'mastery learning'. Mastery learning is about improving your skills, about getting good at something; this is the sort of learning children need to acquire secondary knowledge.

Young children are all about discovery. They explore, they investigate, they rip apart – and then they move on. Their concentration span is short. They are apt to wander off halfway through a book or get bored and head off to another activity. As my daughter used to say once we had got out the Lego or blocks, 'You can stay here and play, Mummy ... I'm going to do something else.' And off she went to create havoc in the kitchen.

As children get older, this changes. When my son was nine, he decided to learn to cycle. He'd tried before but had never persisted for long. When he fell off, he would give up. But the summer he was nine, he decided that he was going to make it happen. He got on that bike again and again, and he fell off again and again. I tried to advise but it didn't really help. He spent several afternoons falling off, and then he started to stay on for longer and longer. By the end of the summer, he could ride his bicycle all around the cul de sac. Now, he can't remember why it was so hard; riding a bike feels natural to him. Something had changed, meaning that he could now persist, when before he would have given up. He was ready for mastery learning. Many assume that this change is due to formal schooling, but children who do not go to school also make this shift.

This shift can be seen even in children who are have serious problems paying attention at school and who are sent for diagnostic assessments for ADHD. Many of these children are expert in topics which are not valued at school – playing Fortnite, for example; or YouTubers; or football. They are frequently able to apply themselves very well to learning things which interest them. The trouble they have is with concentrating on something which school thinks they should be doing. They can do mastery learning, but not on demand.

This is an important distinction that schools do not make. There's a difference between being capable of learning effectively, and learning what school wants you to learn. If children are in control of their learning, many more of them can learn effectively, including those labelled with learning disabilities. This is because, for many children, their problem is not actually their lack of capacity to learn but their lack of desire to learn what school dictates.

From a developmental perspective, it doesn't actually matter what children choose to focus on as they shift to mastery learning. The higher-order skill they are practising is how to learn effectively. Once they know how to do that, they can apply it to different situations. From an informal appraisal of the self-directed children I know (who are all European or American and come from a range of different ethnic groups), I have observed that when children aren't schooled, many of them develop their ability to engage in mastery learning around the age of nine. It doesn't happen overnight. Gradually, children become more purposeful. They manage their emotions better and are less distractible. They have more of an idea as to how to get themselves from a position of not knowing to a place of knowledge.

Learning Like Sponges

People love to say that young children learn more quickly than adults. 'They soak it up like sponges,' they cry. Young children are indeed often open to learning things which are important in the world around them; they learn very efficiently through play and exploration. They are often creative and great lateral thinkers. They acquire languages through immersion. However, try explaining decimals to your average three-year-old. The likelihood is that they will just wander off. Try to get a five-year-old to memorise a list of spellings, and you won't be waxing lyrical about sponges. Very young children may have fewer blocks to their learning – they do not yet believe that they are bad at maths, or useless at languages, for example, but it isn't actually easier for them to learn the stuff that is taught to them at school.

Don't believe me? Look at some of the workbooks used at primary school. Find a topic you yourself know nothing about, perhaps something from science or information technology. How long would it take you to understand the concepts and correctly answer the questions? Do you need to a teacher to explain, or could you work it out for yourself? Usually, adults can grasp the primary curriculum much more quickly than primary-aged children, not because they are more intelligent, but because their brains are more developed, and they have more experience of learning.

This process of development means that humans learn in different ways at different stages of life. I find it very difficult to learn through exploratory play now. Hands-on play just isn't my natural medium. I prefer to read, talk to people or watch videos . . . unlike my nephew, who never stops playing. That's not due simply to my having more knowledge and experience than a three-year-old; it's down to a difference in how our brains work.

Over the last twenty years, the research on brain development has mushroomed, as functional MRI scans have allowed scientists to look at brains working in living people. They can now actually see that brains do indeed change dramatically as people grow. In fact, it seems that brain development continues for far longer than we had assumed, perhaps even into our forties. Even when development stops, our brains visibly change through the process of learning.

One of my favourite research studies is by Katharine Mullet and Eleanor Maguire and looks at exactly this. They were interested in how our brain changes when we learn, and they realised that taxi drivers provided the perfect natural experiment. In order to become a black cab driver in London, you have to pass 'The Knowledge'. This involves memorising a highly detailed layout of London streets. It takes several years of studying for most people to pass and many never do.

The researchers scanned the brains of the drivers before and after they did the studying. Learning The Knowledge successfully resulted in an observable difference in the hippocampal regions in the brains of the aspiring taxi drivers. This ability of the brain to change is called 'neuroplasticity'. Our neurology is shaped by the life we live, starting from before birth. This is why any claims that something is 'hard-wired' should be taken with a pinch of salt. Human brains are exquisitely sensitive to their environment and all of our 'wiring' develops in the context of the life we live.

When Development Clashes with the School System

When I worked in a neurodevelopmental clinic, many children were referred at particular points in their school careers. These children were being sent for diagnostic assessments for autism and ADHD. The main referral points were: aged six, after they had started Year 1 and the curriculum had shifted away from play towards formal instruction; aged eleven, after they had begun secondary school; and aged fourteen, when GCSE courses were beginning.

Are children more developmentally vulnerable at these ages? Do neurodevelopmental problems show up at six, eleven and fourteen, just because that's how it is? Or is it more likely that these were the ages when the school system demanded more, and some of the children simply weren't ready?

We know that a child's level of development matters in the school system. When children start school, each school year group varies in age by almost an entire year. Some children will start school on their fifth birthday, while others will start the day after their fourth. When looked at as a group, these 'summer-born' children do less well in academic tests than their autumn-born peers, and these differences persist right the way through the education system. When they take GCSEs at the age of sixteen, August-born children are 6.4 per cent less likely than September-born children to get five good GCSEs, and 2 per cent less likely to go to university. Since there is really no reason at all to think that children born in August are less capable than those born in September, the difference must be due to the effect of being younger in the school system, and perhaps taking exams when they are younger, too.

Perhaps even more concerning is a study in America which found that summer-born children are 34 per cent more likely to be diagnosed with ADHD than their autumn-born counterparts. We can't really argue that being born in August is more likely to make you hyperactive than being born in September. Immaturity, it seems, is something which counts against you in the school system.

It's worth reflecting on the fact that significant proportion of those summer-born children with ADHD diagnoses will be prescribed drugs. Children are being drugged for being too young for school.

What's the Damage?

Schools impose mastery learning on children who are still at the discovery stage. They give children repetitive exercises, and tasks designed to improve specific skills. They do this because they think the children need it and will not become educated without it. Not doing so seems like a high-risk strategy.

Unfortunately, the process of forcing mastery learning on to children isn't without consequences. It could be seen as a high-risk strategy in its own right. For many, it seriously affects their intrinsic motivation and it prevents them from learning how to manage their own learning during the best chance most people ever get – the teenage years.

The teenage years are special, because this is when young people are becoming capable of intentional, deliberate learning and, in most cases, they do not yet have any responsibilities. By adulthood, most people have to support themselves financially. Adult life is dominated by the need to earn money. Adults quickly acquire other people they need to support too, or other responsibilities such as rent or a mortgage. Learning for yourself, and about yourself, becomes something to squeeze into snatched moments, late at night when the children are asleep, or early in the morning before you have to go to work.

Not so for teenagers; the lucky ones, whose parents can support them, are able to dive into their passions without worrying about whether it will make them any money, and they can try out new things without worrying that they can't pay the rent. They can spend their teenage years working out what makes them feel alive, and how they can manage their own peculiarities and quirks. Many teenagers (although absolutely not all) can get part-time work and use the money for their interests, rather than to pay the bills. If young people can use their teenage years to learn how to live with themselves then, when they become adults, they will not have to start with trying to reconnect with what really matters to them.

This is why the dichotomy which is sometimes drawn between play-based discovery learning and forced learning is a false one. When children can choose how they learn, their learning takes many forms, just as it does with adults. Children don't need to be made to move on from the discovery stage, because they will do it naturally in their own time. This may well take much longer than school allows. Children who are not schooled often play for years longer and acquire skills such as reading and maths years later. It doesn't matter. They can and do acquire the ability to learn in a variety of different ways.

Unstandardised Children

How are children different when they don't go to school? There aren't formal studies which look at this question in Western children. While school is seen as the natural environment of children, no one looks at what happens when it's not there – except for cross-cultural psychologists whose work is often not taken very seriously by those in developmental psychology laboratories in the UK and USA. It is hard to draw conclusions from cross-cultural studies because, when children come from very different cultures, their development may well be different due to environmental differences which go beyond the absence of school. Assessing development outside of school has the added problem of how exactly we should do this.

Cross-cultural studies tell us that many of the tests which are assumed to be free of cultural bias are, in fact, anything but. Even the most basic test-taking skill – answering questions – is culturally influenced. When a child takes a test, they must answer questions which are not 'real'. The tester isn't asking because they want to know the answer; they are asking because they want to know if the child knows the answer. There are cultures where adults do not ask questions of children to which they already know the answer, whereas in Western culture, this type of question is deeply embedded in the way we interact with children. Think of how much of early conversation with young children in Western culture consists of questions to which the adult knows the answer – 'Where's your nose?' we ask of tiny children – thus preparing them for a world where adults ask silly questions and their job is to guess what they want in response.

Close observational studies of children at school show us a process where children's behaviour is constantly and intentionally moulded. Carla Shalaby, author of *Troublemakers* (in which she observed four young children in their early years of school), calls this 'learning school'. It's an environment where compliance and approval-seeking are highly valued, and where creativity and originality are only welcome within the constraints set out by school. Children's success at school is largely dependent on how well they learn the implicit rules of schools – how to talk to teachers, when it's OK to run and when you have to sit quietly, for example.

In contrast, the moulding of behaviour that goes on outside school is much more idiosyncratic, because children do not all have to be coaxed to behave in the same way in order to be manageable at school. There is more space for their personality and preferences to drive their environment. Parents often find this out the hard way, when they try to follow school practices at home and discover that their child does not comply.

The result of this more malleable environment is diversity. Your average home-education group or self-directed learning community is extraordinarily diverse. There will be those who had learnt to read and write aged three, and those who still aren't reading aged thirteen. There are children who never leave their mother's side, and those who run off without a backwards glance. Some children will speak three languages, while others can hardly speak one. There are children who want to do imaginative play, all the time, and others whose whole life is about travelling on buses and who know all the bus routes by heart. Some children spend their whole time on a device listening to headphones, while others are social butterflies.

The structure of school is at odds with the developmental pathways of children. Far from helping children to create an internal structure, imposing formal learning on children who aren't interested or ready leaves many of them confused and anxious. School insists that children sit down and concentrate when they really want to play all day, and tells them that adding fractions is more important than drawing the perfect Pikachu. This can be particularly damaging for children whose developmental trajectories are different to the norm – perhaps they learn to read very early, but don't start imaginative play until they are five. We can't easily go back to earlier developmental stages. Playing like a young child is something that only other young children are really good at. Adults may try hard, but they're pretending to pretend. They're doing it for their child's benefit, rather than because they love to pretend for its own sake. This is much harder work, as any parent of a young child quickly discovers.

The development of children outside school often has a different pace to schooled children. They come back to things over a long period of time. They play for longer. Sometimes they revisit early passions when they are much older, watching *Peppa Pig* or playing with Duplo and playdough aged eight or nine. Because we are used to thinking in standardised school years, the way that we see a child who is different is as having deficits. If a child doesn't do something at the same time as others, then they are thought of as 'behind' and may be offered remedial help so they can 'catch up'. The evidence from children educated outside school indicates that doing things in a different order or at a different pace does not have to be a problem unless a child's environment makes it so. Instead of demanding more conformity from children, we need to demand more flexibility from their education.

As a society, we have very little idea of how diverse human development is outside a school context. We see diversity as a problem, rather than locating the problem in the standardised and narrow environment offered to most children.

When children are in control of their lives and learning, they make highly varied choices and consequently the environments they create around themselves are different. The result is that initial small variations in children become very visible. School requires all children to do similar things at similar ages. Getting an education does not.

Further Reading

Blakemore, Sarah-Jayne – *Inventing Ourselves: The Secret Life of the Teenage Brain*, Black Swan (2019)

Gopnik, Alison – *The Gardener and the Carpenter: What the New Science of Child Development Tells Us about the Relationship between Parents and Children*, Vintage (2017)

Lareau, Annette – *Unequal Childhoods: Class, Race and Family Life*, University of California Press (2011)

Pope, Denise – *Doing School: How We Are Creating a Generation of Stressed Out, Materialistic and Miseducated Students*, Yale University Press (2003)

Rogoff, Barbara – *The Cultural Nature of Human Development*, OUP USA (2003)

Rothermel, Paula – (edited volume) *International Perspectives on Home Education: Do We Still Need Schools?*, Palgrave Macmillan (2015)

Shalaby, Carla – *Troublemakers: Lessons in Freedom from Young Children at School*, The New Press (2017)

6

Outcomes – How Can We Measure Education?

It's summer, which means exam results are out! The papers are full of pictures of jubilant teenagers, literally jumping for joy. Underneath are the articles of statistics, telling us what is different about this particular year group. Some years, girls do better than boys, and some years there's despair about how no one is choosing Physics while too many choose Psychology.

That's it, then – compulsory schooling is over for this set of school-leavers. They've been awarded the set of marks which will follow them around for the rest of their lives, defining them as high achievers, average, or failures. These results will be used to divide up students, deciding who will be allowed to go on to further study and where. But more than that, they will also be used to evaluate the schools and the teachers. No one wants poor exam results.

Exams are the outcome of the school system. They are how we judge whether a young person has succeeded on not and, on a wider level, whether their school is any good. Parents compare schools based on how many 'A's their students acquire, while newspapers rank different schools on how well their students perform. There are even special exams called the Programme for International Student Assessment (PISA) which are carried out every three years in order to compare school systems across countries. Tests like PISA are taken very seriously by the countries who take part, and PISA themselves claim that they are all about inclusivity and improving education for the most deprived students.

It seems to be taken for granted that the way to assess education should be through a competitive test. No one ever mentions that it isn't possible for everyone to be the best, that for every student who does well, another will be disappointed. This goes for countries too. As one country rises in the PISA ranks, another will fall. This is inevitable, because a test which does not result in failure for some is not a good test. Tests are designed to discriminate.

In this chapter, I will first discuss how testing is used in schools and show how standardised testing affects behaviour. I'll then discuss the problem of assessing self-directed education, and why tests designed to assess schooled children cannot be fairly used. Finally, I'll discuss the research which looks at the outcomes for young people who had a self-directed education.

A Culture of Testing

The teenagers receiving their results each year won't be new to formal assessment. Throughout their years of school, they will have been thoroughly tested and monitored. Their teachers were expected to show that they were progressing at a consistent pace, starting before they were potty-trained. In many countries, nurseries for the under-threes are now expected to have plans for what children are meant to be learning, and to constantly assess whether they are performing adequately. Assessment has been woven through the fabric of how the school system works. It's called accountability – for young people, teachers and institutions.

Education should be getting better and better if assessment like this works. Yet there's also a regular panic in the papers about how ill-prepared young people are, how they are stubbornly choosing the wrong subjects (usually those that they find interesting, rather than those which are perceived to be difficult and useful for later life) and how they lack the skills necessary for employment.

It's rare for anyone to ask whether the end point of an education system should be competitive exams. We take that for granted. Exams are a way to categorise people. School-leaving exams sort young people into successes and failures and determine who will be allowed to access further education and professional jobs. Putting competition at the heart of education has consequences for everyone. When the point of education is to do well in the exams at the end, then we are focused on test results, rather than high-quality learning. And, as I'll show in this chapter, these aren't actually the same thing at all.

In the celebratory joy of exam results, some people are missing. Where are those who failed their exams, or those who weren't put in for them at all? You won't see them jumping for joy in the newspapers. In fact, their presence is defined by their invisibility. Alongside the articles about exam success, the *Guardian* reported in September 2019 that 10,000 young people had disappeared from the state school system during their last two years of school, raising suspicions of schools taking students off their registers (or 'off-rolling') to avoid having to count their results.

Gaming the System

Off-rolling is a logical thing to do in a system where schools are judged on their exam results. Humans are extremely good at working out how to make a system work for them. When I had to choose exam subjects at age fourteen, I chose Music. I really wanted to choose Art and I thought it would be more interesting, but I was worried I would only get a 'B' or even a 'C' in Art, and I knew I could get an 'A' in Music. So I did Music for two years, learnt nothing at all, and got an 'A'. When I got to the sixth form, I did it again – I chose French instead of Russian or Japanese, because I thought I would do better. It turns out I was wrong about that one; I was bored out of my mind in French for two years and did badly. Gaming the system doesn't always work out as you intend.

Research has shown that students do this all the time. If you tell them that their performance will be judged and the result is what matters, they will go for the easiest option. If you tell them it's an opportunity to learn and they won't be assessed on it, they will choose more challenging (and interesting) ones. If grades are seen as the point of school, then it's logical to go for the highest grades you can get, even if that means learning nothing at all.

The effect of this on education and learning, however, is to focus children's attention on how to get the best grades rather than how to learn and develop skills. The school system assumes that the desire to get the best grades will motivate better learning, but that isn't what the evidence shows.

An Abnormal Distribution

So how do we measure whether an education is working or not? Usually, the answer is by testing the children. However, test results are a funny thing, for it turns out that when you start testing children, everyone's behaviour changes. It's not just children who start to focus on results rather than learning. Parents and teachers do it, too.

In England, six-year-olds have to take a Phonics test at the end of Year 1. It's a pass/fail test, with the pass mark set at around 32. Because this test is used for accountability – meaning it is used to evaluate schools and teachers, as well as children – the data is collected and collated across the country, and the results published, as shown below in Figure 6.1.

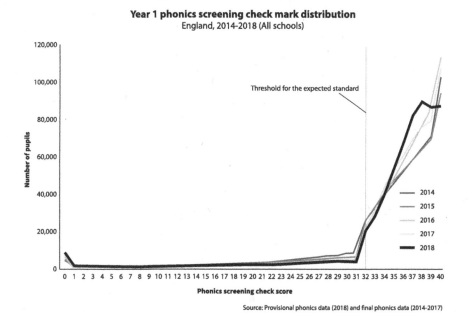

Figure 6.1 – Phonics screening scores

The data in the graph includes hundreds of thousands of children; each line represents the scores on the test for a particular year. Notice anything strange?

This graph shows that a very similar number of children get all the scores below the pass mark – that's why the graph is almost flat – and then suddenly, around the pass mark, the number of children soars upwards and stays up. It has done this every year from 2014–18. Teachers aren't told the pass mark in advance, by the way, but it's always around 32.

A word about statistics. Most meaningful things that we measure to do with human behaviour are something called 'normally distributed'. This means that most people will score somewhere in the middle, with fewer and fewer people doing either very badly or very well. Think of height. Most people are of similar height, but a few are much shorter, and a few are very tall. The peak of the graph is the average. This results in a graph which looks like Figure 6.2.

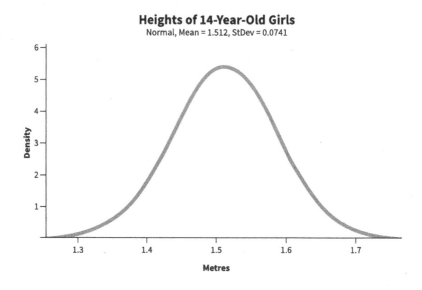

Figure 6.2 – A normal distribution of the heights
of 14-year-old girls

We'd expect reading ability in six-year-olds to be distributed something like this. Most of them will be around the average, with some being exceptionally good and some not really having started reading at all. A test which assessed their reading ability well would reflect this. Scores would raise gradually as they got towards the middle, which represents the average, and then would drop off again.

The phonics test graph is very different. It shows a dramatic change at the pass mark. There's no gradual rise. The number of children who get 28 is very different to the number who get 33, every year.

What to make of the phonics graph? Well, the best explanation is that this isn't a graph which shows reading ability or phonics ability at all. It's a graph which shows what happens when you tell teachers that they must divide six-year-old children into successes and failures. Many of them don't want to do it. They think it is educationally unjustified and unhelpful. So they do everything they can to 'help' children over the pass mark. They may well not be doing this consciously; they may just be giving children the benefit of the doubt, or even mouthing the answers to themselves without noticing – but when thousands of teachers are doing this, with tens of thousands of children, you can see the results in the graphs.

The More You Test, the Less They Learn

Alfie Kohn has made a career out of pointing out the downsides of the standardised testing and assessments which dominate our education system. He argues that when teachers and students are focused on standards, the quality of their learning always diminishes. He calls this 'the difference between focusing on *how well* you're doing something and focusing on *what* you're doing'. As more testing is introduced, schooling has shifted towards how well children are doing, at every level. They cannot help but be conscious of it, just as their teachers and parents are.

All of this is a serious problem for those who want to assess learning rather than test performance. For when children can make choices about their education, their choices are generally all about *what* they do, at least for the first few years. They are far less bothered about how well they are doing it, unless an adult (or another child) starts telling them that this is important. They learn through doing, and they develop excellence through practice. The moment that we introduce a standardised assessment at the end and tell the child that this is going to happen, their learning will change.

A Training in Test-Taking

Performance on tests is related to schooling. Even if we put aside the actual content of the test, there are whole sets of cultural assumptions around test-taking which children acquire at school. For example, the edict that tests must be completed alone, with no questions asked of other people. You can't look up any answers. You must finish in a certain time period. The questions are not 'real'; the examiners already know what they think the answers are. No one actually cares what you think, and it won't make any difference to the world, but you need to demonstrate that you know the answers, nevertheless.

Then there's a whole additional set of skills around multiple choice tests, or short answer questions – test-taking is a specialist subject in itself. It's one that most children outside school aren't learning, and there is no way for them to pick up the skill from their environment because test-taking is not a normal part of most people's lives (unless they develop a particular interest in taking tests – I guess it's possible).

Sometimes, when a family embarks on self-directed education, the parents secretly hope that, after a while, the child will get out the textbooks and start working through the courses they would have been doing at school, but at home. They imagine a child who is self-motivated and doesn't need to be nagged, choosing to learn the same subjects their peers are doing at school.

This may happen sometimes; I wouldn't like to rule it out. But I haven't yet met this child. I've met children who think they should be doing that, usually because they have been to school. Children do use school materials or explore topics which come up at school sometimes, but it's unusual for them to work systematically through a textbook unless they have a higher purpose (like taking the exam at the end so they can do something they want to do and need a qualification for). It's even rarer for them to work through a set of nine or ten different textbooks so they keep up all the school subjects. They can pick and choose, and so they do. As an adult, if I want to learn something, my first call won't be a textbook; I'd prefer to go to primary sources, to talk to people or find videos. Why wouldn't children do the same?

A self-directed education is not simply a different route to the same outcome as school. Children are spending their time in a very different way, and that will have an impact on what they learn. It also has an impact on how we assess them. We can't simply give them the tests children have in school and pretend that these are a good assessment of their education. In fact, we could argue that tests such as children take in school aren't really a good assessment of much that is meaningful, except how good the child is at taking tests.

The earliest study to look directly at informally educated children neatly (and unintentionally) illustrates this. Martin-Chang, Gould and Meuse (2011) looked at children aged between five and ten and compared children who were at conventional school, those being schooled at home and those who were being unschooled. They used standard school academic tests and found that the unschooled children performed worse than both the schooled children and the schooled-at-home children (who outperformed the schooled children). Since the unschooled children were not being taught academic subjects, this is unsurprising. Testing them on this is about as useful as testing all the children in Japan on the history and geography of Djibouti and then using their scores to declare that none of them were being properly educated.

Practical and Academic Knowledge
Aren't the Same Thing

Mathematics is all around us, particularly if you work with money in some way, like the child street vendors of Brazil. These children sell small items to help support their families. In order to make sure that they are not cheated, they need to have a good mathematical knowledge. Most of them learn the mathematics necessary for this informally, even if they also go to school. In order to look at their practical and academic mathematical ability, researchers posed as customers and tested the children on mathematics through buying things from them.

A week later, they tested their abilities on the same problems in a formal Maths test. They found that in a practical situation, the children were able to do complex maths which they could not demonstrate in a test. When solving written problems, the children tried to use algorithms they had learnt at school. When solving practical problems, they did the calculations in their heads without using the algorithms, and they did better. Many studies have found that school maths does not help children with practical maths and, conversely, practical mathematical experience does not help with school mathematics.

But If We Don't Test Them, What Do We Do Instead?

Amanda is eight. She spends her days playing, drawing elaborate pictures of houses she plans to live in when she grows up and making costumes for the shows she plans to put on. She loves playing with other children and isn't really interested in reading books, although she listens to audio books at night. Amanda is happy.

Her parents are uneasy. At eight, shouldn't she be reading and writing? Isn't she falling behind the other children? She'd seemed so bright when she was younger, learning to talk early – and now the other children they know can read and write, and Amanda seems like she is still at an earlier stage of childhood. They worry that they are failing her.

When you see your child climbing trees and drawing cats while other children their age are reading and doing mathematics, it's very hard not to start to panic. Parents often start the process of self-directed education with a vague idea that their children will naturally acquire the same skills as schooled children in a similar timeframe, just without being taught. The reality of a child who is uninterested in the subjects they would be studying at school can be hard to accept.

Any child not attending school triggers adult anxieties, because most of us believe very deeply that school – or something very like school – is necessary for success. Almost all home-educating parents have had the experience of a concerned stranger quizzing them on how exactly they educate their child, and whether they are a qualified teacher. Even more anxiety-provoking is a child who had attended school and who wants to stop. They can be defined as a 'dropout', which doesn't mean anything good.

There is an extensive body of research on the problem of school dropouts and absenteeism, all of which find negative effects of not attending school. Schoeneberger (2012), in a study of how students become dropouts, states in his summary, '. . . the potential exists for children either to follow a course of healthy development associated with positive outcomes or to experience frustration and incompetence associated with disengagement and disinterest in school'.

The course of healthy development he's talking about? He means going to school. Again and again through the literature, we find the assumption that going to school is the best option for every child, and that not going to school is associated with poor outcomes in almost every way. Schoeneberger, in fact, suggests in his review section that dropping out of school is associated in the literature with increased chances of imprisonment and early death, alongside poor employment prospects – and I have no reason not to believe him.

No wonder many parents are desperate to keep their children in school. The alternative seems bleak. And if they aren't in school, how do we know they're going to be OK? What substitute do we have for the regular feedback systems of school, the parent-teacher meetings, the report cards and certificates?

How Do We Know That They're Learning?

Think back to when your children were small. How did you know that they were learning? Did you need to test them in order to check out their progress in talking? I'm guessing not, although in some countries parents are encouraged to take this approach with their children.

When my children were babies and toddlers, the health visitor gave me lists with the abilities children should be showing at each stage, the number of words they should be able to speak at age two, the age at which they should be able to pick up a pea between thumb and finger (not something either of my toddlers ever tried to do) and so on. This certainly increases parental anxiety, and I'm not sure it has much of a positive effect on the children's learning.

Peter Gray is someone who has thought deeply about the problem of evaluating self-directed learning, both in terms of whether the environment is good enough, and whether the child is learning. He explained the central paradox in using tests to evaluate self-directed education.

'The normal way of evaluating is, are the children learning certain things at certain times? You can't evaluate a Sudbury [self-directed democratic] school that way, because children learn different things at different times. Ultimately, my experience is that everybody learns to read but they don't all learn to read at age five or six or seven or eight. Some of them don't learn to read until even later than eight. So if you are assessing learning and you're trying to assess the school on the basis of how well the seven-year-olds can read, that's not going to be a reasonable assessment of such a school. And if you change the school so that they all will read at seven, then it's no longer a self-directed educational setting.'

He went on to explain how he thinks self-directed educational settings can be evaluated. 'The first way is: are the children happy? Do they look like they are having fun and doing things? If they aren't happy, then right off we can say about the school that it's a failure. Any school that makes children unhappy is a failure. So that's the immediate criteria.'

The same applies to children at home. We need to look at whether they are engaged, happy and doing things.

The other way is to follow up adults who were educated in this way, not to see how many exams they passed, but to see what happens to them. Did their self-directed education prepare them for a meaningful adult life? Are they happy with their education? Are they able to do what they want, as adults?

Graduates of Self-Directed Schools

Back in 1983, Gray started off with an independent study of, at the time, all the Sudbury Valley School graduates. They tracked them down by whatever means possible and located 76 (out of 82) graduates, of whom 69 completed a survey questionnaire. They found that about 75 per cent of them had gone on to higher education, and that they were pursuing a wide variety of occupations, often related to what they had done at SVS as children. None of the sample said they regretted having gone to SVS instead of a more conventional school.

In this paper, published in 1986, Gray and David Chanoff suggested that an environment such as SVS fulfils two requirements which enable the students to educate themselves. Educational resources are made available (but not imposed on the children) and an environment is created in which young people are expected to make their own decisions about their education.

Twenty years later, a different independent interviewer contacted SVS graduates and asked them detailed questions about their lives (published in Greenberg, Sadofsky and Lempka, 2005). The findings were similar to Chanoff and Gray. Of the 119 respondents, 82 per cent went on to formal study after SVS, and those who didn't made it clear that they had made the choice because they felt able to go directly into the work they wanted to do. SVS students did not feel held back by their lack of formal schooling. Over half of the alumni interviewed had a lifelong passion that developed into a way of earning a living. These included farming, music performance, ballet or work which supported a cause they believed in, such as the pro-choice alumni who worked for Planned Parenthood. Other themes which stood out were activities that added meaning to their lives, challenge, work that served others.

It doesn't seem possible that students could go from playing all day to college without having been taught anything formally, but that is indeed what they did. It wasn't always easy, though. Several of the alumni described not understanding the expectations of the college system. For example, one student said that they had to learn how to do essay exams and write a paper, while others found it hard to adjust to grading. They also described feeling out of step with the other students, whose behaviour was more disruptive and less mature than anything at their democratic school.

There are other informal studies. Summerhill is a school in the UK, founded in 1921, where children are not obliged to attend lessons.

As far back as 1968, Emmanuel Bernstein visited fifty Summerhill alumni and found that they had gone on to careers as demanding as medicine and academia. In 2011, Hussein Lucas also followed up Summerhillians and found that they reported mostly being able to live the lives they wanted to live, and that they felt their education had fostered independence and adaptability.

These studies have no control group; they can't tell us whether self-directed learning works for everyone, nor whether it was more or less effective than conventional schooling. We can't go back in time to see what would have happened if a particular person had gone to school. What they tell us is that, for many young people, a self-directed education right up to the end of their schooling does not mean that they cannot achieve in later life, nor that they cannot manage the demands of higher education. The studies tell us what can be possible, and they show that school is not necessary for a young person to succeed in higher education.

Unschooled Adults

Democratic, self-directed schools are one thing, but it's significantly more complicated to look at the outcomes of self-directed, home-educated or unschooled adults. For one thing, there's no alumni list. For another, it's not always clear how similar their experiences actually were. Each family will have approached education differently, and what one person calls 'self-directed' education, another person might call 'semi-structured' learning.

Undaunted by this, Peter Gray and Gina Riley (Gray and Riley, 2015; Riley and Gray, 2015) waded in, surveying 75 young adult unschoolers about their experiences. Their sample is particularly interesting because a high proportion of them could be defined as 'dropouts' – 51 of the 75 did attend some school, with 24 having some schooling past the sixth grade.

What did Gray and Riley find? Well, their sample of young adults showed most of them doing well. Over 75 per cent of them were financially independent (in their early to mid-20s), and around 80 per cent had gone on to some higher education. Over 90 per cent intended to unschool their own children. Out of the 24 young adults who had not gone to school at all, 58 per cent of them were either working on a Bachelor of Arts degree or had one already.

For some adults at least, a lack of formal schooling as children did not seem to have blighted their opportunities as adults. Three of their sample were not pleased with their education and felt that unschooling had put them at a major disadvantage in life. They told stories of not being allowed to choose to go to school, and of families who kept them at home in order to limit their experiences or due to their mother's mental health problems. These participants described unschooling as a result of not managing to do schoolwork at home as opposed to a positive choice. An absence of school, rather than a different approach to education.

When asked about disadvantages of unschooling, the most frequent problem was the attitudes of other people towards unschooling; 28 per cent of participants said that was a problem for them. Eight of the participants (all of those with school-age children) were already unschooling their own children, and only five participants out of the whole sample said that they would definitely not unschool their own children.

Judy Arnall, who unschooled five children herself, also looked at what happens to grown unschoolers, particularly the transition to higher education. She surveyed thirty children who were unschooled for a minimum of three and a maximum of twelve school years. Her definition of unschooling meant that we know that these children were self-directed during those years. She unschooled her own children and found her study participants from among their peers. All thirty of them were offered places in higher education, going into fields as diverse as Engineering, Bioscience, Fashion Design and Asian Studies. Twenty had graduated by the time her book went to press in 2018.

None of these studies can prove that an individual child will be OK. However, they show that it can work and, in particular, that it is possible to access higher education without having done the preceding years of school. They also show that there are circumstances within which it doesn't work, where it isn't a solution for all. This may be particularly true if the family is dealing with extra stressors which restrict the child's environment and give the children fewer choices.

For self-directed education to work well, the environment needs to be one full of opportunities to learn. The family needs to be support-ive of the child and they need some resources available to them. This doesn't mean they need to be wealthy, but the child needs to be able to access opportunities beyond their home. Resources could include other adults who take an interest, free museums, online resources and friends.

Dropping In, Not Dropping Out

The results of these studies are far from the restricted life prospects associated with dropping out of conventional school. Yet by many definitions, these students are dropouts. They certainly didn't spend most of their education being schooled. This implies that self-directed education is something quite different to just dropping out of school, and that difference is something which affects the self-directed learn-ers for the rest of their life.

This raises the intriguing question of whether the way we respond to dropouts might be more important than the actual fact of dropping out. We know that how people think about themselves affects their lives. It affects what they think they are capable of, the goals they set for themselves and how they feel about their potential. Perhaps the way we talk about dropouts leads young people to feel that they are now failures with little hope for the future. If, instead, we talked about leaving school as a chance to drop *into* self-directed education, we might mitigate some of the negative outcomes and give young people a more hopeful way to think about themselves and their education.

Scott Gray, who 'dropped out' of conventional school aged around nine, graduated from Sudbury Valley School in 1987 and then from Boston College in 1991. He wrote about the transition in a *Washington Post* article in 1993.

'Many assume that it's difficult to survive the structured environ-ment of college after SVS, but I found the opposite. Most freshmen are accustomed to being told what to do and when, but I was used to directing myself. While other students had to learn how to discover answers on their own, I had never known any other way. People some-times critique SVS as an "unstructured" school – but without formal discipline, people learn to discipline themselves. I spent eight years playing games, thinking thoughts, making things and interacting with people. Doing things, rather than being told how to do them.'

Perhaps it's appropriate to end this chapter with Peter Gray, who has devoted so much time and effort to seeing what happens to adults who were self-directed as children. He's clear about what he thinks the research shows: 'The most important thing – the most important basic finding – is that you don't need to do school in order to succeed in our society.'

Further Reading

Arnall, Judy – *Unschooling to University; Relationships Matter Most in a World Crammed with Information*, Perfect Paperbacks (2018)

Bernstein, Emmanuel – Summerhill: 'A Follow-Up Study of Its Students', *Journal of Humanistic Psychology* 8(2):123–136, April 1968

Gray, P & Chanoff, D – 'Democratic Schooling: What Happens to Young People Who Have Charge of Their Own Education?' *American Journal of Education*, 94(2), 182–213 (1986)

Gray, P & Riley, G – 'Grown Unschoolers' Evaluations of Their Unschooling Experiences: Report I on a Survey of 75 Unschooled Adults', *Other Education: The Journal of Educational Alternatives*, Volume 4 (2015), Issue 2, pp. 8–32

Gray, P & Riley, G – 'Grown Unschooler's Evaluations of Their Unschooling Experiences: Report II on a Survey of 75 Unschooled Adults', *Other Education: The Journal of Educational Alternatives*, Volume 4 (2015), Issue 2, pp. 33–52

Gray, P & Riley, G – 'The Challenges and Benefits of Unschooling, According to 232 Families Who Have Chosen that Route', *Journal of Unschooling and Alternative Learning* Vol. 7 Issue 14 (2013)

Greenberg, D, Sadofsky, M & Lempka, J – *The Pursuit of Happiness: The Lives of Sudbury Valley Alumni, Framingham, MA*, Sudbury Valley School Press (2005)

Kohn, Alfie – *What Does It Mean to Be Well-Educated?*, Beacon Press (2004)

Lucas, H – *After Summerhill*, Herbert Adler (2011)

Martin-Chang, S, Gould, ON, & Meuse, RE – 'The Impact of Schooling on Academic Achievement: Evidence from Homeschooled and Traditionally Schooled Students', *Canadian Journal of Behavioral Science*, 43, 195–202 (2011)

Nunes, Terezina et al – *Street Mathematics v School Mathematics*, CUP (1993)

Schoeneberger, JA – 'Longitudinal Attendance Patterns: Developing High School Dropouts', *The Clearing House: A Journal of Educational Strategies, Issues and Ideas*, 85:1, 7–14 (2012)

Whitaker, Freddie – 'Phonics Check Needs Rethink After Data Shows Something Dodgy', *Schools Week* (2016)

7

Parenting – Magical Counting, Attachment and Control

Schools separate 'learning' from 'life'. While doing this, they also assume that what children do at school is more important than what they do at home, and that school activities have the right to invade home life. The same is not true in reverse. Parents are not able to send in 'schoolwork' activities for children to complete at school, nor are they free to take their child out of school during term time. Parents may spend more time with their children than a teacher, but it's the teacher who tells the parent how the children are doing on Parents' Evening.

Most books on education ignore parenting, except in a sort of adjunct role for schools. They see education as something that happens at school. Any advice about parenting is likely to be about how to support a child at school. You can, in fact, buy many books promising to tell you how to make your children smarter, or to guarantee school success.

There's a certain irony to the fact that giving a child more control over their education inevitably requires more parental involvement. Parents are the people who know a child best, and they will be the ones who decide what resources a child has available to them. Yet at the same time as playing a more active role, parents also need deliberately to step back and allow the child space to develop.

There's no shortage of people telling us how to parent. It has assumed such importance that hundreds of books are devoted to it, alongside courses, websites and seminars. You can hire a parenting coach, download podcasts telling you how to be a more responsive parent, and attend courses with 'certified parenting instructors'. Parenting is assumed to be a set of skills to be acquired.

It's understandable that we look for help. Many of us, before we have children, have very little experience of looking after babies or small children beyond a few hours' babysitting. Media representations of parenthood focus on the joy and fulfilment, particularly for women, of having children. Celebrity mothers appear with a photogenic child or two at their side, expensively dressed and freshly washed. They tell us it's the most rewarding thing they ever did and hope we won't notice the nannies hovering in the background.

Then when our own child arrives, reality comes too. Photogenic moments, yes, but also exhaustion, poo and the terrifying recognition that you are responsible for keeping this new person alive. I can't be the only new mother who would wake every hour with a shock if my baby didn't wake up, convinced he must have stopped breathing. It's not surprising that we turn to parenting experts in the hope that someone else has the answers.

In this chapter, I'll invite you to think about parenting culture, and the beliefs you may hold about parenting without even being aware of it. I'll trace how our modern-day concept of parenting has evolved over the last sixty years and ask who it serves.

The Culture of Parenting

The parenting industry seems to have started in the 1960s with Diana Baumrind, a Harvard developmental psychologist who described three styles of parenting. Channelling the Three Bears, Baumrind suggested that 'authoritarian' (also known as controlling and emotionally detached) parenting was too hard; 'permissive' parenting (not controlling and emotionally involved) too soft; and 'authoritative' parenting was just right. Permissive parenting was later divided into 'indulgent' parenting (emotionally responsive with low control) and 'neglectful' parenting (emotionally detached with low control).

Baumrind's research indicated that a large part of children's success in later life was down to how they were parented, and one style of parenting, according to her, was far and away the best – authoritative.

Authoritative parenting comprised high control with high emotional responsiveness. With the ideal style of parenting for all identified, the field was wide open for the flood of parenting advice, courses, books and experts which followed.

Baumrind's work has been criticised as confirming her own biases and endorsing a controlling model of parenting. She approved of spanking, assumed that high control was necessary for children, and she found what she set out to see. Nevertheless, her ideas are ubiquitous in the world of parenting, where it is often accepted without question that being 'authoritative' is the ideal. Firm boundaries, with loving warmth. The spanking is now usually quietly left out.

With this was established the basic principle of parenting culture, which could be summarised as saying that the job of parents is to mould their children into the best adults they can be. Parenting became a verb, and the child was the object.

Seeking Secure Attachment

Soon afterwards came Mary Ainsworth. Another American psychologist, Ainsworth designed an observational assessment called 'The Strange Situation'. You can find many examples on YouTube. It's a way to measure the quality of attachment between a mother and baby, by putting babies aged between one and two into a 'strange situation' where their mother and a stranger keep coming back and forth from the room they are in. The child's responses as their mothers and the stranger leave and arrive again are observed, rated and then their attachment style is decided. Seventy per cent of the babies Ainsworth saw were rated as having secure attachment, while the others were evenly split between insecure-avoidant and insecure-ambivalent.

Again, it was always clear that there was one best way to be, and Ainsworth suggested that high-quality attachment (which was associated with a whole range of positive outcomes) was due to maternal responsiveness in that first year of life.

It later turned out that perhaps it wasn't quite as clear as it first seemed. When the Strange Situation was used with babies outside the United States, they found that Japanese babies reacted so badly to being left alone that they had to abandon that part of the Strange Situation test, and no Japanese babies at all were rated as insecure-avoidant; 35 per cent of German babies, on the other hand, apparently had insecure-avoidant attachment. Cultural differences like these raise the possibility that at least some of the behaviour seen in these observations reflects culturally specific social learning, rather than fundamental attachment differences.

No matter, the attachment parenting industry has mushroomed. Practices such as co-sleeping, carrying babies in slings and breast-feeding are promoted as the right sort of behaviour to promote that all-important secure attachment, even though there's no evidence that they actually are necessary. And with it we have seen the parallel rise of maternal anxiety about the attachment, with mothers desperate to get it right, and devastated when their baby dislikes the sling, or when they can't breastfeed.

Neuroparenting

The most recent form of 'ideal' parenting centres around neuroscience. Using brain scan images of severely neglected children, parents are told that the first three years are a crucial time in brain development, and if their child doesn't receive adequate stimulation then they will never reach their full potential. These claims are used to sell 'developmental toys' and parenting programmes which purport to show parents the best way to interact with their very young children, to maximise brain development.

This is a distortion of the facts. Severe neglect in the first three years of life (being confined to a cot in a Romanian orphanage, for example) can indeed lead to children having life-long disabilities. However, there is no evidence that your average caring family need to be paying more attention to stimulating their baby's brains, nor that if they don't buy the right toys their child's development will be blighted for ever. Brains are very flexible and dynamic. They change as we learn new skills throughout the lifespan, and there's no need to cram everything into the first three years. Even the children from Romanian orphanages made great progress once they were adopted into caring families.

This mentality is what Jan Macvarish, founding associate of the Centre of Parenting Culture Studies at the University of Kent, calls 'neuroparenting'. It has led to campaigns urging parents to interact more with their children to build their brain synapses and has contributed to widespread paranoia about getting parenting wrong. When every day counts, and you're told that if you make a mistake your child's entire life and brain will be blighted, it's not surprising how anxious new parents are.

The problem with defining one style of parenting as the best is that suddenly many parents who were previously just doing what came naturally or what was normal in their culture become deficient parents. Something that was natural becomes a set of skills to be learnt. With so many different ways to get it wrong, it seems easier to miss the mark than ever before.

Blame Blame Blame

In fact, there are so many ways to get it wrong that many women secretly fear that they are failing at motherhood. The responsibility of motherhood is lifelong.

As Jan Macvarish argues, all this emphasis on how important parenting (and mothering, in particular) is for the long-term development of children may actually be making it more difficult for parents to bring up their children. It raises anxiety, and makes the stakes very high.

By this focus on the child as a product of parenting, we turn everything the parent does into something they have to think about. Are they cooing enough? Is their expression genuine as they tickle their baby's tummy? Are they gazing at their baby as they feed? What was natural for generations before has now been analysed, and the result is that what comes naturally may now be found wanting.

Parenting as an Intervention

Alison Gopnik, the developmental psychologist I introduced in Chapter 3, is equally concerned about parenting. She argues that the term 'parenting' leads parents to think that they should be consciously controlling their children's learning, in a similar way to how school attempts to control children's learning. She points out that most middle-class parents have very little experience of childcare when they have children, but have years of schooling and work, and so they approach their children in a similar manner. Everything is planned and purposeful.

Pat Farenga worked with John Holt, an educator and author who many credit with starting the unschooling movement. Farenga has worked ever since as an advocate of unschooling. He gives talks and, when we chatted, he told me about a conference he spoke at in the 1990s.

'I remember I spoke in London in the 1990s, it was a conference with John [Taylor] Gatto and I. For years, I started off doing what John Holt did, which was to start with saying, "How many of you here taught your child to walk or talk?"

'No one would [usually] raise their hands.

'But in London, they did! Some of them raised their hands. Now I just did it again in Calgary in mid-September, and about a quarter of them raised their hands. And to me that is a sea-change. People feel responsible and they are bold enough to say, "I taught my child to talk." We're always giving credit to the teacher, the instructor. The learner is never the centre, he or she is always the object.'

This focus on teaching and moulding children is everywhere, and the atmosphere it creates is one of pressure for children and parents.

When my children were very young, a friend told me she had spent the summer focusing on her two-year-old's fine motor skills, as she was concerned that he was behind. I was amazed, I had spent the summer focusing on keeping my two-year-old from pushing his baby sister off the sofa. It hadn't occurred to me to assess his fine motor skills, but I was immediately worried; should I have been spending the summer threading beads on to laces and picking up beans one by one? Is that what good parents do? How would I even know if my son was behind?

For some middle-class children, everything that they do is carefully orchestrated by adults and there for a purpose. Sports are to develop co-ordination and team co-operation. Arts and crafts are for fine motor skills and to develop colour awareness. Martial arts are for emotion regulation and confidence. Even messy play is now a planned activity, promoted for its sensory benefits, rather than a canny child taking the opportunity to pour the flour out all over the kitchen floor when their parent isn't looking.

Sometimes it seems as if children's whole lives are one long improvement project. Nothing is done just because it's fun.

Intensive Motherhood

Over the last thirty years, several authors have described the culture of 'intensive motherhood' which dominates discussions about parenting in the twenty-first century. Sharon Hays, a sociologist who studies motherhood and mothering, argues that there are a set of culturally accepted beliefs in Western culture about what makes a good mother, and that these are remarkably similar across mothers who work for money and mothers who stay at home. They generally involve being devoted to your child, putting their needs first and sublimating the mother's needs and wants.

One of the most damaging parts of this culture is the emphasis on children as the outcome of their mothers' mothering. In this deterministic world, almost every feature of children's lives can be said to be decided by how well attached they are, by how emotionally present their mothers were when they were infants, and how emotionally connected their mothers remain with them as they get older.

Into this have leapt parenting brands, who sell us a particular form of high-quality interaction with our child. This, they promise, will solve all our problems and create happy well-balanced adults. Whether it's *Obedience on the Count of Three*, *Superlative Parenting for a Magical Childhood* or *Your Toddler Can Be a Genius*, they all claim to have the knowledge that the rest of us lack. And it's really important information, apparently, which will transform our families and get our children to finally do what we want without complaining.

In order to sell us a product, we first need to believe that we need it. Confident, happy parents won't pay for advice. So while their websites burble on about supporting parents and wanting a better world, the only way to really convince us to pay for parenting advice is to make us feel that our current level of parenting is inadequate. We need to be convinced that there is a superior sort of parenting out there, and we'll only learn how to do it if we are coached or trained.

It also makes for a particular sort of parent-child relationship. From this perspective, it's not enough to feed, clothe, cuddle and play with a child. The parent has to have one eye on the goal, whether that's brain stimulation and synapse building or interacting with their children so as to promote a secure attachment.

Of course, the irony of all campaigns like this is that the families who take it to heart are almost entirely the loving families who were doing fine. Those who are severely neglecting or abusing their young children are extremely unlikely to respond to calls to build better brains through developmentally appropriate play. Their parenting problems are much deeper than a lack of skill.

Children Create Parents

One of the really interesting psychological findings in recent years is that parents don't just influence their children; children influence their parents, too. Right from birth, parents respond to the child they have in front of them. A calm and easy-to-soothe baby gets a calmer parent than a colicky and hard-to-settle one.

This goes on throughout children's lives. Children are not simply recipients of parenting; they are an active participant in their relationships. They affect their parents' behaviour and create their own environment. This calls into question the research which claims to show that parenting style affects children in later life. It also might make us re-evaluate some of the attachment research. That's because it means that parenting style might be a reaction to the child's personality and behaviour, rather than something which is solely a choice of the parent.

These findings are backed up by behavioural genetics research, which shows that people are never passive recipients of an environment. Their individual characteristics interact with the environment, meaning that two children can be in what is apparently the same situation and have entirely different experiences. This also means that children will always learn different things, no matter how standardised their environments.

Meet Rufus and Raya. Rufus is relaxed and calm, right from birth. He smiles a lot and is friendly to strangers. He sleeps well and without fuss. Rufus's parents are always being congratulated on his behaviour and they carry on with their lives, just taking him along with them. He goes to adult parties and they put him down to sleep upstairs. They go to music festivals and he falls asleep among the crowds. Rufus's parents tell other people they think it must be because they've always expected him to come along with them and so he accepts it. Rufus's parents are loving, and he complies when told to do something in a firm voice.

Raya is a totally different personality. From day one, she is unsettled and restless. She seems constantly on high alert. She never sleeps alone, preferring a parental chest, and rarely sleeps for more than forty-five minutes. She avoids looking at strangers and screams if someone coos at her, resulting in them rapidly backing off. As she gets older, she won't let her parents talk to other adults when she is around, covering their mouths with her hands. When Raya is told to do something firmly, she becomes extremely distressed, screaming and crying and refusing. It seems the firmer her parents are, the worse things get. Raya's parents love her dearly but the lack of sleep and constant attending to Raya's needs wears them down and they are often snappy and irritable with her.

Rufus and Raya have very different parents. Rufus's are calm, warm and loving, with firm boundaries – the authoritative ideal. Raya's are irritable, inconsistent and loving, with very few firm boundaries. Perhaps they might be called permissive. Diana Baumrind would not be impressed.

The children are siblings.

Rufus and Raya's parents look back on life before Raya was born and laugh wryly at their naïveté. They thought they had parenting worked out, when actually Rufus's temperament had given them an easy ride. They are able to be warm and firm with him, because he responded in a way which made that easy. Raya was a whole different story and required another set of skills, primary of which was flexibility to respond to her individual needs. Reducing their behaviour to parenting style misses this subtle interactive dance.

Parents create children, and then children create their parents.

Alternative Parenting Culture

When you choose a very different educational path for your child, your parenting will immediately come under scrutiny. As you step away from school, you step away from the path of 'good parenting' sanctioned by our society. In fact, allowing your child not to go to school is right up there with not feeding them or not buying them shoes in some people's minds.

There are, of course, alternative parenting experts who step in to fill the gap, selling their personal brand of advice about nurturing children without school. Many of these alternative experts based their expertise solely on their experience with their own children, which they will then sell to the rest of us via coaching sessions or online courses.

It takes a lot of courage to step away from seeing your children as a reflection of yourself and your parenting skills. Facing the reality that there are no guarantees with parenting, no matter how much you want to get it right, is a frightening thing. Everyone wants certainty deep down, and to know that they aren't screwing their kids up. Doing this without school requires particular courage.

Parenting Choices

The choices we make define who we are and how we live our lives. Rebecca English, a home-educating mother and academic at Queensland Institute of Technology, Australia, told me how in her research with home-educating parents, she found that their educational choices formed part of their view of what 'good parenting' was. She explained to me that just as some parents will choose a private school for their children because of their values, unschooling parents make decisions for similar reasons.

'I wanted to see how much these families who were unschooling were identifying with a particular ideology of "good mothering", "attachment parenting" (à la Sears et al) and whether, and, if yes, how their beliefs about family life were tied up in choices. My hypothesis is always that you can't understand a school (or, in the case of home ed, a choice that eschews formal schools) choice without understanding what parents believe good mothers (and, research says it's principally mothers) do and how they educate.'

She found that unschoolers were particularly able to explain why they had made the educational choices they did, unlike other parents. In her research with unschooling parents, they would tell her about the books they had read and the path they had taken to that decision. It's not a decision that anyone takes without significant thought, because it's so far from the norm.

English also became aware of how choosing unschooling became part of a family's narrative, and often provided a chance for parents who had strongly disliked school to have a reparative experience.

'For many of my participants, and people I've met since, unschooling was restorative in a way they didn't think anything could be. More than therapy or other systems that they'd tried to heal their child's – and their own – abuses, the decision to unschool helped not only their child but also them to heal from school trauma.'

What's Different about Parenting a Self-Directed Child?

Most conventional parenting techniques focus on how to control your child most effectively. Whether they suggest strict discipline or empathic listening, their bottom line is how to gain co-operation from your child so that they will do what you want. Successful parenting is managing this without a fuss from the child.

Even if the parents themselves tend towards a less controlling approach in the early years; when school starts, they are co-opted into the system. Parents are expected to support the school through controlling what clothes their child can wear, how they can cut their hair and what time they get up in the morning. They are expected to monitor homework and complete reading diaries. If a child doesn't behave as expected at school, their parents will be called in and told they need to control their children more. The basic paradigm is one where the parent and school wields power over the child, no matter how nice they are about it or how co-operative the child is.

In order for a self-directed child to optimise their learning, they need to be able genuinely to choose what they do. Their parents need to prepare the ground and allow that to happen. This is at odds with parenting by control and is a big change in mindset for many parents.

Freedom of choice for children is more complicated that it might first appear. Children literally spend years absorbing their parents' values, and then their schools' values. Even if they don't go to school, they learn from books and TV shows which activities are considered useful, and what's a waste of time. Their choices are inevitably affected by this. They can't choose equally if they know that one choice will result in a happy parent, while the other choice results in disappointment. This is particularly true if those parental preferences are unspoken. Make it explicit, and then everyone can discuss it. Keep it quiet, and the children will know, but they won't feel able to bring it up.

Control is Easiest When People Consent

Some talk about educating and parenting by consent. I don't actually like this idea, because I think it is too easy to manipulate people into consent. While giving birth, for example, I gave consent for medical procedures that I didn't want because I was told that otherwise my child risked brain damage. In retrospect, I don't know if that was true, but at the time it made it effectively impossible for me to withhold consent. Schools tell children all the time that if they don't co-operate with school, their future will be bleak. Most of the children then consent to what school asks of them.

People are easiest to control by consent. Religious cults have long realised that if you can get inside someone's head and manipulate how they think, they will control themselves. This makes your task far easier. What's more, cult members will tell everyone that it's their choice and they love it. They even look happy. If you can convince a person that their future salvation is dependent on complying with your demands, you will have no trouble at all convincing them to do what you say.

Religious cults typically promise eternal life to those who live a godly life, and fire and brimstone (or Armageddon) for those who don't. Schools don't usually go quite this far. But they do start very early to talk about the benefits of doing well at school, and the consequences of not conforming. These are long-term: exam failure, boring jobs and a wasted life. Or short-term: detentions, suspension and expulsion. They show how Maths and English are more important than rock climbing and pottery, and they demonstrate how the choices of adults are more important than the choices of children. Most parents will reinforce these beliefs at home. They were taught the same thing in their time.

This means that, by the time a child is seven or eight, their choices have already been strongly influenced for years by people who think they know what is best for them. They know what they have to do to get approval, and many of them do it without question. Many children consent to school because they do not think they have a genuine choice to do otherwise. The only options are to consent, or to get into trouble.

As children go through school, many of them forget that there was ever a choice not to consent. Their wish to meet the expectations of the adults around them becomes merged with their own desires, and consequently they lose touch with their own motivation and curiosity. They don't know what they want for themselves anymore, and so they consent to what others want for them. This means that consent is not enough as a basis for learning and future wellbeing. For that, children need to feel their own power and autonomy. They need to exercise their ability to make meaningful choices about their own lives.

Revising by Consent

When I was fifteen, I took a set of school exams. It was the year before our GCSEs, and while our teachers were telling us how important it was to do well in these final exams before GCSEs, in fact the exams counted for nothing at all. That didn't stop most of us from drawing up revision timetables and settling down with our books at weekends. This was a grammar school – we had all thoroughly bought into the system and wanted to do well, whatever it took.

Out of my group of studious friends, one stood out. Clara. She was quiet, but she had a rebellious streak. 'This is the last time I will ever take exams that mean nothing at all,' she said. 'I'm not going to revise at all. I want to see what it's like.'

We were horrified, she was going to face the public humiliation of bad grades, a poor school report, the potential wrath of her parents – for what? For the experience of taking exams with no preparation?

Yes, she was. Clara was the clearest-minded of the lot of us. She could see that there really was nothing riding on these exams. At the time, I secretly wished I was as brave as Clara, and now I wonder how she managed to maintain that clarity of vision, in a world where we were told constantly how important every test was, every exam. Our school didn't need to control us, because they had got inside our heads. We governed ourselves, as the school wanted us to.

But not Clara. I don't remember how those exams went, nor if Clara did worse than the rest of us. It turns out she was right, that they meant nothing at all. I do remember that the following year, after GCSEs, Clara refused to stay on at our academic selective school and instead escaped to the local sixth-form college, where there were boys, and subjects like Media Studies and Psychology. We thought she was ruining her future.

We all chose to study for those exams. No one forced us and, as Clara showed, it was possible to choose not to. But she was the exception. Most children will consent to what they think will make their parents happy, and they may not even be aware that this is the reason why they are making the choice.

For this reason, there is furious debate between alternative educators about exactly what adult input a self-directed child requires. Is it acceptable for an adult to suggest something, or is that in itself pressuring for the child? For just because a child says 'yes' doesn't mean that they chose freely; it could just mean that the control is hidden. In fact, hidden control is harder to combat, because we don't even notice that it's there.

When an adult is being strict or authoritarian, then a child has a clear edict to rebel against. If someone is telling you that you absolutely cannot go out this evening, then you know that you are being controlled. You can sneak out, feeling righteous anger that they try to restrict you like that. However, if someone says, 'Well, of course you can go out, but it will make your mother very sad . . .' then the emotional manipulation is much harder to defy. If you sneak out, you'll feel guilty.

If the parent has created an atmosphere where the child feels too scared or shamed to even try to go out, then the control becomes invisible. That child won't sneak out. They might not even think of it.

To Suggest, or Not to Suggest?

To get around this problem, some self-directed educational environments prevent adults from making any suggestions to children. They say that this in itself can be controlling, and so it's best avoided. This is controversial, with others saying that it can lead to stagnation, particularly in small, self-directed schools where children may not make many suggestions themselves. Others argue that they can provide a timetable of lessons within an atmosphere of non-compulsion. The COVID-19 crisis brought this issue into stark relief; schools closed across the world. Suddenly, millions of children were at home, with no access to other children except for their siblings.

Some self-directed schools continued with the approach they use in their buildings, of not providing any adult suggestions at all. In a building full of children and adults, ideas are generated and projects start. When this model was applied to children stuck at home due to lockdown, most of the children under twelve did not reach out to other children, except those with whom they already played online games. Without the structure of the school community, there were no informal interactions, and ideas did not spark between children. They did not connect with children other that those they already knew well. Interaction was only possible through online meetings, which had to be intentionally organised and which the youngest children could not take part in without parental input. Lack of adult suggestion resulted in lack of community, and lack of interaction for the children. It was an absence, rather than an alternative.

Other self-directed schools took a different approach and created a structure for children to meet online with offerings from adults, and adults who helped them to organise group activities. They tried to offer more than they would usually, recognising that many children had lost much of what was fun and stimulating from their everyday lives. These schools managed to keep their communities together, but with a huge amount of effort from staff. Flexibility in the face of crisis is essential, and self-directed education should always be about what works in a particular situation, rather than following dogma.

This balance is much harder for home-educating parents than for a self-directed school. Parents do have strong preferences, and children will know about them, because children are highly attuned to their parents' emotions. Parents make suggestions and provide opportunities to their children all the time. If they don't, their home will become intensely dull. So, the question is, how can parents allow their children the freedom to choose, while also creating a rich educational environment?

Hidden agendas are always harder to challenge. Openly saying 'Part of me would like you to work through a maths book and I think that's because I learnt at school that you had to use textbooks to learn maths,' can be less controlling than pretending that you don't care if the child ever picks up a maths book while secretly losing sleep with worry (and leaving maths books around 'just in case'). If it's out in the open, the child can disagree, and you can discuss it. If it's secret, they'll feel the disapproval but may not be able to put their finger on exactly what it is.

For self-directed education to flourish, parents and educators need to foster an atmosphere where it's OK to disagree with other people and make your own choices. Too many children grow up trying to please others, without ever quite knowing what they really want or what really interests them. A truly unconditional relationship is one where you can say what you think and how you feel, knowing that you will be accepted for who you are. That goes two ways, for parents and children.

Further Reading

Baunrind, D – 'Child Care Practices Anteceding Three Patterns of Preschool Behaviour', *Genetic Psychology Monographs*, 75(1), 43–88 (1967)

Goodwin, Daisy – *Bringing Up Baby, A New Mother's Companion*, Hodder & Stoughton (2007)

Hays, S – *The Cultural Contradictions of Motherhood*, Yale University Press (1998)

Kohn, A – *Unconditional Parenting*, Atria Books (2007)

Lee, E, Jennie Bristow, et al – *Parenting Culture Studies*, Palgrave Macmillan (2014)

McLeod, SA, Mary Ainsworth – *Simply Psychology* (5 Aug 2018): https://www.simplypsychology.org/mary-ainsworth.html

Macvarish, Jan – *Stop Putting Pressure on New Mums* (2018): https://www.spiked-online.com/2018/07/31/stop-putting-pressure-on-new-mums/#.W2AGPNhKh-U

8

Differences – Being Yourself

There have always been children who don't conform to the expectations of the adults and culture surrounding them. Depending on when and where they were born, these children have been declared to be possessed by demons, full of original sin, in need of firm boundaries, in need of more love, 'just being boys', naughty, out of control, in need of a male role model, in need of more mothering, in need of less mothering, in need of boarding school . . . the list goes on. Many of these children do not thrive at school, leaving their parents unsure of what to do. Do they continue to push their children through a system which clearly doesn't make them happy, or do they pull them out and try something different?

Popular culture for children is full of references to 'being yourself'. Elsa from *Frozen* belts out how she's going to 'let it go' (and show everyone who she really is) and Tinkerbell the fairy learns to be happy with her natural talents and to stop trying to be someone else. We feed children a stream of aspirational messages about embracing who you really are, even if you are a small elephant with enormous ears.

At the same time, most children are in an environment which very rarely enables them to be genuinely themselves. The school environment rewards conformity. 'Being yourself' is only allowed within strictly drawn parameters. Children pick up on this very quickly and enforce it on their peers. A six-year-old girl with short hair or a boy who likes playing with dolls will be quickly pushed into place by other children, and will often be excluded from play. A child whose uniqueness involves preferring to jump while doing maths rather than sit still, or who likes to spend long periods sitting under or on the table will not be encouraged to embrace this part of their personality.

Becoming Different

Many people think of difference as something which is located in particular individuals. A child might be different to the majority of their peers because of their behaviour, their ability, a disability, their skin colour, their cultural background, the language they speak at home – the list goes on. Of course, people do differ on these attributes. But whether any particular difference prevents a child from thriving depends on their environment.

As a white British girl, I immediately became 'different' when my family moved to the Democratic Republic of Congo (then Zaire) when I was ten. Suddenly, my skin colour went from being unremarkable to unusual. I stood out wherever I went. Children called out 'mundele' (white person) in the street and came up to feel my hair and touch my skin. At the international school I attended, being white-skinned was less rare but being British put me into a tiny minority. Every time I opened my mouth, everyone could hear my accent and soon that included me. My own voice sounded strange. I could never blend into the background or go unnoticed, but that didn't matter particularly because, at that school, everyone was in the same boat. We were all far away from our home countries, we all sounded and looked different to each other and to the Congolese people, of whom there were very few in our school. In an environment of others who were all in a minority for various reasons, I learnt to feel at home with being unusual. I made friends, did well at school and felt good about myself.

Three years later, we moved back to Britain and I become different in a new way. Now I was apparently 'back home' and my skin colour and accent were no longer exceptional. It turned out, however, that the culture of my classmates was a world away from that which I was used to. They had been in the same class together since they were five, since the school had a policy of keeping classes from primary school together. Being unusual was not valued. On my first day at comprehensive school, I explained that my father had worked for Oxfam when we lived in the Congo, and the class fell about laughing. To me, Oxfam meant international development. To them, it meant second-hand clothes, and my reputation never recovered. Every day, comments were made about the (apparently second-hand and musty) smell of my clothes. I was the girl no one wanted to talk to, the one that no one wanted to sit next to or be partners with. If I joined a group, they would run off giggling and holding their noses. Even the teachers seemed surprised if I did something well.

The school appeared sympathetic and made the right noises but 'Why can't you just fit in?' was the message I got. I didn't know the answer.

I didn't change. I was me throughout. I was different in both places, but the difference affected me in completely different ways because of the people around me.

While we tell children through popular culture to embrace and celebrate their differences, the world around them tells them to keep quiet and pretend to fit in. Adults tell children they must stay true to themselves without taking on the challenge of changing the system to enable them to do so. We put all of the onus on the children, telling them to remain themselves while the world is telling them otherwise.

Self-directed education provides us with the chance to do things very differently. This doesn't mean that individual differences disappear. In fact, when education is responsive and individualised, the result is increased diversity. Many self-directed children are more 'different' than they might have been if they had gone to school, because their environment has allowed them to develop their individuality without censure. Self-directed education gives every child the opportunity to discover and develop their differences, and therefore to become fully themselves.

In this chapter, I'll focus on how we respond to differences in behaviour in our society, and the impact of this on children. I'll describe the 'brain or blame' dilemma and discuss alternatives. I'll talk about seeing behaviour as communication, and what children's behaviour is telling us about their experiences at school.

Medicalising Behaviour

In Western society, when a child's behaviour is causing concern, the first stop for a worried parent is often their GP. If the GP thinks there's 'enough there', then they send the child off to be assessed 'to see if we can find out what is going on'. Demand for services is high and parents are desperate. In some parts of the UK, there is a two-year waiting list for diagnoses of attention deficit/hyperactivity disorder (ADHD) and autism. In the United States, around 10 per cent of children are diagnosed with ADHD, which rises to over 20 per cent of boys in some areas. Despite media coverage which claims that French children 'don't have ADHD' or 'don't have autism', it's pretty clear that French children do demonstrate the behaviours which in other countries result in diagnoses of autism and ADHD, but that the French respond differently – often by saying that the children need long-term psychiatric or psychoanalytic care and admitting them to day hospitals.

The basic assumption is that there is something wrong with the child – if we identify exactly what it is, we can treat and remediate. Behaviour is seen as symptomatic of a disorder.

This approach is the medical model. It sees behavioural or psychological problems as the direct result of a medical or neurological problem, which can be diagnosed in a similar way to any other medical disease.

These assumptions are now so deeply rooted that most of us don't even realise there are alternatives. We see a child reacting in an unusual way, and we start thinking about diagnoses: late reading – dyslexia; clumsiness – dyspraxia; hand-flapping or socially awkward – autism; can't pay attention and distractible – ADHD.

For children, the medical model is winning out as our way of seeing their behaviour. So much so that, to many, the medical model seems like it is the only way to think about difference and that those who question it just don't get it. They think the problem is lack of awareness and stigma.

This has all sorts of implications. Let's accept for a moment that at least 10 per cent of children apparently have something medically wrong with their brains while being biologically healthy. How do we know where to draw the line? Who is disordered, and who isn't? There are no biological tests for behavioural problems.

The way that professionals do it is using a diagnostic manual. This has lists of symptoms, which are compared to the child's behaviour. This process is highly subjective, and it's been shown that different professionals will give different diagnoses, depending on their personal preferences, and that the same people often get different diagnoses at different times. Over the last forty years, the number of children diagnosed with autism and ADHD has risen steeply, and diagnostic criteria have widened. Children who would previously have been deemed to be within the normal range are no longer considered to be so. Some people think this is progress and reflects increased awareness, while others think that it's pathologising difference and diversity.

There are some developmental disabilities which are clearly distinct categories. Down's Syndrome is caused by a chromosomal difference; a child either has Down's Syndrome or they don't, and we can determine that with a biological test. Many children have cerebral palsy and there are a range of less common genetic disorders which cause physical and learning disabilities. Some children do not learn to talk or use the toilet until they are much older than others; these children have particular challenges and may require specialist interventions to help them learn. There are also many children with physical disabilities such as visual and hearing impairments.

It's likely that if your child falls into one of these categories, then you already know a lot about it and have a very good understanding of their needs. These children can also take more control of their education, but they may also need specialist therapies and interventions to help them learn. As with all children, they will only be able to learn what is accessible to them in their environment. If people around a deaf child aren't using sign language, that child may not acquire language and will not be able to access Deaf culture. If a visually impaired child doesn't have access to Braille, they won't learn how to read it. This means that their learning environment needs to be thought about even more carefully and the adults around them may need to acquire specialist skills. However, this should never be forced. The child should feel valued and listened to. Therapy should not feel coercive or controlling.

Special Educational Needs

Daniel Greenberg, founder of Sudbury Valley School, one of the most famous self-directed democratic schools in the world, famously said that there are no special needs at SVS. They have plenty of children with diagnoses, but they don't look at the documents to see what they are. It's hard from the outside to understand what he means, but now, having had my children at a Sudbury-model school and having also used self-directed education at home, I think I get it. 'Special educational needs' are not things that exist just within a child. They are diagnosed when a child is unable or unwilling to meet the demands made by other people. Specifically, in this case, by school.

Special educational needs, therefore, are never something which a child has in isolation. They are a product of an interaction between a child and the expectations of the world around them. Something which is a 'special need' in one context isn't a problem at all in another.

Let's think about reading. Late reading in the school system is a big problem. If you can't read by the time you're six or seven, concerns will be raised and you will be sent for assessments of various types, to see if they can work out what's wrong. Not reading by your third year of school will mean that you can't participate in the rest of the school curriculum, and that you may well come to see yourself as stupid or lazy. Even if you learn by the time you're eleven, you will already have had years of struggle behind you. A diagnosis of dyslexia may give you some relief, as out of the alternatives you'd rather be dyslexic than stupid or lazy.

Self-directed children often learn to read later than schooled children. Some of them don't learn to read until they are teenagers. However, it doesn't stop them participating in their education in the meantime, because they have other methods open to them. When they do learn, they quickly catch up with others of their age. This research suggests that perhaps there is nothing inherently wrong with those children who take longer to learn to read than others. It also suggests that the school system may be creating disability, by requiring that all children learn things at the same times. My nine-year-old daughter cannot yet read fluently but, in her life spent at a self-directed school or at home, that isn't a disability. She manages fine without fluent reading and is able to pursue her interests regardless. Most importantly, her self-esteem is not determined by her reading ability. If she was at a conventional school, the story would be quite different.

Viewed from this perspective, the expectations of the school system – in particular, the expectation of standardised progression based on age – creates a lot of avoidable problems.

Neurodiversity

Neurodiversity is the idea that some children and adults have naturally different brains, and these differences should not be thought of as a disorder. This is sometimes talked about as 'differently wired' or a 'peculiar neurology'. Neurodiversity includes autism, ADHD, dyslexia, dyspraxia, dyscalculia, sensory processing disorder and more.

Neurodiversity is an anti-stigma movement and it comes from the social model of disability. This sees disability as a product of the inaccessible world, rather than something which is located in a person. For example, if a person cannot walk, the degree of their disability is determined by the world around them. If they have a good wheelchair and live in an accessible area, they may only be mildly disabled. If they have no money for a wheelchair and therefore cannot leave their bed without crawling, they will be severely disabled.

The principle in neurodiversity is that some people should be recognised as different (not disordered) and accommodations made in order to reduce their level of disability. Those who aren't 'neurodiverse' are sometimes called 'neurotypical', and the life of the neurotypical is assumed more straightforward in our society. In the neurodiversity movement, many people self-diagnose with autism and ADHD as adults.

Neurodiversity has many important insights. It is sometimes presented as a non-medicalised approach. However, there are problems with it, mostly to do with how in many cases it divides people into distinct groups: the neurodiverse, and the neurotypical.

Neurodiversity accepts the basic premise of the medical model. It assumes that there are some people who are qualitatively different to everyone else and this is because of a discernible difference in their brains. It rejects the term 'disordered' but replaces it with 'difference'. There is no evidence for this. All of the behaviours which make a person neurodiverse vary on a continuum, not categorically. It's not at all clear where the line between typical and diverse should be drawn. Neurodiversity runs through the whole population, not only in a subset.

Genetic research has found that differences associated with diagnoses of 'mental disorders' are made up of thousands of differences in common genetic variants. These genetic differences aren't specific – it seems that people who are at high genetic risk of ADHD and autism are also at risk of developing a wide range of mental health problems throughout their life. Genetic research doesn't back up claims of there being a separate group of neurodiverse people with 'different wiring'.

A problem with the neurodiversity framework is that it can encourage us to think that problems are fixed. The idea is that we can identify those who are neurodiverse (usually by diagnosis or self-diagnosis) and that we know then that they will be different to other people for their entire lives. This isn't based on evidence. We simply don't know what will happen to many of the children who are currently being diagnosed with developmental disorders. We do know that they would not have been diagnosed twenty or thirty years ago, because the diagnostic criteria have changed and widened. What used to be a rare diagnosis indicating a severe level of disability (such as autism) has become so common that most classrooms will have several children with diagnoses.

So when a child is given a diagnosis, and their family is told that that they have a lifelong disability, we don't actually know if that is true. We know that some children do stop meeting diagnostic criteria as they develop; we also know that some adults who had apparently 'normal' childhoods developed severe problems later on, including some of the difficulties which are associated with developmental disorders. We don't know that people can be divided into fixed categories of neurodiverse and the neurotypical on the basis of a diagnosis. It is much less clear than that.

The other problem with this approach is that it assumes that there are people who do not have the same struggles and who will never have them. If this is true, then the so-called neurotypicals are a very small group. A large-scale study in Dunedin, New Zealand, followed all the babies born in a particular hospital between 1972–73. They found that fewer than 20 per cent of their sample had not met diagnostic criteria for one or other 'mental disorder' at some point by the time they were in their late thirties.

De-stigmatising unusual behaviour is important and necessary. We need to learn to listen to behaviour, and to see it in context. However, we can't do that by designating a group of people as fundamentally different, and therefore as allowed to behave differently. By doing this, we still stigmatise the behaviour in everyone else. This leads to people feeling pressured to get a diagnosis as it's the only way that their behaviour can be acceptable to themselves and others. We need to recognise the neurodiversity in all of us and accept unusual behaviour whoever it comes from.

The Business of Diagnosis

Have you ever wished you had an excuse for your inadequacies? An explanation for your incompetence and a reason why life is such hard work sometimes? Then look no further. The Internet is heaving with online quizzes which will help you self-diagnose with one of a range of disorders, all of which will apparently help you accept yourself in a way you couldn't without a diagnosis.

Have a look at *ADDitude* magazine, the online resource whose tagline is 'Inside the ADHD Mind'. Readers of *ADDitude* are told that a diagnosis of ADHD can be 'transformative at any age', and the articles tell of how their diagnosis has promoted self-acceptance – while also warning of the dreadful consequences of undiagnosed and untreated ADHD. There are several quizzes and I'd be surprised if you don't start to wonder if you or your child might have ADHD after you complete them. Articles like this get into the mainstream press too; a recent *Guardian* article tells us how 'magical' a diagnosis of ADHD in your forties can be.

You might start to think that maybe something is up here – and you'd be right. When people are encouraged to think about themselves as disordered or ill, they become a lucrative market. They can be offered treatments – which are mostly drugs. In the USA, drugs can be marketed straight to consumers, who are told that the drugs such as anti-depressants will fix chemical imbalances in their brain, despite there being no evidence to show that depression is caused by a chemical imbalance.

In most of Europe, it's illegal for pharmaceutical companies to market drugs directly to consumers. However, it's not illegal for them to promote the diagnoses themselves, and so this is what they do, a process documented by Ray Moynihan and Alan Cassels in their book *Selling Sickness*. Diagnoses are marketed directly to consumers as a solution to all their problems, as an explanation for the parts of their lives that they wished were different. That's what is happening in those articles about the magical and transformative process of being diagnosed with ADHD. The approach used isn't that different to selling anything else, just that instead of claiming your life will be transformed by a new vacuum cleaner or lipstick, they're selling a diagnosis.

If you look carefully, you'll find that many awareness and anti-stigma campaigns are funded by the companies who sell the drugs. They promote the idea that 'mental disorders' are common, under-diagnosed and treatable. They also promote the idea that, without a diagnosis, you can't be helped. They promote the medical model.

Apart from drugs, there is no intervention for ADHD that can't be used without a diagnosis. 'Untreated' ADHD simply means 'unmedicated'. All the alarmist articles sounding the klaxon about the time bomb of 'untreated ADHD' are really calling for more people to be given drugs to control their behaviour.

Canaries in the Mine

It's not unusual in self-directed schools for a meeting between parents and teachers to involve at least one parent breaking down in tears. It's usually when they are telling the story of what life was like before they found the school. At one meeting I attended, one father told us how his eight-year-old son had been declared ineducable, and they had been told that he would have to spend his childhood at a psychiatric day hospital rather than at school. Another told of how his teenage son had hardly left his bedroom for two years, completely refusing to go to school, and had tried to kill himself. One mother told of how her daughter fought each morning not to go to school, scratching and biting them, for over a year.

These children are now members of the self-directed learning community, engaged in a wide range of activities. They are still the same people as before, with the same characteristics, but the pressure has been lifted and so they are able to flourish. Many of these children will have diagnoses. Home-educating parents tell similar stories – children whose behaviour at school was uncontrollable who start to behave differently when they are allowed to follow their interests and are treated with respect.

Something happens when children are in an environment in which they are valued and accepted for who they are. They see themselves as capable and as contributors to their community, and they develop and learn. That's why the respectful and non-judgemental way that adults relate to children in self-directed environments is important. It doesn't happen overnight. When you've spend years fighting a system, you can't just forget all the strategies you learnt to survive.

These children are experiencing the shift from a system which sees their personalities as a problem, to one which genuinely accommodates difference. Because when children are really allowed to choose what they do, difference stops being such a problem.

Something in the Air

Viewed through the lens of disorder, disruptive behaviour is a symptom. Viewed from a different perspective, it's a sign that something isn't right in the world around the child. It's those children who are considered to be troublemakers, the 'problem children', who shine a light into corners which the rest of us might prefer to avoid.

Carla Shalaby, who I mentioned in Chapter 5, is a former teacher who closely observed some of these children. Her participants had been identified by their teachers as disruptive to the class in their first two years of school. She describes them as 'canaries in the mine'. To explain, as recently as 1986, canaries were sent down mines in order to detect harmful gases. The small, vulnerable birds would succumb before the miners, thereby giving the miners an early warning system and a chance to get out.

Viewed from this perspective, children who refuse or who are unable to comply with school expectations could be telling us that there's something really wrong – the toxic gases of the mine. They are the sensitive ones, showing us how harmful the environment is. We ignore them at our peril, for all children are breathing the same air.

Shalaby describes how the children she observes are being social-ised (or are resisting being socialised) into a culture with specific rules for behaviour. She calls this 'white bread Americana'. Success is acquiring these rules, and inequality is built into the system, because some children come from that culture and are learning it at home, while others don't. She asks if we should really see resistance to this as a disorder, and whether we should be telling children that obedi-ence is more valuable than protest?

All of the children Shalaby follows are being prescribed drugs by the time they finish the second grade (age seven). The pressure for children at school to behave in a certain way is so strong that their parents will medicate them to help them comply.

Sami Timimi is a child and adolescent psychiatrist working in the UK. He makes an impassioned case for seeing the diagnoses of disorders such as ADHD in a colonial context, where healthcare pro-fessionals 'represent Western white, middle-class institutions and their values. Indeed, we carry these values with us, mostly unconsciously, and our practices are steeped in the racial, cultural and class history of the Western training we have had to undertake.'

Shalaby suggests the same goes for schools. Children are bearing the weight of colonial cultural expectations, and we are telling them that if they don't like it, the problem is them, not the system.

When we decide that children who do not fit into the school system must be disordered, we enable the system to continue unchanged while ignoring its own dysfunctionality.

What's the alternative?

If we don't think that a child's behaviour is due to a medical disorder, how might we understand it instead? It's undeniably true that some children have very different behaviour to others and some are much more challenging to parents. Some children just cannot pay attention and never sit still, while others struggle with social interactions and communication. Others struggle to learn to read and write. Some hit other children or adults. Difference doesn't disappear outside the school system.

The problem with the medical model is that it directs our attention to the child's brain, away from the social context.

Even medics have noticed this problem. In the 1970s, George Engel, a doctor, proposed that a 'biopsychosocial' model provided a more useful way of thinking about problems (Figure 8.1). This model includes biology, psychology and the social environment.

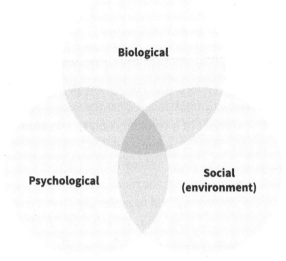

Figure 8.1 – The Biopsychosocial Model

This model says that any behaviour or problem should be thought about from all three perspectives – biology, psychology and the social world around us (or environment) – and only by understanding how these three things interact can we hope to understand what is going on.

Meet Sidney. Sidney (who is a composite of children I have seen) came to see me in an NHS clinic, referred by his school and accompanied by his mother.

Sidney is ten and in his sixth year of school. Two weeks before I saw him, he and three other boys planned an escape from a school trip. When no one was looking, two of the boys opened the door at the back of the coach and ran off. Sidney was caught before he could join them. The school suspended him and told his whole class that they were doing so. When Sidney returned to school, his classmates avoided him, the bad boy who tried to get away.

When Sidney gets angry, he'll smash things, including windows or doors. He tries to run but there's nowhere to run.

Sidney and his mum were reading a story about circus animals who were kept in cages all day. Sidney looked at the picture of a sad animal in a cage. 'That's me at school,' he said.

Sidney is one of only two Black children in his class, and sometimes the other boys shout racist insults at him in the playground. Then Sidney gets so angry that he hits them, and it's always Sidney who ends up in trouble because he has a reputation. Sidney feels that everyone thinks he's bad.

When Sidney gets angry, his school responds immediately because their behaviour policy is zero-tolerance. Sidney is put in isolation, sometimes for a whole day. In isolation, he has to sit outside the headteacher's office, and no one speaks to him. When he's not in isolation, he's being kept inside at breaktime and lunchtime for not finishing his work, distracting other children in class or saying 'silly things'. He generally misses his breaktime three or four times a week 'to catch up'. But he's not catching up. He's miserable.

When I talk to Sidney, he is lively and friendly. He tells me about the things he enjoys, playing Minecraft and football. But withdrawal of his Minecraft time is used to punish him when he gets in trouble at school, and his problems with other boys at school is spilling over into football, where the others are refusing to play with him on the team.

Sidney starts secondary school next year and his mum is worried that things will get worse.

Sidney's school want him diagnosed with ADHD and perhaps autism as well. Sidney's mum doesn't know what to do; school calls her up regularly to come and get Sidney and tell her that he's 'out of control'. She feels it must be her fault and lies awake wondering where she's gone wrong.

A Diagnosis Isn't an Explanation

The medical approach is to diagnose Sidney. There's a checklist of symptoms to look at, which Sidney meets. These symptoms are highly related to the demands of the school environment. They include failing to finish tasks, fidgeting, or trouble focusing on tasks they find boring. Once Sidney is diagnosed, he could be offered drugs. He will certainly be told that there is something different about his brain and that he just can't help behaving the way he does. He may be told that he's not naughty or lazy, but he has ADHD.

Everyone will feel relieved. Sidney's mum has been told it's not her fault, Sidney has a reason now why he dislikes school so much, and school has a label for it which they can use for their records. The diagnosis will follow Sidney through his education.

But ADHD isn't actually a reason. No one has identified what ADHD is, beyond a list of symptoms. There is no brain scan, genetic test or blood test which shows you have ADHD. ADHD itself has no explanatory power, because we don't know what 'it' actually is. It really is just a description.

This means that the reasoning gets very circular, very fast. Sidney can't sit still in class, is inattentive and overactive, so he gets a diagnosis of ADHD. The next time Sidney doesn't sit still in class, he will say, 'Oh, that's because of my ADHD.' But it's *because* of not sitting still in class that he got the diagnosis of ADHD. Which came first, the not sitting still or the ADHD? And which explains which?

Behaviour is Communication

An alternative is to ask what Sidney's behaviour is telling us. Rather than seeing his behaviour as a symptom, we could see it as communication. Let's think about Sidney's experience.

Sidney is someone who loves to be active, he has a tendency to move around a lot and is happiest when he's running not walking. That could be the biological part of his behaviour – note, there's nothing wrong with these preferences, they aren't a disorder.

Sidney is quick to get angry and doesn't like being bored. He prefers to make decisions for himself rather than being told what to do. He's quick to feel enclosed and doesn't like feeling trapped. He also prefers to have a few close friends rather than spend his time in a large class. Again, this isn't disordered, it's just who Sidney is right now.

And then the social environment. This is the part about which many assessments of this type hardly ask.

Sidney's school has a good reputation and an excellent inspection report. It prides itself on its 'high standards' and 'zero tolerance'. This means that compliance is highly valued, and any behaviour which deviates from what they want is quickly stamped on. Sidney is expected to do what he's told when he's told it, with no fussing. Sidney's wish to run in the corridors gets him into a lot of trouble in this environment, as does his hatred of waiting to be told what to do before getting on with something. The school environment also encourages peer pressure, as whole classes are punished when one class member does something wrong. Sidney is a visible minority, and easy to blame. He's experiencing racism from the other children but it's always him who gets in trouble. Sidney is quickly the least popular member of his class, since he gets them regularly in whole class detention. Sidney is struggling before he even starts thinking about academic work.

It all adds up to a miserable life for Sidney, and a stressful time for his parents.

But it's not inevitable. His school doesn't have to be that way. If Sidney was at a school where running around was possible and where he could leave and go outside whenever he was feeling trapped, his need to be active wouldn't cause such problems. If Sidney was in a school which listened to why he got so angry, then they might realise that the other children are provoking Sidney on purpose and that they need to address the racism.

Brain or Blame

The medical model, on the other hand, says there is something wrong, and it's with Sidney, not with the school. It sets up a trap for his mother in particular, because the only two explanations that seem to be available are either Sidney has something wrong with his brain, or that his mother is an inadequate parent. She's desperately worried that she's doing something wrong, and diagnosing Sidney means that instead of being a failure, she can be a parent struggling with a disabled child. This situation has been called the 'brain or blame' dilemma by eminent clinical psychologist Mary Boyle.

Self-directed educational environments change the social environment quite radically. They remove many of the demands which children find challenging. These include behaviour policies about things like what you wear and how you walk, an imposed curriculum, having to sit in a classroom with many others, being shouted at and rules you have no control over, which are all quite apart from the academic demands of a traditional school.

By changing the environment, for many children their biological and psychological characteristics are no longer a serious problem. They can thrive in a way they couldn't before. That doesn't mean that they themselves have changed. It also doesn't mean that their behaviour isn't real. Sidney will still want to run in the corridors, whatever type of school he's at. It just means it's no longer a problem for the school and therefore no one is going to punish him for it. If Sidney could be in an environment where he doesn't constantly feel bad about himself, things might be very different.

Look for the Interactions

Even schools which think of themselves as child-centred and progressive may not be a good fit for individual children. They are not immune to the cultural pressure to locate any problems in the child, rather than in the interaction between the child and their environment.

Let's meet Luke.

Luke was someone who worried when he didn't feel in control. That worry made him visibly shake and sometimes cry. When upset, he would refuse to comply with any request and would sometimes run out of the room. Luke loved playing Fortnite on his iPad and this helped calm him down. He also liked having time alone when he felt overwhelmed and was well able to calm himself down if he could get out of a stressful situation.

Luke went to a small school that prided itself on its individual-ised, empathic approach. However, this approach did not extend to allowing Luke to take his iPad to school. In fact, the school frowned on the use of technology by children and Luke lived in fear that teach-ers would tell his parents he shouldn't use his iPad at home either.

Each day, all the children spent hours outside in the forest in unstructured play time. The school did not tell the children when this time would end, and they frequently extended the time if a teacher was delayed or busy.

Luke found this situation intolerable. He did not enjoy unstruc-tured time in the forest and wanted to know when it would come to an end, something the adults could not tell him since they did not know. He found joining in with other children in this setting very hard, as his co-ordination was poor, and he couldn't climb trees or play football as they were all doing. He became very anxious and upset and tried to run away.

The school met with Luke's mother and said that they felt Luke had complex special needs and probably mental health problems as well. They recommended that he was referred to a neurodevelopmen-tal team and that they looked for a specialist school. They could no longer educate him.

Luke's school has a rigid model of what they think childhood should be. For some children, this works well, while for others it doesn't. Unfortunately for Luke, the school's strategy when things don't work well is to say there is a problem with the child, rather than look at how the school environment could change to work with Luke's personality, rather than against it. For another child, hours in the forest might be perfect. For Luke, it was like torture. When an inflexible environment meets a child with particular needs, then trouble ensues.

Sometimes, alternative schools talk about 'freedom', but they mean a very particular sort of freedom. Freedom to play in the forest, but not freedom to play on a computer. Freedom to play outdoors, but not freedom to come back in. For some children, these environments are perfect. For others, they feel stifling and controlling. A school that can't take this into account isn't a self-directed learning environment, no matter how alternative they think they are.

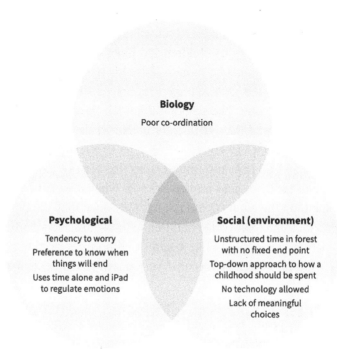

Biology
Poor co-ordination

Psychological
Tendency to worry
Preference to know when things will end
Uses time alone and iPad to regulate emotions

Social (environment)
Unstructured time in forest with no fixed end point
Top-down approach to how a childhood should be spent
No technology allowed
Lack of meaningful choices

Figure 8.2 – A biopsychosocial model of Luke's experience at school

Benefits of Diagnosis

There are good reasons for parents to seek out a diagnosis for their child; they validate the experience that this child is indeed, challenging to parent. For some families, a diagnosis gives them access to extra funds. They often provide an immediate support group and identity. Children may need a diagnosis in order to be able to access the right sort of education if they want to attend classes or lessons. A diagnosis provides a quick explanation for other people who don't understand why a child's behaviour is unusual.

Parents often feel blamed for their children's behaviour, and this can be even worse for parents who have chosen a self-directed education. They've made a radical choice and it can feel like their child is the test case. So if their child is refusing to greet people or sit down while adults talk at social gatherings, it feels like a judgement, not only on their parenting, but on their choice of education. A diagnosis gives a reason they can offer to others as to why that child isn't behaving like the others.

A diagnosis can help a child if they go back into formal education, as it means they may be able to access extra support from the start rather than the school having to go through a process when it becomes apparent that they cannot manage.

Cultural Differences

Soon after we moved to France, I was dismayed to realise that we were getting dirty looks as we went about our lives. People refused to talk to me in shops when I asked for assistance, and the neighbours would look askance as we passed them in the hallway. It took a while for me to work out why. In France, it's the culture to greet people politely each time you see them. People say '*Bonjour*' all the time. Every time they go into a shop, every time they pass a neighbour in the hallway. Once you've said '*Bonjour*', you can say something else. But if you start with something else (even something polite like, 'Excuse me, where can I find the butter?') they think you're rude. Even if you see the same person again later in the day, you say '*Re-bonjour*' before you say anything else. The same applies to leaving. You say '*Au revoir*' and '*Bonne journée*' as you leave. And then there are no dirty looks.

All this is completely different in England, where I come from. The English don't make such a big deal out of greetings. There, it's normal simply to nod to a neighbour in passing, or to walk into a shop without greeting the assistant. And as for leaving, we English tend to sidle off, not liking to draw attention to our arrivals and departures. It turns out the French have noticed this. They have a special term for sneaking off without saying goodbye which commemorates this English tendency – '*filer à l'anglaise*'.

My family and I were failing the French test of good manners, without even knowing that we were taking it. We were showing ourselves to be rude and badly brought up, while behaving in a way which, when we were in England, was perfectly acceptable.

Of course, this happens to every family that moves countries and culture. They come up against their own cultural assumptions, and suddenly discover that they are just that, assumptions. Cultural norms become visible when we are no longer surrounded by people who do things like us. We get things wrong without ever knowing why.

A similar thing can happen to self-directed children when they are tested and compared to schooled children. All assessments assume that children have been schooled. The tests are standardised on schooled samples. The small amount of research which has been done on the measurement of psychological wellbeing and behaviour of home-educated children found that they are likely to overestimate their problems. School is a process of enculturation, and self-directed children don't learn the school norms.

Take a child who likes to jump, flap their hands and make loud noises when excited. Lots of young children do this. If they jump at school, they'll quickly be told when it's inappropriate. Jumping and noise is OK in the playground but not indoors. Flapping will get you laughed at by other children. Those children who can control their jumping and flapping will stop in order to avoid being mocked or told off. In school, this will leave a group of children who either can't yet control their behaviour or who don't respond well to being told what to do. These children are likely to be quickly flagged as having special educational needs.

Outside of school, jumping, flapping and noise isn't really a problem, and so the child isn't repeatedly told to stop it unless it annoys their parents. Their parent won't take them to places where it might be an issue and will often prevent other children from making fun of them. More children will continue with this behaviour, because there is no pressure not to. This means that your average gathering of self-directed children will exhibit a greater range of unusual behaviours than a schooled group. Just like their learning is more variable and individualised, so is their behaviour. There simply isn't the same pressure to conform.

If a self-directed child comes in to a clinic for an assessment, the professional assessing them is going to assume that they have been socialised in a large group with certain norms, such as sitting still when asked, talking respectfully to strangers, doing your work when told to, putting your hand up to speak and not running out of the class-room when you want to leave in the middle of a lesson.

Meet Amina.

Amina is a self-directed eight-year-old who has a phobia of dogs. Her parents take her to see a psychologist, who discovers in passing that she can't read. She is immediately concerned. The psychologist assumes that Amina has had several years of reading tuition, as she would have had if she had attended school. When Amina's parents explain that they home-educate, the psychologist imagines Amina at the kitchen table working through workbooks. Even as Amina's parents try to explain self-directed education, the psychologist still assumes that some lessons must be taking place (because how else could an education work, right?). The psychologist suggests that Amina has a specific learning disability and should be sent for diagnostic tests.

Research on self-directed acquisition of reading suggests that children are highly variable as to when they acquire different skills. Amina may learn to read next month, with or without intervention. Assessments, even ones which purport to be objective, are unlikely to mean the same thing when applied to a self-directed child as to a schooled child.

Conversely, it's also true that parents of self-directed children can struggle to get professionals to take their concerns seriously because the children don't seem to be distressed enough about their difficul-ties. Professionals are used to looking for those layers of anxiety and shame. If they aren't there, then they may assume that the parents are overstating the issue.

Creating Layers of Anxiety and Shame

When I was at primary school, I strongly disliked playtime. We were obliged to go outside and play, for what seemed like for ever. Our playground was a concrete slab. The boys played football and the girls skipped. I wanted to read. I took my library books and sat on the concrete floor and read. This strange behaviour soon elicited concern from the playground attendants who thought I should be joining in. The other children also thought it was weird and would aim their football at my head. Soon, I become ashamed of my playground reading. I didn't want to skip, and I wasn't welcome on the football pitch, but now I felt like I couldn't read openly either. Playtime became a time of worry – where would I go? What would I do? How long could I hide in the toilets?

I was developing shame and anxiety about my desire to read, which on the face of it was not that big a deal and was, in fact, something that most of the time my school was keen to nurture. A small individual difference was becoming a much larger issue because of the reactions of others.

This happens in schools all the time. For many schooled children, their behaviour is buried under layers of worry, embarrassment and self-criticism. They aren't just a very active child any more – they're an active child who feels bad about being active. They aren't just a child who can't yet read – they're a child who feels that they are stupid and will never learn to read. Or they're a child who feels ashamed of the language they speak at home, their skin colour or the food their family eats, because they feel they should be the same as everyone else.

This doesn't have to happen. It's a product of how schools reward conformity, even as they say they celebrate diversity. True diversity isn't a strength when everyone has to follow the same standardised path through education. One of the most obvious differences you see with self-directed children is that they are far less ashamed of their individual differences, because no one has ever made it an issue. They are as they are.

Unusual behaviour is very common in self-directed educational communities, and so diversity is accepted as part of life. There is no pressure to conform to school standards, and a child is not made to feel bad about their inability to sit still, or their late start in reading. This means that the developmental differences can be just that – a difference.

This lack of pressure early on means that children get the chance to learn skills in their own time. I know several self-directed children who didn't start imaginative play until they were five or six – years after most children. I also know children whose independence in daily living developed much more slowly than other children. Others developed the ability to manage their emotions long after the time when most children stopped having tantrums.

We simply don't know what potential each child has, and just because they struggle in one setting does not mean they cannot thrive in another. Differences can be a strength when they are given space to develop. For this to happen, the environment, not the child, needs to change.

Further Reading

ADDitude magazine – retrieved 15 Feb 2020: https://www.additudemag.com/adhd-Wsymptoms-test-adults/

Dowty, T & Cowlishaw, K – *Home Educating Our Autistic Spectrum Children: Paths are Made by Walking*, Jessica Kingsley Press (2001)

Frances, Allen – *Saving Normal: An Insider's Revolt against Out-of-Control Psychiatric Diagnosis, DSM-5, Big Pharma, and the Medicalization of Ordinary Life*, William Morrow (2013)

Moynihan, Ray & Cassels, *Alan – Selling Sickness: How Drug Companies Are Turning Us All into Patients*, Allen & Unwin (2005)

Rothermel, Paula – *Home Educated Children's Psychological Wellbeing*, Estudios Sobre Educación, 22. 13–36 (2012)

Schwarz, Alan – *ADHD Nation: the Disorder, the Drugs, the Inside Story*, Little Brown Book Group (2016)

Shalaby, Carla – *Troublemakers: Lessons in Freedom from Young Children at School*, The New Press (2017)

Timimi, Sami – *Naughty Boys: Anti-Social Behaviour, ADHD and the Role of Culture*, Palgrave Macmillan (2005)

Watson, Jason – 'Being Diagnosed with ADHD in My 40s Has Given Me Something Quite Magical', the *Guardian* (15 Jan 2020), retrieved 15 Feb 2020

9

Deschooling – Leaving School Behind You

By this stage in the book, you probably have a good understanding of what self-directed learning can look like. You know that children can learn in different ways, and you understand how extrinsic and intrinsic motivation can affect learning. We've seen how destructive testing and pressure can be in education. You might be sure that you want to try something different.

Taking the next step can be surprisingly difficult.

The process of psychologically and practically moving away from school and towards alternative forms of education is called 'deschooling'. Deschooling is a time of transition; you're leaving the certainties of schooling for a new, generally less certain, normal. It's a time of excitement – but also a time of anxiety and uncertainty – as you try to work out what your future will look like if school isn't part of it.

Almost everything about self-directed education is idiosyncratic. No one can predict what your family's path is going to be or where you will end up. The one piece of common ground is that the transition between schooling and self-directed learning is rarely entirely smooth. Some have likened it to peeling back the layers of an onion. Just as you think you've finished, you discover another whole layer underneath.

In this chapter, I will start by talking about the cultural beliefs about school and education which we acquire simply by living in our society. I'll talk about what deschooling is, and what needs to be in place for it to happen. Then I'll present a cognitive model of deschooling, and examples of families deschooling. I'll include some practical exercises to get your own deschooling under way.

School Culture Is Invisible

I often meet parents who tell me that they don't need to deschool. They usually say that they were a rebel at school and didn't ever conform there; they're sure that they will be fine with however their children choose to learn. I watch as they start their journey to self-directed education, confident they know exactly how this will go.

A year later, when I meet them again, the story is always different. Some will say that they didn't realise just how much deschooling they had to do, while others will say that it didn't work out for them and the children are back at school, or they have a tutor to catch them up while they wait for a place at their local school. Their children just didn't take to self-directed education, they say.

It's often the most gung-ho ones who are in this second category. What they mean is that self-directed education didn't look like they were expecting it to. The more people are convinced they have nothing to learn, the less likely they are to open themselves up to the learning they need to do.

School is part of our culture in the Western world. No one asks whether your child goes to school, they ask which school they go to. Most people were schooled as children, and they school their children in turn. It doesn't occur to them to do anything differently. Rather like offering people tea when they come to visit, or saying 'please' and 'thank you'.

This doesn't mean that school is always thought of as good, or that everyone has a good experience of school. It's culturally acceptable to have hated school; being bullied at school is common; feeling that you didn't learn anything at school isn't unusual; grumbling about school or listing its limitations is totally normal. These are all familiar cultural narratives. But not sending your child to school at all, *by design*, puts you in a different category altogether.

We don't have a comfortable cultural category for those who choose self-directed education. Parents who don't send their children to school are thought of as neglectful. Teenagers who stop attending are dropouts. Those who home-educate are caricatured as hot-housing their children, grooming a future chess or tennis star. Those who choose to opt out of school because they want to take a very different approach to education? There isn't a handy box for them.

People find it easiest to make sense of the world by connecting new information to what they already know. Our network of information expands gradually, as we acquire new experiences which we perceive through the filter of what we knew already. Self-directed education is so far from most people's experience that they lose their bearings, not knowing how to fit it in to their world view.

This cultural gap explains why families who choose self-directed education find themselves explaining their choices again and again. Often to the same people, answering the same questions. 'Is it a bit like Montessori?' they say. 'Or more like Steiner?' People can't feel at peace with it because, to them, it doesn't really make sense.

School Provides Safety and Structure

The structure of school provides a roadmap for childhood (Figure 9.1). It structures not only children's days but their years. Without that roadmap, the landscape is unpredictable. Suddenly, it is up to you to draw your own map, setting your own milestones. There will be no school reports for each year, tracking progress and recording failures.

Figure 9.1 – School provides an apparently linear structure for childhood

Self-directed education, in contrast, is definitely non-linear, progressing in leaps and starts, and is very unlikely to follow a neat pathway (Figure 9.2).

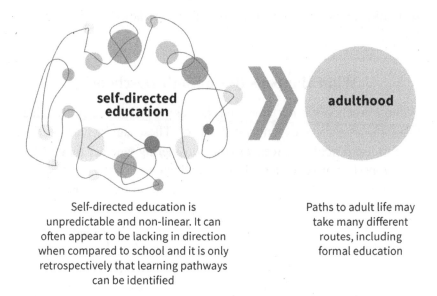

Self-directed education is unpredictable and non-linear. It can often appear to be lacking in direction when compared to school and it is only retrospectively that learning pathways can be identified

Paths to adult life may take many different routes, including formal education

Figure 9.2 – Self-directed education is unpredictable
and can appear to be lacking in direction compared to school

What's Deschooling Like?

No matter how much preparation parents have done in advance, the deschooling period is the time when the reality of self-directed learning kicks in. For most parents, it's a time when they have to give up some of the control they had been wielding over their child. For others, it's a time when they realise just what a lot of effort this will require, and how unhappy their child was at school.

For many of the parents I have spoken to, the deschooling period is when they worry that perhaps their children do need school in order to learn. They had all these dreams and ideas about how self-directed education would be. Perhaps they envisioned their child deciding to study astrophysics or Arabic and, in reality, it turns out that they just want to watch the entire eight seasons of *Full House* on Netflix.

This period of uncertainty is an important part of the process towards self-directed education. Stepping outside our comfort zone does provoke anxiety. Realising that there are choices where before you only saw inevitability shakes your world view. For a while, it can seem like nothing is stable any more. You lose the certainties in your life.

What Happens If We Don't Deschool?

Without deschooling, decisions and choices are still driven by schooled assumptions and the experience of school. These can include continuing to use school practices without considering whether they really are the best. It also includes decisions which are made in opposition to school. While decisions are still being made in reaction to school, self-directed learning won't flow as effectively.

A child whose experience of school was bad will make choices which are informed by that. Some refuse to read at all because they were made to do so at school. Or they may be uninterested in anything which reminds them of school – workshops at museums, for example, or TV programmes about history. Particular topics are out-of-bounds, because they learnt them at school. Words like 'maths' may induce panic. They want to take the long way round to avoid walking past schools at playtime. Their decisions aren't being made because they dislike reading or workshops; they're made because the pressure of school has triggered anxiety and therefore resistance, and this continues, even though school isn't there any more.

In the opposite scenario, a family sits down to lessons every day from 9 a.m.–3 p.m., with playtime and lunch break, because that's what they assume should happen. They buy age-graded workbooks and make their way through them, because that's how they think learning works best. They may follow the national curriculum, because that's what schools do. In this case, the family continues to accept the assumptions of a schooled education, and to use them in their home. They end up doing 'school at home'.

Without deschooling, the shadow of school continues to dictate a child's education, long after they have left the building.

How Do We Start Deschooling?

The first and most important part is to decide that your child will not be going back to school unless they themselves want to. You can't deschool over the holidays to try it out. While everyone in your family knows that school starts again in a few weeks' time, deschooling won't really begin. Some decompression can happen, but schooled assumptions will continue to be accepted as truth.

The next thing is to back off. Children who have had a difficult time at school particularly need a period when they are not being pressured. The aim is to reduce their anxiety about learning and their abilities, so that they can start to learn freely from their environment and the people around them again. Children are born with this ability and the younger they are, the easier it is for them to reconnect with it. This can take a strong nerve on the part of parents, as children may initially choose to stop getting dressed each day, to stop brushing their hair and may not want to contact their old friends. They may be quite withdrawn, and they may sleep a lot; or, conversely, they may be always on the go, never sitting still for more than a few moments. Parents who are used to a schooled lifestyle often struggle with their children choosing activities that appear to be a 'waste of time'.

What Blocks Deschooling?

Deschooling is often talked about as something that happens for children as they get used to life without school. In fact, it is parents for whom deschooling is crucial. For if parents don't deschool, their children won't get the chance to.

Deschooling can be a particular challenge for parents whose children are in a self-directed school setting, rather than home-educated. It's also more of a challenge for parents who work full-time outside the home and therefore are not the main educators. This is simply because they see their child less than a stay-at-home parent who is there full-time.

Home-educating parents are with their children a lot. They see their learning up close and they quickly acquire a knowledge of their child's strengths and weaknesses. They see the learning *in vivo*. Parents whose children are at a self-directed school, in contrast, may know very little about what they actually do all day. These schools often do not report much detail back to parents. For these parents, trusting that their children are learning can feel like a blind leap of faith. It can feel like their life hasn't changed much – the children still go to school as they did before, yet all the predictability and security has gone.

Of course, the predictability is a mirage. School doesn't guarantee results, and good school results don't guarantee a fulfilled life. Nevertheless, school usually feels safer to people because it is familiar and structured. This is the place to start challenging your thoughts. If you can't get beyond thoughts of how, really, they should be learning to read now that they are six, your children's freedom to learn will be affected. This doesn't mean that you have censor yourself or try to suppress your thoughts. It does mean that you need to start to reflect on your thought processes and to catch yourself in schooled thinking. By becoming aware of your thoughts, you can be more conscious about your behaviour.

Deliberately Changing Your Mind

In this chapter, I am going to present a way of reflecting on your thoughts and feelings which is based on cognitive behavioural therapy (CBT). CBT was first developed by a psychiatrist called Aaron Beck. It's a framework you can use to reflect on your own experiences and how these have formed your internal world.

CBT assumes that, while growing up, we form beliefs about ourselves, the world and other people. These beliefs influence how we interact with the world around us. Many of these beliefs are at a level where we aren't aware of them from day to day. These are called 'Underlying Assumptions', or 'Rules for Living'.

It's easiest to understand through an example. So, meet Anya and Elise.

Anya had planned to home-educate for years and didn't intend to send her daughter Elise to school at all. She enthusiastically planned the busy and happy life they would have together. Then, as the date when Elise would have started school drew nearer, she started having feelings that she hadn't expected – feelings of fear. What if Elise failed to learn and blamed her? And of loss and loneliness – of her little friendship group of local mums. All the others were sending their children to school. Already their focus was on meeting people at the new school and they were less available for meet-ups. Anya suddenly had a sense of being left behind. She wondered whether, in fact, she should be sending Elise to school with her local friends.

Anya was schooled herself and, while she was at school, had acquired some typical assumptions about education. Anya's experience of school was not bad, but it was uninspiring. She left unsure of what she wanted to do and with little idea of what she enjoyed. She wanted something different for Elise.

Anya's Early Experiences of School

Anya mostly enjoyed the social side of school and had friends there. She didn't have friends outside school.	Anya worked hard at school and did well, but never really enjoyed it. She left as soon as she could and never went back to formal education, but always felt that she hadn't fulfilled her potential because she had left early.

Underlying Assumptions/Rules for Living

If you don't go to school, you won't make friends.	If you don't go to school, you won't learn.

Automatic Thoughts

Elise will be lonely and friendless.	Elise will be a failure and it will be my fault.

Automatic thoughts are the ones we are most aware of; they pop into our heads throughout the day. Anya's automatic thoughts take her by surprise. She is really confident that she's making the right decision, and yet it's like she's ambushed by thoughts which come out of the blue. These thoughts are driven by her underlying assumptions. Underlying assumptions usually take the form 'If . . . then', or else 'I must . . .' or 'I should . . .' These assumptions will be different for each person, depending on their life experiences.

Sandy, another mother, had a very different perspective. She had never thought about self-directed education, but her son's years at school hadn't gone well. He had been suspended several times for punching other children and was starting to refuse to go. She decided to take Ben out of school to send him to a part-time, self-directed learning centre and home-educate the rest of the time. Ben was keen to leave. But once Ben stopped going to school, Sandy found that she was worrying all the time about whether he was falling behind his former class at school. At the learning centre, he would play and chat with his friends and, at home, he wanted to play on his Xbox. He was doing nothing that Sandy considered to be 'learning'. She was in despair and was considering sending him back to school.

Sandy's Experiences of School

Sandy disliked school and was bullied there.	Sandy was made to go to school by her father who told her that he loved her too much to allow her to drop out.

Underlying Assumptions/Rules for Living

School is so important that it's OK for children to be unhappy there.	If you love people, you force them to do things.

Automatic Thoughts

Ben should still be at school and needs to learn to behave.	I should be forcing Ben to go to school or he'll never learn.

Both Sandy and Anya are reacting to the situation right now, but their thoughts and feelings about it are based on their experiences in the past. Because they aren't aware of their underlying assumptions, all they are consciously aware of are the automatic thoughts.

Underlying assumptions are general and apply to lots of situations, while automatic thoughts are specific and more individualised.

These automatic thoughts make them feel anxious and, when they are anxious, they put pressure on their children. The children react by resisting, which makes their parents more anxious, creating a vicious cycle. The only way to change that is for the parents to apply less pressure, allowing everyone to relax. But this is easier said than done.

Identifying Your Own Assumptions about Education

What was school like for you? What memories come into your head when you think about your school experiences? Was it a happy or unhappy time?

Whether it was good or bad, you will have learnt lessons there about how the world works, and particularly how education works. What were the fundamental things that you learnt about yourself, learning and school? These are your underlying assumptions. They are usually in quite general terms, and therefore can apply to lots of situations. For example:

If you stop going to school, you're a loser
If you fail your exams, you'll never amount to anything
If people think you're too clever, they won't like you
If you work hard, you'll be successful
Other people know better than you do
In our family, we do well at school
If you go to school, you can fulfil your potential
If you play all day, you'll never learn
All children should go to school
People who do well at school are better people than those who fail
It's important to do better than everyone else
The judgements of others really matter

Then choose a situation where you have felt uncomfortable about your child's education. Imagine the situation – perhaps it's seeing your child playing on a video game; or perhaps a teacher is telling you that you really need to make sure your child does their homework. Let yourself focus on it and notice the thoughts that come into your head. Write them all down, without judgement.

They might include:

He's wasting his life and I'm facilitating it
He'll never amount to anything
I'm failing him
I need to make him read a book
He's addicted to video games

These are your automatic thoughts. Do they make sense in the context of your early experience and underlying assumptions? If not, you might need to dig deeper, asking yourself what is so uncomfortable about the situation.

Try filling in the chart below.

Early Experiences (What happened to you?)

Underlying Assumptions (What did you learn from it?)

Automatic Thoughts (What thoughts pop into your head now?)

Cycles of Thinking, Feeling and Behaviour

Automatic thoughts are, in fact, only the start of another cycle, because when we have thoughts, feelings and behaviour quickly follow. When Sandy thinks, for example, 'I must make Ben learn', this makes her feel tense and anxious inside. In order to relieve these feelings, she tries to force Ben to do a maths workbook. Ben resists, and so Sandy's anxiety gets worse.

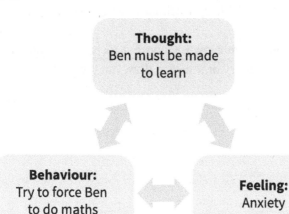

Getting stuck in cycles of our thoughts, feelings and behaviour is very common. We try to avoid the feelings, and so we act in a way which assumes that our thoughts are true. Doing this can often make things worse, and so our feelings get more intense. All of our attempts to change our thoughts don't help, because the thoughts are driven by underlying assumptions.

Here's an example from Anya.

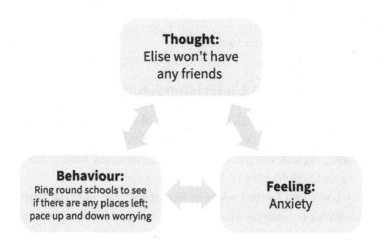

The problem here is that Anya is behaving as if her thought is true for the situation now, whereas, in fact, her thought is based on her past experiences. She rings round schools, but she knows that she doesn't want to send Elise to school so she gets more anxious and feels trapped.

Now try one of your own. Choose a recent situation where you have felt anxious, angry or low, and draw out the cycle.

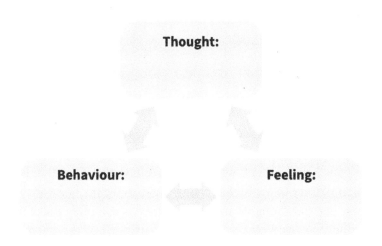

Thought:

Behaviour: **Feeling:**

The deschooling process is one of challenging those underlying assumptions and breaking the cycles. We need to make our choices based on the actual situation right now, not on our fears for the future based on our experiences in the past.

Shifting Underlying Assumptions

As you watch your child deschool, some of those underlying assumptions may shift by themselves. There are few things more powerful than seeing a child learn something for themselves which you previously thought could only be learnt at school.

My son learnt to read when he was eight, just as I was starting to have automatic thoughts like 'He'll never learn if I don't teach him' and 'I've failed him'. From my own experience at school, I had strong beliefs about the importance of learning to read. I learnt to read myself at age three, and being a voracious reader was one of my identities as a child. I had always assumed that my own children would follow suit. Then along came my son. He wouldn't even sit down to allow me to read to him, let alone try to read a book for himself.

I had managed to keep these concerns to myself when he was small and it became clear he wasn't going to learn to read at age three . . . or four . . . or five. At six, schooled friends we knew had mostly learnt to read, and I kept quiet about his lack of progress. At seven, I was watching him secretly for signs that he might be able to read at least some words. There were none.

Then one day when he was eight, he looked out the window of the car.

'Does that say Zombie?' he asked.

It said 'Zone'. And from that day forwards, it started. He read road signs, he read adverts, he read shop names as we went past. His first words were 'Way Out', 'Tesco', 'Stop' and 'Free'. I could almost feel my assumptions changing as I watched him. It really was true; he hadn't needed to be taught. He was putting all the pieces together in his own way, and when he was ready, out it all came.

Now I feel totally differently about my daughter, who hasn't yet learnt to read. I have every confidence that she will read when she's ready, even though right now she says she can only read 'Pizza'. I've had similar experiences watching both my children learn to swim, which they also did without lessons.

Seeing the Learning

Learning to read only happens once for each child, and your child might already have learnt at school. You don't need to wait for a similarly life-changing experience. There are things you can do to help yourself focus on the learning that is in front of you.

What follows are some practical ways for you to start to shift your perspective away from schooled thinking.

Exercise: Learning Log Book

You need to tune yourself into ways of learning which previously you might not have even noticed. One way to do this is to keep a log of times when your children have surprised you, questions they have asked which show that they are thinking, insights that they offer you. It's very easy to get bogged down in anxiety and to lose contact with the moments of wonder. Get a notebook now, jot them down.

To do this, you need to widen your perspective, because your schooling will lead you to look for evidence of reading, maths and other school subjects. The purpose of this isn't to evaluate your children, this is to help you see learning everywhere.

Self-directed learning is far wider than school learning, and part of deschooling is learning to see all learning. For example, you might see your child effectively negotiating with other children. Or you might see them improving their ability to build a house in Minecraft. You might see them becoming able to buy things at the shop and work out the change. They might be learning how to manage their emotional reactions, and how to deal with difficult situations.

If you feel you can't see any learning, jot down what they are doing each day. Wait a few months and do it again. What are the changes?

Places to look for learning:

Questions
Observations
Increasing complexity and variety of play
Social interactions
Relationships with others
Ability to manage in new situations
Increased independence
New types of play
Video games
Physical skills
Arts and crafts
Music
Cookery
Self-care
And more . . .

Seeing the learning isn't always easy, because our schooled minds think that learning must look a particular way. We assume that there is a right way to do things and, therefore, a wrong way, too. Matthew's story below shows how he was schooled to think of history in a certain way, and therefore missed the way in which his daughter was actually learning.

Matthew had recently taken his children out of school, and he was worried. They didn't seem to be learning anything. Matthew himself loved history and was trying to share this love with his daughters. He took them to exhibitions about the Vikings and the Romans, he read them books about the Egyptians. His eldest daughter, Rose, was interested, but in a completely different way to how Matthew had expected. Rose wanted to know what had happened to the family of the Viking with the red beard, whether the Egyptian slave had children and whether the Roman boy in the picture had liked tomatoes. Matthew was worried – this wasn't what he thought of as history. He thought Rose was missing the point entirely.

Matthew started noting down Rose's surprising questions, and then he noticed that Rose was interested in the human element of history. She wanted to know people's stories, and that was how she made sense of what had happened. So Matthew started asking Rose what she thought about the people. They started looking for books and videos which told the story of individual lives in the past. Rose started writing her own stories of historical characters. For Rose, the individual was the whole point. Out of school, she could explore history in whatever way was most meaningful for her. Once Matthew saw this, he was able to relax and enjoy exploring the history of ordinary people with Rose.

Experimenting with New Assumptions

Exercise: Acting As-If

Sometimes, seeing our underlying assumptions written out can be helpful in itself and can lead to change. However, sometimes you need to be more proactive. If you have identified an underlying assumption which you think is causing problems in your deschooling process, you can actively try to change it.

One way to do this is to identify an alternative that you think is more applicable to this current situation, and which you would prefer.

So, for example, if the underlying assumption you're trying to change is:

If you don't force children, they won't learn

You might prefer to believe:

If you don't force children, they can start to learn in unexpected ways

What you do is give yourself a challenge to behave AS IF you believed this new underlying assumption. Imagine how you might behave differently, if that was what you believed.

At first, you might want to try this just for an afternoon or day. Write down the new underlying assumption on an index card or make a note of it on your phone. If you find yourself behaving as if the first underlying assumption is true, get out your index card, read it to yourself, and ask yourself what someone who believed that would do.

In the world of cognitive therapy, this is called a behavioural experiment. Try it out, see what happens, see how things go. If it doesn't work, tweak the situation and try again.

Let's look at an example.

Janice was frustrated with her teenage daughter Maisie. She'd been out of school for four months and all she had done was lie around in her pyjamas texting her old friends. It drove Janice up the wall. She was worried that she was letting Maisie get away with bad behaviour, that she was getting addicted to her phone and that she would never amount to anything.

Janice swung between forcing Maisie to get up, get dressed and complete schoolwork, and giving up the fight and leaving her to lie in bed all day. Whichever she did, she felt terrible.

As a child, Janice had never been allowed to choose what she did. Every part of her day was regimented. She was only allowed to spend her time doing activities her parents approved of, such as sports teams and music lessons. Janice identified her underlying assumption in this case as this:

If you let children choose, they will waste their time.

She decided she would prefer to believe:

If you let children choose, they will do what is important to them.

Janice recognised that by forcing Maisie and making her dissatis-faction known, she was preventing her daughter from feeling free to choose. Maisie's choices were in reaction to the pressure by Janice. So she backed off; but she also decided that she did not like doing all the work in the house while her daughter did nothing, and she didn't feel this was fair. She put this to her daughter, and they made a plan – Janice wouldn't interfere with Maisie's texting, and Maisie would help with online grocery shopping and would cook a meal every other day.

Once the pressure was off, Maisie decided she would like to do something else other than texting and signed up to volunteer in the local charity shop as well as starting to learn how to play the guitar by herself.

But What About the Children?

So far, I have focused on deschooling for the adult – that's because adults usually have more deschooling to do than children. They have typically spent least a decade of their lives in school.

However, there's another reason why I focus on adults – it's because I assume that you, the reader of this book, are an adult. One of the central premises of this book is that children need to be able to choose how they learn and what they learn, and so it would be contradictory for me to suggest to you formal methods to help children deschool. I haven't yet met a child who tells me that they need to deschool and they don't need worksheets to help them with it. What they need is the right environmental circumstances for deschooling.

Talking About School

That doesn't mean that I haven't met children who have acquired schooled assumptions. In fact, most schooled children I meet over the age of about six openly express their newly learnt beliefs about schools and are horrified by the challenge to the status quo represented by children who don't do lessons. 'You have to go to school or you'll never get a job!' they tell my children with utter conviction; or 'Now I'm seven, I'm too old to play all day . . . it's time for serious work.'

Schooled assumptions in children are more amenable to change than in adults because they are more open about them. By adulthood, these assumptions have gone underground and become part of our psychological make-up. In childhood, it's much easier to see how children are acquiring these beliefs and adding them to their world view. Ask some children what school is for and why they have to go, and you'll see.

A Deschooling Environment

Since adults are in the position of creating an environment for children, they can create an environment which is conducive to deschooling. You can also create an environment which will totally stop deschooling from happening. That's quite easy to do, in fact; buy an expensive curriculum or sign up for online school and tell your children they have to do it or else go back to school.

For effective deschooling to occur, children need to be sure that they won't be made to go back to school if they do something wrong.

They need to know that taking them out of school was not a punishment, and they need to know that they are now able to make choices in a way they could not before. They need to be able to relax. This can take a long time. Children may well not believe that they can really stay out of school and that this isn't just a temporary blip on their educational journey.

You might need to start with taking back some of the things you have said to your children about school. For example, if you told your children they have to go to school or they'll never get a job, you need to go back and say you were wrong. If you did things you regret, like forcing them into school or leaving them begging you not to go, apologise. It's OK to have changed your mind and made mistakes. It's important for the children to be able to express how upsetting that period was for them, even if it's hard for you to hear. Be prepared to apologise, and to listen.

Talk About Your Own Deschooling

It might be useful to talk openly about the process of deschooling you are going through, about how you used to think, and what you think now. Children can also benefit from seeing the learning in everything. If you've been someone who would comment favourably on their schoolwork, can you comment on their online gaming skills instead? Can you join them in their playing, rather than telling them it's time to put their toys away and do something more productive?

Don't Rush In

If you're going to plan things to do, start with what your child enjoys, not with what you think they should be learning: go to the park; go swimming; find new adventure playgrounds or escape rooms; find new music to listen to; make stop-motion movies; go trampolining or rock climbing; visit charity shops and try out new games. Look up videos of things they find interesting and try out things you see. Listen to audiobooks and watch films; customise old toys or paint yourself a t-shirt; watch TV together. And even with all these ideas, take any pressure off; make things available but don't insist. Don't sign up for long courses for which you have to pay in advance and don't buy expensive curriculums. You may then feel obliged to force the child to keep going in order to get your money's worth.

Give It Time

The deschooling process is slow. School requires that children and families behave in a certain way. When school stops, a child can gradually find their own way of being in the world. Some of this is quick and other parts are much more gradual. The role of the educator or parent is to provide a safe, containing space for that to happen.

This takes months, not days. You can't rush it, because by doing so you introduce pressure, which will cause anxiety, which will stop deschooling from happening.

Further Reading

There is very little written about the process of deschooling. The following suggestions are books which will help you to challenge your assumptions about education and learning but which aren't specifically about deschooling:

Gatto, John Taylor – *Dumbing Us Down, 25th Anniversary Edition: The Hidden Curriculum of Compulsory Schooling*, New Society Publishers (2017)

Gatto, John Taylor – *Weapons of Mass Instruction*, New Society Publishers (2010)

Holt, John – *How Children Learn, 50th Anniversary Edition*, Da Capo Lifelong Books (2017)

Holt, John – *How Children Fail* (Rev Ed), Da Capo Press (1995)

Kohn, A – *Feel-Bad Education: Contrarian Essays on Children and Schooling*, Beacon Press (2011)

10

Supporting Self-Directed Learners

At the adventure playground, there are four rope swings. The lowest is for small children, the biggest is really quite scary. They are huge wooden frames with a rope hanging from them; you have to climb up in order to jump off. When we arrived, my son was dismayed.

'I can't do that,' he said. Even the lowest one seemed too much. He couldn't get on to the rope knot before jumping and he didn't have the confidence to jump off and hope that he'd land on the knot.

Then a smaller child came along, leapt off the side on to the rope knot and swung. My son's face changed.

'I can do that,' he said. And he jumped and swung. And again . . . and again. Then he moved on to the next highest rope swing, which was quite a lot scarier. At first, he got to the top and couldn't jump. He climbed down and tried clambering on in the middle – much harder to get swinging. Then he decided he was going to do it. He climbed up and jumped off and swung. His face was alight with pride.

'Did you see me? . . . Did you see me? . . . Did you see me?'

'Yes, I saw. You did it.'

'I don't think I'll do the biggest one,' he said, 'It's too high.'

Then he climbed up to the top and looked down. 'Too high,' he said and came down again. And up and down. Up and down. Another child came running past and jumped on. He watched carefully.

'OK,' he said, 'I'll do it.' And in a moment of pure exhilaration he jumped . . . and caught the rope . . . and swung and swung. He ran a victory lap of the playground.

'I think if I can do that, I can do anything,' he said.

***

You've probably turned to this chapter hoping for lists of school subjects, with hints as to how you can encourage mathematics and reading without destroying your child's intrinsic motivation. Your comfort zone is Maths, English and Science, and you want to know how to make sure your child learns those, even while you nurture their autonomy and competence. You really want self-directed, with an insurance policy.

I'm sorry, but there is no insurance available. You can't have it both ways. You can't make a child learn particular things and yet also tell them that they are in charge of their education (well, you can, but it won't result in a self-directed learner). They may well choose to learn subjects you consider important at some point, if they also think they are important. You will be able to make suggestions down the line and, if they respect your opinion, they will listen, and they may agree with you. But if you want to give your child control over their learning, you can't start with a list of things they have to do.

In this chapter, I'm going to talk about the process of self-directed learning – what it looks like, and what the adults' role is. Take a deep breath, take a step back, and start with yourself.

From Content to Process

Moving to self-directed education means a shift from dictating content to appreciating process. School is all about content and outcome; there are plans for what knowledge and skills children should acquire, and teachers devise strategies to help them learn it. The process of learning matters less than retaining information and showing that you know it. Rote learning the night before the exam can be as effective for this as in-depth study. Rewards and punishments may destroy intrinsic motivation in the longer term, but if they lead to short-term improvements in test scores, they'll be used.

When I talk to adults about self-directed education, they often tell me the things that they wish they had learnt at school. They do this to show me how important they think school is. Several successful professionals have told me they wish they had been forced to learn their times tables and that they have always felt the lack. Others have told me they wish they had been made to learn a musical instrument or a language, while others lament the gaps in their scientific and geographical knowledge. They all talk as if this information was only available to them at school and, as if, having missed it at school, they were then doomed to lack it for ever.

To the self-directed learner, such an attitude makes no sense. For if someone wishes they knew their times tables or how to play the trombone, why not just go and learn? Why should school be the only place where such skills can be acquired?

In Chapter 1, I talked about the Victorian roots of our education system. In Victorian times, knowledge was indeed harder to access and school (or the library) might have been the only place people could find out about science and mathematics. Now, however, most households will have several devices which are capable of finding information on an infinite range of questions. If you don't know your times tables, it's not because you don't know where to look them up.

Self-directed education, in contrast, is about the learning process itself. Content is less important than how children are learning. When children acquire a skill, from this perspective it doesn't really matter what that skill is. They may not know about Pythagoras' theorem, but they will know how to look it up when they come across it. They will be very unlikely to complain that they don't know about Pythagoras because no one ever taught it to them. For them, learning is an active rather than a passive process. Self-directed children are doing what they care about and are learning about themselves in the process.

Of course, from the child's perspective, this means the content is very important. It's why they do what they do. They are interested, and so they learn. But from an educational perspective, it really doesn't matter if they are learning about particle physics, World War II or how to play the harmonica. They are learning how to learn.

Remember how self-directed learning was described by Sugata Mitra, Alan Thomas and others? They describe a synergy between a child and their environment. The interactions lead to learning and understanding, but these are never forced. This doesn't mean that adults can't provide things in the environment – without those computers stuck in holes in the wall, the children in Mitra's studies would never have learnt how to use them. It does mean that the adult needs to prepare the ground, make it accessible, and then step back.

The strategies needed to enable this are respectful and available (but not intrusive) adults, coupled with an environment full of opportunity and challenge. I'll talk about these two aspects separately, although they are always intertwined.

Available (but Not Intrusive) Adults

This last weekend, my sister came to visit with her two-year-old. He was a non-stop bundle of activity. Watching him move seamlessly from stacking pots to singing a song to making a video to jumping up and down, I was struck by how he effortlessly took control of his learning, and how unpredictable it was. We took him up a tall tower to see Paris, and he spent most of his time trying to get his ticket to fit into the slot in the telescopes. We pointed out the Eiffel Tower, and he asked where the trains were. The main point of conversation on the way home was how traffic lights in Paris (unlike those in London) have no button to press for pedestrians to cross, you just have to wait.

I'm pretty sure his take home message from Paris will not be anything I tried to show him, but something he noticed by himself. Most parents of two-year-olds accept this, since it's very hard to convince young children to focus on anything they find boring.

As children get older, however, we refocus their attention again and again. We pull them away from what they find interesting, towards what we find worthwhile. Many of us do this unconsciously, because it was done to us. We genuinely believe we are doing the right thing, getting them to focus on mathematics rather than Fortnite, or geography rather than TikTok. In order to convince them, we tell them that their choices are not as good as our choices.

Each time an adult tells a child that their passions are unimportant, that child will find it harder to tune into their own preferences next time. Important adults in children's lives have a massive influence; their voices will be those that the children carry forwards with them into adult life, in an internalised form. Telling a child that their choices are pointless results in young adults who don't know what they like to do. The two-year-olds who were fascinated by life become sixteen-year-olds who have no interest in anything. They have had so many experiences of being told that they should be doing something else instead that they've lost the ability to connect with their own preferences.

In self-directed education, we are nurturing high-quality motivation. We want children to grow up knowing what it feels like to do something because you choose to, rather than because you are made to. To do this, we really do have to let them choose. You can't do this if at the same time you are undermining the child by telling them that their choices are frivolous.

That doesn't mean that adults have to be fascinated by the things their children are intrigued by. It's fine to be bored by traffic light buttons. But being bored and dismissing something as trivial and unimportant is a different thing. You can still talk about traffic light buttons, even if it bores you to tears. You never know, you might learn something new.

The children are learning to listen to themselves. Or rather, if they start young enough, they never have to forget. They can remain as in touch with their interests as a two-year-old but, as they grow, those interests will develop and become more sophisticated.

Painting Roses

There's a story in *Alice through the Looking-glass*, where the Red Queen required red roses, but her gardeners have planted white. Their only option, as they saw it, was to paint the roses red and it was this that they did. They were terrified of being found out and having their heads chopped off as frauds, for they knew that white roses painted red are not the same thing at all as roses that grew red.

> *'Would you tell me,' said Alice, a little timidly, 'why you are painting those roses?'*
>
> *Five and Seven said nothing, but looked at Two. Two began in a low voice, 'Why the fact is, you see, Miss, this here ought to have been a red rose-tree, and we put a white*

*one in by mistake; and if the Queen was to find it out, we
should all have our heads cut off, you know. So you see,
Miss, we're doing our best, afore she comes, to . . .'*

*At this moment Five, who had been anxiously looking
across the garden, called out, 'The Queen! The Queen!'
and the three gardeners instantly threw themselves flat
upon their faces. There was a sound of many footsteps, and
Alice looked round, eager to see the Queen.*

Alice through the Looking-glass *by Lewis Carroll*

This is what we do to our children, when we try to force them into a mould that is not of their choosing. We leave them terrified of exposure even as they are doing their best, desperately trying to pretend that they are the person they think we want them to be. They learn to present a façade to the world and to hide who they really are. And there is no reason at all why the garden couldn't be full of roses of all shades, and other flowers, too.

Follow the Questions

Children ask questions. Young children ask all the time, to the exhaustion of their parents. Their curiosity drives their learning, and so they need opportunities to find answers, whether that is through their own research or discussions with others. One key difference between self-directed learning and schooling is that the focus never shifts away from the child's questions, and so they continue to ask. Their sophistication grows as they grow, but the curiosity remains the same.

The questions asked at school are different and children quickly learn this. At school, questions must be kept on topic. You can't ask how rainbows are formed during a History lesson. You're allowed to ask a question which helps you understand what someone else is trying to teach you, but not to ask about why you have to learn this information at all and why you have to spend so many years at school. School asks questions of children, but these questions, too, are different. When a teacher asks a question, they know what answer they want. It's not a question of enquiry, it's a test. The child knows this and is put in the position of trying to guess the teacher's desired answer.

Responding to questions is an essential part of facilitating a self-directed education. This doesn't mean you always need to know the answers, but it does mean that you need to encourage the process.

We were once on the motorway, driving home in the rain.

'Naomi,' my nine-year-old said (he chooses to calls me by my name and has done since he was about seven). 'You know Henry VIII? Why didn't he divorce all the others ... why did he behead numbers two and five?'

A brief history primer, for those not familiar with English history: Henry VIII was a Tudor king of England; he was married six times and, in order to divorce his first wife, he broke off with the Catholic church, thus turning the whole of England Protestant, and declared himself Head of the Church of England, a position which the monarch holds to this day. This meant he could get a divorce, something which the Catholic Church did not allow.

So he went to quite extreme measures in order to be able to get a divorce. But yet when he decided he didn't want to be married to his second wife, rather than simply divorcing her, he beheaded her. And he did it again with wife number five, having divorced wife number four (wife number three died in childbirth).

All in all, a reasonable question to ask. But one which it had never occurred to me to think about. I'd done projects on Henry VIII at school, memorised the mnemonic 'Divorced, beheaded, died ... divorced, beheaded, survived', visited Hampton Court Palace (where Henry VIII lived) multiple times; but I had never wondered why he went to the trouble of murdering two wives when he could have divorced them.

Now why did I never think of that? Perhaps because I'd never really thought deeply about Henry VIII at all. I just worried about what I needed to know about him, and what someone else might ask me. Self-directed children are in a different position; free from the need to retain information for a test, they think about it from unexpected angles.

And, of course, I didn't know the answer. I came up with a few possible hypotheses, and my son came up with a couple more. Then my daughter (aged six) piped up, 'But it was all because he wanted a boy.' I had had no idea she knew who Henry VIII was.

Our discussion of Henry VIII moved quickly on to why males inherited the throne over females, how Henry VIII never knew that his daughter Elizabeth I was such a successful queen, and how he had been so focused on having a son when actually it was his second daughter who was the successful monarch. Then to why the monarchy was so sexist, and then on to long-reigning queens, Victoria and Elizabeth II. Then we moved on to names and why the royal family use the same names again and again and how the latest heir to the throne would be yet another George.

By this point, I was worried we would miss our turning and asked for a moment of quiet. A few moments later, as I was about to go back to the monarchy, another question.

'Do you think, if you made an absolutely perfectly symmetrical disk, it would be possible for it to rotate very fast without you being able to see it was turning?'

I watched the neighbouring car's wheels turn outside the car windows and I could see where this line of enquiry came from. It had never occurred to me to wonder about that either. My head started to spin with the wheels.

My mother has a brief record of questions I asked aged three. 'Why do we have chins?' and 'What does the sun have for breakfast?' I never found the answer to either of them. I assume after that the questions came too fast for her to keep up with writing them down.

Self-directed children continue to ask questions of open enquiry way beyond when schooled children have stopped. Adults don't have to know all the answers, but they do need to listen and take the questions seriously. People who are with a self-directed child are important resources. When a child can't yet read or look things up, the adult or an older child will need to play that role, perhaps finding videos which explain answers to questions like 'How do fish have babies?' and 'Why was Apple floated on the stock exchange?' Children soon become able to ask Siri or Alexa for answers even if they can't yet type, but pursuing the answer to a question with someone else has a special quality. In the relationship, new ideas are generated.

Anything can be the trigger for a question. A phrase on an advert, a chance comment by someone, and then you're off, asking questions, investigating answers and sharing hypotheses. Those questions are important – they are the spark that starts a cycle of self-directed learning. They show a desire to connect and learn from others.

As children grow, the answers they require are more detailed. For previous generations, this might have been a problem, but for most children of the twenty-first century, the Internet is never too far away. Ask your own questions, too, and let them see you looking for answers.

Some children ask very repetitive questions. This can be because they aren't getting the answer they want, but also for some it can be that they struggle to move on from a question to something else. It can help to record the answer or write it down, and then say, 'You've asked that question lots of times . . . can we think of another one?' As they get older, they will be able to reflect on the process and perhaps to talk about why they ask the same question, and what answer they are hoping for. Asking repetitive questions can also be a sign of anxiety, in which case you might need to think about what the child might be anxious about, and whether there are ways you could help.

Seeing Others Learn

This last year, I decided to learn to crochet. I totally failed to learn to knit as a child; holes everywhere in anything I attempted. So I got a crochet hook and some wool, and watched some YouTube videos. My daughter was immediately interested and came along to watch, too. I talked about how hard I was finding it and how I had no idea how to start. She was encouraging and told me she thought I could do it, but it might take some practice. We made a chain together. Then I thought perhaps she would learn to crochet and tried to teach her. She wasn't interested in doing it herself; she'd rather watch me. So I struggled on, and managed to make her a hat, with only intentional holes. She was proud of me, she said.

Children need to see adults learning, and adults being incompetent. Adults are typically so good at things like reading, cooking and searching on the Internet. It can feel to children like adults are always capable and that they never had to learn. Make the process explicit; talk about how you learnt to do things and, even better, find something to start learning from scratch. Show your children that you're not afraid of being a novice. Talk about your thought processes so they can hear what it's like for you. We need to create an environment where learning involves making mistakes, and not knowing how to start, but doing it anyway. An environment where the process, not the end point, is what it's all about.

Connections

An important part of self-directed education is connecting with others. It's here that lots of learning happens, particularly when children can meet people outside their immediate family and cultural background. Again, the aim with self-directed education is always to open up the world, create opportunities.

Close relationships with other people are important for all human beings. With self-directed education, some argue that connection is an essential part of the process. Unschoolers, in particular, tend to think less about practical features of their environment, and more about emotional and relational aspects. They see the family as a key part of the child's environment. Research such as Pattison's and Thomas's looks at the interaction between children and parents, and what needs to happen in that relationship so that a child can learn. This sort of close learning relationship is unique to home-educating families, where parents know exactly where their child's learning is at, not because they have tested them, but because they talk to them every day, all day long.

Some unschoolers use the analogy of a dance between parents and children, where the parent knows just where to step and when to support the child, and so is able to make the right interventions at appropriate times. This sounds complicated, but it's intuitive – all parents do this with their small children. They adapt their speech and behaviour to the child's level of development without having to think about it. We talk to our two-year-olds and ten-year-olds entirely differently, and it's not something we have to plan.

Parents may need to think deliberately about finding wider connections for their children, particularly when they are younger. It's important for children to have other trusted adults to talk to and learn from, no matter how good their relationships with their parents is. These people could be extended family, family friends, scout or activity leaders or other members of the community. They need to be open to building an ongoing relationship with the child.

Respecting Boundaries

Boundaries can be a bit of a dirty word for some parents. That's because 'boundaries' is used by some behavioural experts to mean putting arbitrary limits in place for children and then sticking to them inflexibly. So a 'boundary' might be that a child must sleep in their own bed alone, or that they have to leave the playground when you say so.

Boundaries don't have to be arbitrary or controlling. They can be thought of as each person's psychological space; the invisible lines which define what someone can tolerate without harm to themselves. Those boundaries could include how much sleep a person needs, how much alone time someone needs, and how much exercise they need to stay healthy. They also include how someone wants to be treated by other people, and how much a person takes on the feelings of other people. Babies usually trample all over the boundaries of their parents, because their needs are so intense, and they haven't yet learnt that they can wait. Toddlers will hit their parents, sit on their faces and generally treat them however they please. This is normal.

What can happen next, however, is that some parents don't reestablish their boundaries as the children grow. School provides a break between the dependence of early childhood and the independence of middle childhood for most families. When this break doesn't happen, some parents continue sacrificing their own needs. It becomes second nature. Some alternative parenting experts encourage this. There's a type of parenting and unschooling which urges parents to say 'no' as little as possible, and always to say 'yes'.

Children learn from what we do. We want them to grow up to be able to hold their boundaries and say 'no', but also to respect the 'no's' of others. It isn't enough to respect their 'no' – we need to help them to respect ours, too.

It's often tempting for parents to prioritise peace and calm over the needs of the whole family. This means that the loudest member of the family has the most power because they keep protesting for longest. Part of creating an environment for learning is making sure that everyone's voices are heard.

Saying 'no', or insisting on all voices being heard, can lead to intense distress for some children. How you react to that depends on the developmental age of the child, and why you think they are so distressed. Many children become distressed because they are anxious, and the best way to reduce anxiety is to practise doing what makes you anxious. If you consistently make decisions on the basis of avoiding distress and anxiety, the child doesn't get the chance to learn how to manage those feelings.

Part of effective self-directed learning is knowing what your boundaries are and protecting the boundaries and needs of each person in the family.

No Division Between Learning and Play

Before a child starts school, everything they do may be experienced as play and fun. Once they start school, the world is divided up into 'learning' or 'less important'. 'Learning' invariably involves doing something that an adult has planned for a child. School prioritises this sort of learning over everything else, to the extent of preventing children from going on holiday with their families because more learning is assumed to take place sitting in a classroom.

This over-valuing of school-based learning means that schools feel justified in pulling a child away from what they would prefer to do in order to require them to do something else. Younger children resist this more strongly, and so the activities they are offered at school are closer to things they would have chosen themselves. This is called 'play-based learning'. Older children, however, typically spend much of their time doing things which others have chosen for them. They are told that the things they choose to do are less worthwhile than the things that school chooses for them.

Parenting can easily fall into the same pattern, as parents try to move their children away from activities they deem worthless. For example, even play-focused parents often prefer crafts, board games and outdoor play to video games and cops and robbers. Persuading children not to engage in the games they prefer becomes a daily battle in which parents use a range of strategies.

Meet Hannah.

Hannah loved to play that she was a gangster. She would grab any item, turn it into a gun and shoot other children. If there was no 'gun' to hand, she'd use her fingers. She and her friends would run around shouting 'Bang! . . . Bang!' and falling to the floor. Her parents were gentle and peace-loving, and they were horrified. This wasn't what they had thought imaginative play would be like at all. They set up a 'home' corner and gave Hannah dolls. They bought her dress-up doctors' outfits and encouraged her to play hospitals. Hannah shot the dolls and then staged a gory death scene while wearing a doctor's outfit.

Hannah's parents had several chats with her about how serious shooting was and how death wasn't something to play about. Hannah realised that this meant they disapproved of gangster play. She took her playing underground; she would do it quietly when her parents weren't looking or when she was at a friend's house.

In despair, her parents banned gangster play. The next day, Hannah was shooting at people again. When her dad reminded her that Gangsters was now banned, Hannah explained that her new game was called 'Rescuers'. She was coming in to save people from the baddies and, of course, in order to do that, she needed to shoot at them. What could possibly be wrong with that?

Violent play is particularly hard for parents to embrace. Many parents fear that, by allowing violent play, they will encourage their children to be violent in real life. They ban violent video games. Some primary schools do not even allow children to point their fingers at each other and say 'Bang!' in the playground, saying that shooting is not something which should be trivialised by play.

This misses the point of play, in my opinion. Children's play isn't trivial or frivolous. It is the way that children interact with the world. It's how they explore ideas and concepts, and how they deal with difficult events in the world around them. Saying that a child shouldn't play about something is analogous to saying that an adult shouldn't talk about something. We can learn about what a child is thinking through their play but, when we stop it, we prevent them from communicating.

Children in refugee camps play about their experiences; children in concentration camps played about what they saw there; children who have experienced terrible things will play about them. This is how they make sense of events.

Engaging in violent play doesn't necessarily mean that a child is traumatised, however. It may mean that they are exploring the idea of death and injury. It may be that having a pretend gun helps them feel more powerful. It may be that they are copying shows they have seen on TV. The adults around them may not understand what purpose the play has for the child but, if the child is driven to do it, then there is a purpose.

Joining the Child

The opposite of pulling children away is joining. Joining simply involves staying with the child where they are. If they are playing Minecraft, you play with them. If they are making jewellery, you learn how to do that too, or just watch them doing it. If they want to learn Arabic, then try it too. Just sitting down next to the child and being curious – but not judgemental – is a start. Don't tell them it's time to put the tablet away; don't criticise their choice of game; don't ask them how long they've been sitting there; don't demand that they instruct you or explain anything – just observe and comment rather than question.

It's hard for some parents to shift from questioning. We're used to trying to get children to tell us things and to explain why they are doing something. Sometimes, we are looking for an opportunity to teach them something. But for children it can feel like they are endlessly put on the spot and asked to account for themselves. To avoid this, say things which don't require an answer. Instead of asking, 'What are you doing?' try saying, 'That looks like a fun game.' Instead of 'Why are you playing that?' try saying, 'That bit looks tricky.'

Through joining the child, you help them feel valued; you show them that you are interested in the things which interest them. You also build a relationship which isn't based on them doing what you want. In the future, they can use that experience to establish relationships with others.

Doing, Rather than Learning to Do

John Holt, the educator and author I introduced in Chapter 4, whom many regard as the founding father of unschooling, describes in his books how children learn through doing the things they want to do. At first, they may appear to an adult to be incompetent, but they are always doing. They learn to read by looking at books and turning the pages, or by working out what a road sign says. They learn to talk by hearing others talk and joining in themselves, at first with babble and later with words. School teaches children skills out of context in the belief that later on they will be able to do what they want to do. In self-directed education, children do what they want to do right now and, through doing so, they learn the skills that they need to become competent.

One morning, my daughter returned to her French self-directed school after being off for a week with chickenpox. She wasn't infectious any more but she still had a few spots. Before she left, I tried to teach her a word I thought she might find useful – '*contagieux*' or 'infectious' in English, as in 'I am not infectious any more.' She looked at me with some incredulity. 'I learn when people say things, that's how I know words. They say them and then I say them. That's how I learn. I don't need you to tell me.'

I took the hint and shut up. She learns French through doing. My attempt at helpful preparation wasn't welcome or necessary.

An Environment of Opportunities

Children learn from what is around them. They don't need lots of expensive toys, but they do need opportunities. They need chances to go outside their family and learn from the wider world.

Children need an environment which evolves as they grow. Self-directed schools can provide a changing environment as long as there is a wide enough age range, but home-educating parents need to think proactively one step ahead. Moving to the countryside may seem ideal when children are under eight and love nothing more than building dens in the woods, but it will feel very different when they are fourteen and there are only two buses a day to town.

Limiting and Restricting

Well-meaning adults often spend a great deal of energy limiting their children's learning environment. They restrict children's access to electronic devices or tell them they can only read the books which are right for their level. I've met parents who limit how much time their children can spend playing outdoors, worrying that they should be spending time doing more 'worthwhile' activities like reading and mathematics. Schools, of course, limit everything; limiting outside time to break time, exercise time to PE and reading fiction to English lessons. They create an environment of restrictions, of things that you cannot do.

While some restrictions are necessary for safety reasons, it's useful for an adult always to consider why they are stopping a child from doing something. If it's due to a belief that they are 'wasting their time', then it's probably time to step back and join their child rather than restrict them.

Parents who try to prevent their children from doing something very rarely take the time to watch what their child is actually doing. Parents have told me with conviction that they have to limit Minecraft, Roblox, YouTube, Netflix and 'screen time'. When I ask them how their children use these things, they have no idea. They have never played Minecraft with them or sat down to see what they are using their 'screen time' for. They often don't know how the games their children love work. They have limited without really understanding what they are limiting. They are often surprised to hear that Minecraft, for example, is a 'sandbox' game which is highly creative and social.

I ask them what they notice if they sit down and play with their child, on their terms. What would happen if they looked for really good new games, rather than focusing on restricting them? If they saw the virtual world as a learning environment, what could they put there for their children to discover?

The effect of focusing on restriction is two-fold. One, children and parents are at loggerheads about something which could be an opportunity for connection; and two, children spend the time they have doing lower-quality activities because their parents have rules like 'we don't pay for apps'. If children are only allowed thirty minutes a day of 'screen time', they won't risk exploring new things. They'll stick to the familiar, and thereby limit their experience still further.

We Learn What We Live

When my son was four, all his friends went to school. Suddenly, we were alone at home, or alone at the playground. He didn't seem to mind, but I did. I got lonely very fast. My old friends didn't seem to be interested in meeting up, they had a new group of school mums, and when we went to try and meet new friends it always seemed to go wrong, such as the terrible time that we went to the playground with another local home-ed family. I had thought it had gone well; I was happy to think that we might have made some new friends. Then I got the email the next day, telling me that when I wasn't looking, my son had spat at and kicked the other boy, and he never wanted to see him again. They were the only family close to us who home-educated. I was mortified. When there aren't many other families around who have made similar choices, each incident is a disaster.

It took me a long time to come back from that. I retained the feeling that other families only tolerated us, that we were not really wanted. Unsurprisingly, we didn't make many friends. We didn't attend local groups because my son refused to, and I was scared that he would alienate all the local children.

Then I realised that, by doing this, I was depriving my son of the opportunity to learn how to relate to other children. Children can only learn from what they have available in their environment. We were avoiding other children, and so his social skills weren't improving.

I decided things had to change. I found some new families online and set out to make friends. I set up fun things for their children to do. I invited them round for pizza. I watched my son like a hawk and coached him on how to behave with other children. I persisted, even when the children ignored each other for the whole afternoon. We had a few bad moments. One child got a door slammed in their face; one was told he could play with nothing except a broken brown crayon, but we persevered, apologised and tried again. Genuine friendships started to form, some of which still continue today.

Other people are important; they're particularly important for children who find dealing with them difficult. For some families, sociability is as easy as finding other families to meet up with or joining local groups. For others, it takes a sustained effort. When my son was having a particularly hard time with other children, I found adults who would come to visit. We found a local home-educated teenager who came to see us every week and just played with my son. We invited family round so he could get to know other adults, even when he refused to talk to them. Very slowly, things changed.

The Best Intentions

After I finished school, I went to Botswana to volunteer at a rehabilitation centre for disabled children. We played with the children, we helped with washing and dressing and daily living tasks. The children mostly had cerebral palsy, although some had other problems, such as brittle bones or missing limbs. There was a physiotherapist there called Neo. Neo was firm and no-nonsense, and one day she said to me, 'You know, some of these children can do a lot more than they are doing. You need to stop doing things for them, because you are stealing their one chance to learn.' It was strong language, and I was shocked. Stealing from them ... me? But I just wanted to help! It made me feel good to do it; they were happy, I was happy – what was the problem?

I resisted the urge to mutter quietly that she had no idea what she was talking about and watched her. I soon saw what she meant. She wasn't washing and dressing children. She was giving the children their own socks and showing them how to put them on. Then she expected them to try. There were tears. It's really hard putting your socks on when you have severe cerebral palsy. Some of them begged her to do it for them, but she refused. 'You're here to learn how to be independent,' she said. 'You can't learn to be independent if someone does everything for you.' The children tried, and they were learning. With me, everyone was happy, and no one cried. But they still couldn't put on their socks.

These children were from rural Botswana. They had been brought to live in this rehabilitation centre so they could learn the daily living skills they needed for the rest of their lives. The system of taking children away from their parents to do this had limitations. The staff told stories of children going home and then, when the staff visited them several months later, they discovered that the children had forgotten how to do everything, and their wheelchair was sitting unused in the corner. Their loving parents had gone back to doing everything for them. But while it feels fine to do everything for a sweet six-year-old, it's very different for an eighteen-year-old who can't put on their underpants.

There's a danger with self-directed education. Some parents interpret it as meaning that children never have to do anything they don't want to do. With the best of intentions, these parents create an environment for their children which is so perfectly tailored to that child that there is no space for learning. They bring them food, solve their problems and meet their every need. It seems fine and everyone is happy, except, after a while, the parent who burns out and the child who becomes totally dependent.

In order to develop, we all need to move outside our comfort zone and, for some, this causes distress. Distress isn't always a reason to back off.

With this in mind, meet Alice, who loves peanut butter bagels. Her mother puts them together for her. Alice just says, 'Bagel, please?' and one appears. That's been happening since Alice was two, and she's now ten. Alice is happy with the situation, but her mother has had enough. She tells Alice it's time to learn how to do her own bagels. Alice protests; she likes her mother doing them for her. It makes her feel loved! And it's far too difficult for her to toast her own bagel.

Alice's mother stands firm. Alice storms and cries, and says she'll never eat a bagel again. Alice's mother said fine, but she's ready to help Alice learn to make bagels whenever she wants. The next day, Alice comes and asks if her mother will help her make a bagel. It's hard, she can't work out how to slice the bagel or spread the peanut butter, but each time she does it, it gets a little easier. Two months later, Alice is making her own bagels regularly and is proud of her new ability to make herself snacks.

It is possible for a situation in a family to be perfectly stable, apparently happy and yet also lacking in opportunities for the child to learn. Sometimes, things need to be shaken up. For example, think of all the adults you know (in my case they are all men, but I wouldn't want to generalise) who have never learnt to cook or look after themselves. Their mothers did it when they were younger, then they got married and their wives did it for them. The women always did the cooking and looked after the house, and the men (and possibly the women too) never saw any reason for this to change. As they got older, their daughters stepped in to take up the slack. Everyone accepted that they couldn't do it and this belief became fact. Life was organised around their lack of skill, thus removing the opportunities for learning.

We can do this to our children if we meet their needs without ever considering whether we really should be doing so. It's not supportive of someone's autonomy in the long term to prevent them from learning life skills, even if it is done with a nurturing and caring intention.

The Basic Skills of Self-Directed Education

Blake Boles is someone who has spent years thinking about self-directed learning. His business is Unschool Adventures, which organises trips away from home for unschoolers without their parents. He has written several books about self-directed learning. He and I had a lively chat about unschooling, self-directed learning and what it really is. For him, it's all about learning how to manage your own motivation.

'The special thing that happens for unschoolers is that they get to experience intrinsic motivation in a time when they have no economic responsibilities. As soon as a kid turns eighteen, they, more or less, have economic responsibilities. And that's also when we say, right now you have to be more intrinsically motivated. There's an inflection point. We haven't prepared them to be intrinsically motivated by giving them the long-term immersive experience of dealing with the very real challenges of intrinsic motivation which are the challenges of self-directed learning.'

An immersive experience in dealing with intrinsic motivation? If you think back to Chapter 2, you'll remember that I think that lots of self-directed learning can be thought of as immersive learning, in its full, messy and unpredictable glory. If we also consider that self-directed education is an immersive experience in intrinsic motivation, then that moves us up to another level. Self-directed children are getting repeated experiences of learning how to manage themselves, their desires, their frustrations, and working out how they want to interact with the world. The lack of an imposed curriculum means that they are getting an immersive experience in decision-making and responsibility, for they are the people who are in charge of their own lives.

In this way, we could say that the basic skills of self-directed education, instead of being literacy and numeracy, are the skills of self-regulation. The ability to know what you want to do, the ability to manage your emotions, and the ability to take responsibility for your own life. The ability to say 'no', when all around you are saying 'yes' (or vice versa), because you know yourself and your preferences.

This doesn't always make self-directed children easy to be around. In the group of parents I know, it's accepted that some children will say 'no' to what we think are good suggestions. That 'no' is often respected, even if it's not convenient. There is no assumption that everyone will join in; in every social gathering there will be a child or two in the corner with a tablet. It's only when I go to gatherings of schooling families that I realise how unusual this is. There, there is often as assumption that everyone must participate, particularly if there are organised games. There are also other assumptions, like you shouldn't bring your tablet to social events. Schooled children may accept these implicit rules as just the way things are, but self-directed children will find them strange, because what about all those adults who are on their phones?

Children need to feel emotionally safe or secure in their environment, because learning flows best when a person feels safe. They need to feel unpressured; they need to feel accepted for who they are, even at their worst; they need to know that the love and respect that others have for them isn't dependent on their behaviour; and they need to feel connected to others in their world, that they are a part of something larger than themselves. Only then can they start to explore.

How Do I Know It's Working?

That's all very well, you may be thinking. But how do I know if they're learning in the way they are supposed to? If I can't focus on knowledge and your advice is to back off with the workbooks, what do I do?

Look for exploration, discovery, questioning, practice, using feedback and more exploration. Look for children and teenagers who are engaged with what they are doing, whether that's making a mud pie or learning the trumpet. That's where self-directed success lies, in the way the child relates to the world, and the way the world opens up for them in return.

This learning may well be unexpected and not what you would have chosen. It will definitely take unpredictable paths. It doesn't matter. What matters is the quality of engagement and learning, for they are learning how to find their place in the world. They are learning how to find excellence on their own terms.

If you don't see engagement with anything at all, and you are well outside the deschooling period (which can take at least a month for each year the child was in school or school-at-home), then go back to the basics. For a start, are you dismissing the things they really are engaged with? Are you discounting their friendships, or the ways they choose to pass their time? If you aren't, then what could you change? How can you help them feel autonomous and competent? What are they doing that you could join in with?

And what do they say is the problem, if you ask them and really listen?

Further Reading

Boles, Blake – *The Art of Self-Directed Learning, 23 Tips for Giving Yourself an Unconventional Education*, Tells Peak Press (2014)

Holt, John – *Learning All the Time*, Addison Wesley Longman Publishing Co (1989)

Jones, Gerard – *Killing Monsters – Why Children Need Fantasy, Super Heroes and Make-Believe Violence*, Basic Books (2003)

Llewellyn, Grace – *The Teenage Liberation Handbook: How to Quit School and Get a Real Life and Education*, Thorsons (1997)

Llewellyn, Grace – *Guerrilla Learning: How to Give Your Kids a Real Education with or without School*, John Wiley & Sons (2001)

Rosen, Michael – *Good Ideas: How to Be Your Child's (and Your Own) Best Teacher*, John Murray (2015)

11

Wellbeing – Seeing What the Rest of Us Don't Want to See

Why are modern children so unhappy? It seems like every few months there's another article in the press about anxiety and depression and the failure of child mental health services to keep up with demand. Not only are children said to be unhappy, they're becoming more so. The World Health Organization says that 10–20 per cent of children worldwide experience problems with their mental health. This equates to millions of highly distressed children. What's going on?

There's no lack of people coming forwards to suggest why this might be. Electronic devices, disengaged parents, bullying, divorce, too much testing and pressure, not enough time spent outside, low expectations, addictions to video games . . . it seems that there is very little about a modern childhood which *doesn't* cause unhappiness and anxiety. Everyone has their pet theory, and there is no shortage of experts advising parents on how to change things for their child by banning handheld devices, getting their child more in touch with nature or making sure they have regular one-on-one time.

As is the pattern in our society, we look for explanations on an individual level first. It must be something their parents are doing wrong. Helicopter parents are making kids anxious by being too present and engaged, or parents who are always on their iPhones are not providing enough human interaction. Parents who praise their children too much are said to be setting them up for failure later in life, while those who don't praise are critical and not warm enough. It's not surprising that many parents aren't very happy either.

In this chapter, I'll start by explaining the relationship between stress and control. I'll talk about how school adversely affects the mental wellbeing of some children, and why this happens. I'll then discuss several ways in which children struggle emotionally, with some ideas as to what to do to help.

What's the Problem?

In a *Guardian* article in February 2020, Greta Thunberg's mother wrote about her daughter, who, at the time, was travelling the world and campaigning for governments to modify their policies on climate change. She describes how, since the age of eleven, Greta had been expressing distress. She was crying every day, all day; she stopped eating; she started having panic attacks. She was diagnosed with autism, OCD and almost hospitalised for her eating problems. She was put on drugs. Yet her mother writes: 'What happened to Greta in particular can't be explained simply by a psychiatric label. In the end, she simply couldn't reconcile the contradictions of modern life. Things simply didn't add up. We, who live in an age of historic abundance, who have access to huge shared resources, can't afford to help vulnerable people in flight from war and terror – people like you and me, but who have lost everything . . . She saw what the rest of us did not want to see.'

When Greta started to act, starting a school strike which spread around the world, she started being able to eat and live again. Her mother sums up a dilemma of our time: are very distressed people sick or disordered, or do they see the world more clearly than the rest of us?

When we look at the wider environment, it's unsurprising that children are distressed. Children today have easy access to an enormous amount of information, from all around the world. The news is not hidden from them and much of the news is not reassuring.

In addition, most of them spend their days in an environment which makes very specific competitive requirements of them, and over which they have almost no power. When they refuse to co-operate with this, they are said to be suffering from school refusal, or perhaps school phobia. This is often thought of as an irrational anxiety, a bit like being scared of spiders. But is it irrational to refuse to go to school? Instead of assuming that distressed children must be disordered, let's think about whether school is an environment in which all children can thrive.

Once a child goes through the door of a school, they give up a significant amount of control. They can no longer make choices about when they can eat or use the toilet. They cannot wear their hair how they like or take treasured possessions with them. They are told what to do and assessed on how well they do it. Their only choice is whether to comply or not. If they don't, they are in trouble. There are lots of demands and no privacy at all. Most adults would refuse to tolerate this, particularly with no pay, but we expect children to manage it for their entire childhood. To categorise resistance to this as a mental health problem seems to miss the point.

Control and Stress

When I left school, the first job I got was at Druckers, a handmade cake factory. We made patisserie for cafés all over Birmingham. I thought it would be fine, I'd do the job, earn the money, go home and live my life outside work hours.

When I entered the factory each morning, I first had to put on my uniform – white clogs, blue-and-white checked trousers, white apron and a white mob cap. When I was ready, I could clock in. The supervisor, Dave, who called all the women 'Babs', would tell me where to stand on the conveyor belt. We made fruit tarts, and I was given a huge bowl of mandarin orange segments. As each tart went past, I would carefully place three segments, and then it would pass on to Sara, who was doing the kiwi pieces. At the end, Amanda was on the hot-glaze spray gun, spraying the tarts with gel to keep it all together.

I worked from nine to six, and I had no control over when my breaks were; Dave would decide. Sometimes I would start at nine, and he would send me on my break at ten, and then my lunch at twelve, leaving me working from 12.45 p.m.–6 p.m. without a break.

I soon noticed that there was an unofficial hierarchy of jobs.

Conveyor-belt jobs were the lowest of the low. If the supervisor liked you, you could get promoted to the spray gun. If you missed out the occasional piece of fruit or sometimes got your satsumas the wrong way round, not a chance.

After two weeks of mandarin oranges, I started to dream about cakes. The conveyor belts went faster and faster in my dreams, with me running desperately behind, trying to get the mandarin oranges perfectly straight.

I don't know why Dave decided to move me off the mandarin oranges. Perhaps he noticed my vacant expression and thought I needed a change to perk me up. Or maybe there was some new employee who needed to start out on the oranges. We never chatted in the factory. We couldn't risk missing a cake, and the local radio station blared too loudly anyway. Faces came and went, and we only got to know each other if, by chance, we were sent on our break at the same time.

Anyway, I was moved to the profiterole machine. This was a huge metal cone, filled with cream, with two spikes sticking out at waist level. Profiteroles came along the belt, I had to grab two, put them on the spikes, and – 'thunk' – the machine filled them with cream. Thunk . . . thunk . . . thunk . . . thunk – the machine was set so that it regularly squirted cream out the spikes. You had to keep up the rhythm, or else the cream went all over you.

There I was, eight hours a day, sticking profiteroles on spikes as fast as I could to avoid being covered with cream. If Dave didn't think I was working fast enough, he would come and turn up the machine: thunk-thunk-thunk-thunk-thunk-squirt. 'Keep up, Babs!' he'd bark.

Soon my dreams were filled with 'thunks' and cream. I stopped being able to sleep. I couldn't do anything with the time I had off work. At the same time, I felt anxious and nervous all the time. My weekends were spent dreading Monday. At work, I was reduced to a rather faulty automaton. I had no control over anything.

Much as I needed the money, I just couldn't do it. I lasted four weeks. Dave smiled when I handed in my notice.

Many people assume that the most stressful jobs are the ones at the top, the ones where you have the power to determine the future of thousands of employees, or to steer a company away from bankruptcy.

It suits people in these jobs for everyone to think this, because that justifies their high salaries. It's not uncommon for someone to choose a job where they have few choices and no control, in the belief that this will be less stressful.

In fact, the research shows the opposite. The most stressful work situation to be in is one where you have no control. Leaders experience less stress than those lower down the hierarchy. Feeling like you have some control is more important than other factors, like how demanding your job is.

This tallies neatly with some research I discussed earlier, on self-determination theory (SDT). If you remember, SDT is a theory of motivation, which suggests that autonomy, relatedness and competence underpin intrinsic motivation. Autonomy is the ability to make meaningful choices, to take some control over your life. Take away people's autonomy, and you take away their joy. That's what happened to me at Druckers. I had no control at all, except to leave the job. Children at school don't even have that choice. And yet we wonder why they aren't happy.

People Need Autonomy

Autonomy has been related to increased wellbeing in a large number of studies. When people have choice about what they do, and can stop when they want to, they feel better about the world and themselves. Richard Ryan and colleagues found that wellbeing for college students and workers increases at the weekend; the so-called 'weekend effect'. Even when people work at the weekend, they tend to do it in their own time and in their own way, and therefore have increased autonomy as compared to during the week.

People who report high levels of wellbeing at work tend to be those – you've guessed it – with higher levels of autonomy over what they do.

Of course, some people have to do jobs where their autonomy is low. Sometimes, there is a requirement to just do the job at hand in the same way as everyone else and to very precise requirements. Although, even with these jobs, there are ways in which people can be given more autonomy. When I worked for Druckers, I could have been allowed to choose when I went on my break, or the speed I thought that the profiterole machine should be set at. I could even have been asked if I wanted to place mandarin oranges or strawberry slices.

It's not clear what benefits there are in reproducing this low-autonomy system at school. Just because some jobs have few choices is no reason to spend twelve years making children practise feeling powerless. The school system works by gradually reducing autonomy as children grow. At pre-school and nursery, children are typically allowed to choose between a range of activities and are not made to continue with something once they have lost interest. However, from the age of five onwards, school becomes increasingly more controlling. Children generally have no meaningful choices about what they do all day. Even when, at age fourteen, they do get to make some decisions, it's usually between which classroom they sit in and what information they will be tested on, rather than anything more significant.

In fact, when children leave school to be home-educated, one of the things they often do first is refuse to change out of their pyjamas or refuse to brush their hair. Some of them refuse to put clothes on at all or strip their clothes off the moment they arrive home from anywhere. It couldn't be clearer that they felt that those requirements were externally imposed. When they have choices, they choose not to.

You Can't Promote Wellbeing with Control

Everything we know about wellbeing would suggest that controlling children will not lead to them flourishing. Cast your mind back to the spectrum of motivation from Chapter 4. For the youngest children, intrinsic motivation is allowed to be their guide. They insist upon it. Then, as they get older, not only are their choices narrowed, but the things they like are denigrated. They are told that they need to get on with working, that life's not all fun, and that their future depends on following instructions well. Between the ages of five and sixteen, the regulation moves relentlessly from internal to external. Many children become resentful of this, and those who are most sensitive to control lose their motivation entirely.

Children vary a lot over how sensitive they are to these messages. Some children (I was one of them) enjoy schoolwork and do well enough so that they retain a high quality of motivation throughout school. These children may not even feel controlled, because they have internalised the goals of school and identify with them; they really want to do well. For children like these, external motivation is not necessary because they will work hard for their own satisfaction. Their psychological needs are being fulfilled.

Other children lose all interest. These children can go into a downward spiral, because the response of schools in this situation is typically to try to change their behaviour through increasing control. They might put the child on report, a system where they have to be signed in and out of every lesson by a teacher; they might give the child detention after school or in their breaktime; they might require a child to sit alone doing their work so they can't disrupt the others. All of these interventions act to reduce a child's autonomy, and therefore the quality of their motivation will fall further. The harder the school cracks down, the less motivated the child becomes.

When Psychological Needs Aren't Met

This can mean that, for some children, school is devastating to their wellbeing. It takes away their autonomy, they feel incompetent, and they feel disliked by teachers and other children. Their psychological needs are not being fulfilled on any level and their behaviour deteriorates.

Meet Natalie. When she was eight, she was suspended from school for twenty-eight days in a single term. She has furies. When she's in a rage, she smashes things up. She can fly off the handle when something doesn't go her way – like if she can't find her favourite pencil or if the person sitting next to her jogs his arm. When that happens, she gets suspended. Then she goes back to school, and it's sort of OK until it happens again. Natalie refuses to talk to most people and avoids doing things she might fail at. She says schoolwork is boring and she feels uncomfortable at school. Natalie's mum carries her into school resisting and screaming, and then leaves her in the classroom still protesting. In class, Natalie fidgets all the time and it annoys the other children. Their parents ring up to complain. Natalie might be expelled from school before she's ten.

Natalie's mum is desperate for help. She's been on parenting courses about parenting angry children, about sensory processing disorder and anxiety. Each one helps her a bit, particularly meeting the other parents. But Natalie still carries on having meltdowns, and nothing she does seems to help. School call her in and tell her it has to stop. She feels terrible, because she doesn't know what to do.

Natalie's needs aren't being met at school. She's miserable, and the school are trying to use external regulation to force her to comply with requirements. Unfortunately, their efforts just make Natalie angry and frustrated, which means she gets into trouble again. Natalie is in a downward spiral and the courses that her mum is being sent on are unlikely to help, because they won't question the lack of autonomy in Natalie's life. The onus is on Natalie to change so she can make it through school; no one is considering how the school system itself needs to change to give Natalie more control over her life.

Children like Natalie are likely to look elsewhere to have their psychological needs met – to video games, for example, a place where many children can feel autonomous and competent. Or to a group of peers who are equally disaffected by school, and with whom the child can feel temporarily better about themselves. As they get older, they may also turn to alcohol, drugs or self-harm to get away from the intense distress that they feel.

The school and their parents often see what the children are doing to cope as the problem. A child who plays on video games for thirty hours a week may be diagnosed with a video game addiction, and her parents told to reduce her access to the game. By reducing video game use, we just end up reducing her access to the one place where she feels autonomous and competent. We risk making everything worse unless we think about the whole picture.

Prioritising Wellbeing

There is no way that an education based on control and pressure can genuinely prioritise wellbeing. Strategies such as teaching children mindfulness without addressing their lack of autonomy just gives the message that they need to change to cope better. It doesn't encourage them to think about what they need, nor does it give them the power to change their life. If a child is unhappy at school, then we need to listen to what they are saying and work out with them what isn't working.

With children, behaviour and their emotional wellbeing are closely linked. Many children can't yet express how they are feeling in words, but their behaviour is their way of communicating. Unfortunately, at school, distressed behaviour is often labelled as 'challenging' and is treated as something which needs to be controlled rather than understood.

There are some specific issues which many children experience, and which often lead to distressed behaviour. Understanding these can help us to address the real issue, rather than trying in vain to control a child's expression of distress.

Trauma

The things that happen to us matter. When something traumatic happens to a child, they may continue to feel the effects for years afterwards, but they may not be able to express why this is.

Sajid is fourteen; he talks in a monotone about his life. Nothing seems to excite him or impress him. It's like he's slowed down. Sajid's mum says she misses his smile and they can never have fun together.

Sajid's been put in a special class at school for those who are struggling. He hates it; he feels singled out as stupid. He used to be popular at primary school, he had lots of friends and they would play basketball together. He was really good at basketball. When he was eleven, he broke his arm very badly and had to have several operations on it before it healed. His recovery was really long and painful and he couldn't play basketball. At the same time, his parents split up and there was a lot of arguing. That year seemed to change Sajid. After that, he found it hard to concentrate on school and his marks started falling. He wasn't so good at basketball any more. He became irritable and angry with his friends and they stopped coming round. He began spending a lot of time on his iPad and spent several hundred pounds on his dad's credit card on in-app purchases. His dad was furious and Sajid is still paying the money back with any money he gets given for birthdays or Christmas.

Everyone wants to know what's wrong with Sajid. He's been sent for assessments for dyslexia, dyscalculia, autism and ADHD. His mum thinks he's depressed and his dad thinks he should pull himself together. He spends most of his time on his iPad with headphones on, and doesn't communicate much with anyone. School thinks the iPad should be taken away and his mother does remove it to punish him if he hasn't done his schoolwork. Then he has huge tantrums and will smash things up.

His mother is desperate to reconnect with him before he's an adult. It feels like time is running out for Sajid; he's not going to do many GCSEs and he already thinks his options are limited. He can't think of anything he wants to do in the future.

Sajid's experiences aren't out of the ordinary. He wasn't abused or neglected, but he had a very difficult year and the adults in his life were preoccupied with practicalities. His basic psychological needs weren't being met, and he turned to his iPad. Buying things on the iPad made him feel good, and so he did it more. Now people are seeing his iPad use and saying that that is the problem, but actually it's a way of coping with his distress.

When something traumatic happens to us, it's recorded in our memory in a different way to other memories. We have two places in our brains where memories are stored. In the hippocampus is stored the narrative of our lives, like in a filing cabinet; memories here are organised with dates attached. If you want to remember a particular year, you can do so by thinking about linked memories. For example, I want to remember my friends at the first school I attended. I can mentally take myself back to the classroom, and the image comes to mind of a little girl who had the same blue dress with a red flower on the front as me. Karen. I hadn't thought of Karen for about thirty-five years, but she's there in my memory, next to the Roger Red Hat and Jennifer Yellow Hat reading scheme. When I start to think of that, other memories from early primary come up. The school assemblies where the Year 6 pupils seemed as tall as grown-ups and scraping my knees in the cold concrete playground. I can remember what happened, but the events feel like they are in the past.

Traumatic memories, on the other hand, are encoded along with all the emotions and sensations of the time. If the hippocampus memories are neatly filed away, trauma memories are like screwed up pieces of paper which have been shoved in the cupboard under the stairs. Every so often, the cupboard door bursts open, no matter how hard we try to keep it shut. Out come the memories, just as vivid as the day they happened, with all the feelings still fresh. When I remember the time I fell down the stairs and badly twisted my ankle, I can still feel the terror in my stomach (and a twinge in my ankle), even though it was over twenty years ago. These memories often pop up in flashbacks, nightmares or thoughts that just come into our heads when we don't want them.

Children can experience all sorts of different things as traumatic. Sajid's year sounds pretty awful, but less objectively terrible things can also cause problems. I've met children who have traumatic memories of being left out of a friendship group, wetting themselves in reception or of vomiting in the coach. Some children react to teachers telling them off as if something catastrophic has happened. Adults hope that children are resilient and, if they don't talk about something, they assume that there's no problem.

Many children have memories which distress them and which they don't feel able to talk about. This can mean that they have trouble concentrating at school, they lash out, they are irritable, they are anxious, and they sleep badly. This doesn't mean they all need trauma therapy (although some of them might). They may just need a space to talk about what happened without worrying that they will upset other people. They might need to know that this is a normal reaction to stressful events. They need a chance to express their feelings rather than the focus being on their non-compliance with school requirements.

Emotional Regulation

Young children have trouble managing their emotions. For them, each obstacle in life is a crisis. They become extremely distressed over the wrong colour cup, or utterly furious because someone borrowed their crayon.

From birth, parents help children to regulate their emotions. The mother who soothes her baby through rocking or feeding is helping them to calm down. With toddlers, it's a question of offering regular snacks, naps and sympathy and being there to intervene when tensions run high. Parents very quickly learn what their children can manage emotionally and plan their days accordingly. When they get it wrong and go too far, meltdowns follow.

Children remain dependent on their parents to help them manage their emotions. The child who returns to a parent when they are hurt or feeling unsure is seeking help with emotional regulation. All is well, the parent reassures, and the child moves on. When children go to nursery or childcare, they look for a parent substitute to do the same thing, and settings for young children recognise this need.

Once children are in school 'proper', the focus moves from caring to education. Their teachers cannot provide emotional reassurance for all the children in their classroom; the ratios are simply not high enough and this isn't their role. Children have to manage their own emotions or find other children who help them feel safe. This is one reason why friendships are so important at school. Without them, you're emotionally on your own.

Over time, if all goes well, children become more able to manage their own emotions and need to refer less often to an adult for support. They become able to manage challenging situations without breaking down and are able to stop themselves from screaming and kicking when they are frustrated. They also become more able to reflect on their emotions, and better able to state what they need. Not everyone learns this, and many adults continue to have difficulties with their emotions. Some adults regulate their emotions using drugs, alcohol, eating or self-harm.

Some children find emotion regulation more difficult than others. These children are challenging to parent, because you never know when they are going to lose it. It might happen on the bus or in the queue at the supermarket. They seem to go from zero to a hundred in an instant. Their parents are always on high alert, anticipating how they are going to get out if the situation turns. Days are carefully planned around what a child can manage. The children who develop emotional regulation more slowly are likely to get flagged as having special educational needs at school, because their behaviour is unpredictable and inconsistent. They may hit other child when they are distressed or angry.

Helping children learn emotional regulation is part of the hidden work of parenting. When it goes well, nothing happens. Often one parent, usually the primary carer, will take on the emotion regulation work while the other one remains largely oblivious. When things are going well, the work is literally invisible. It just looks like everyone had a good day, and no one sees the enormous amount of under-the-surface support which is going on to help the child stay calm and regulated.

How Do We Help Children Regulate Their Emotions?

Emotion regulation happens internally and externally. Internal strategies are those which go on inside a person's head, like deep breathing and mindfulness. External strategies involve doing something different or changing the situation. Most people use both to manage their emotions.

At conventional school, children's ability to regulate their emotions externally are limited. They can't use many of the strategies which adults use. They can't decide to go and sit outside for a while; they can't get away from other people. Their options when feeling very distressed or overwhelmed are essentially limited to trying to control their emotions internally or behaving in a way which is likely to get them into trouble. It's not surprising that schools sometimes teach mindfulness or relaxation; these are the only options which don't challenge the school set-up in any way. They encourage the children to stay calm, no matter what is going on around them. The children who can't manage their emotions in the school environment are the children who fight in the playground, or who leave school in the afternoons and are immediately inconsolable or furious. They've been holding it in all day, and they just can't do it any more.

When a child can choose what they do each day, their capacity to develop emotional regulation is increased. Quite simply, they have more options and more chances to practise. Their ability to express their emotions is also increased, which means that younger self-directed children often appear more volatile than their schooled peers. One of the things which I've particularly seen self-directed children learning as they approach puberty is how to reflect on and manage their emotions. Even children who had serious difficulties with their emotions at age seven, eight or nine (and who would therefore be causing serious concern at school), start to develop the capacity for self-reflection as they get older. They become more able to keep calm in stressful situations, and they start to pace themselves so that they don't become overwhelmed. In order to do that, they need to have the space to make choices. Punishing children for their lack of skill in emotion regulation is likely to backfire, as it makes them frustrated and anxious – and it's focusing on something that they cannot help. It's similar to punishing a child who has not yet learnt to read or write. It will create anxiety and shame and is unlikely to result in effective learning.

Learning Strategies on Managing Emotions

Children coming out of school will often have difficulties with their emotions, and some of them can benefit from explicit strategies to help them stay calm. These could include fiddle toys, stress balls and visualisation. There are apps with calming stories which they can listen to, or some children find it helps to play repetitive yet engaging games such as Tetris.

Exercise is a great way to regulate emotions, and a child who gets enough exercise is likely to be calmer through the rest of the day. It's also important that children get enough sleep, and they may need a lot of help to wind down at the end of the day. Some children require the presence of a parent to fall asleep for many years, and this can be because the presence of a parent helps them to feel calm enough to drop off.

Parents sometimes feel that they have to keep up a calm exterior no matter what, but this means that children don't get to see other people managing emotions. When parents talk about their emotions and how they manage them, children can learn by example. For example, if a parent is feeling stressed by a situation, they can tell the children, but with a solution attached. In a queue, a parent could say, 'I find it so difficult waiting and not knowing how long it will be. I'm going to take a few deep breaths and think of something interesting to talk about.' Or they could say, 'I'm feeling angry about the bus running late . . . part of me wants to shout and swear! I'm going to do some running on the spot instead and jump up and down.' By consistently seeing their parents using strategies like this, the children start to follow suit. They can begin to reflect on and name their emotions and they can also suggest strategies to others.

Resistance

Some children are extremely resistant to any suggestions and appear completely unmotivated to do anything which isn't their own idea. Some of these children have come out of school, but there are children like this who have never been to school. These are some of the children who benefit most from a self-directed education.

Just knowing that someone else wants them to do something is enough to stop them doing it. They can be exasperating people to be around. These are the children who reply, 'No, you can't force me!' when you ask if they'd like to go to the cinema or the adventure playground. They are so sensitised to control that everything feels controlling to them, even asking them to get dressed or brush their teeth.

It is very likely that this resistance is driven by fear. They aren't trying to be annoying; they are genuinely scared of doing anything. The zone in which they feel safe is extremely small. They are usually highly anxious, and they use control over their environment to manage their anxiety.

These children need an intensely un-controlling environment in order to find an awareness of their own choices and preferences. It won't be enough to say, 'Now it's your choice.' They won't truly believe it, or they don't know what to choose.

The adults around them need to step back, bite their tongues, and provide choices about everything. Instead of telling them to brush their teeth, tell them their toothbrush is ready and they can clean their teeth whenever they want to. Instead of telling them to get dressed, put the clothes out and say they can get dressed whenever they want to or not at all. Make statements rather than asking questions. Say, 'We could go to the park . . .' and then leave it at that. Drop the reminders and stop worrying that they might be missing out if you don't ask them again. Each time you ask will increase their anxiety, and the more anxious they feel, the more they will resist.

Non-Negotiables

That works for things which they can choose, but what about the non-negotiables? Every family will decide for themselves what these are, partly depending on what causes the most distress. Some families stop insisting on their children coming to the table to eat, for example, or stop insisting that they change out of their pyjamas. Wearing underpants when visitors come might be a non-negotiable, as would be non-violence. By allowing the unimportant battles to cease, you can focus on holding the line where it really matters. It's far less important that they wear clothes than that they stop hitting their sister.

With the non-negotiables, it often helps to make a plan in advance and to agree it with the child. So, for example, you could have a conversation along these lines, when everyone is calm and there is no hitting. 'I can't let you hit your sister. What shall I do to stop you when you look like you're about to hit her?' You can make a list of ideas with the child of what to do. Those could include sitting between the children, a code word, jumping up and doing some exercises, all doing some kick-boxing together, or going for a run. Ask the child how they know they might be getting annoyed and what the signs are. Then watch out for them and intervene quickly. Repeat the boundary: 'I can't let you hit your sister.' Breathe deeply. This is a marathon, not a sprint.

If you do get angry and shout, forgive yourself. Apologise if you have said something you regret and move on.

Nothing is For Ever

It's important to remember that this is a strategy to help them regain their sense of being in control of their own lives. Once they start to relax a bit and become less rigid, you can reintroduce ideas like eating round the table. This can be done in a non-controlling way, so the dinner table is set and you say, 'You can join us when and if you want to,' and leave it at that. The aim is to create an atmosphere of positivity, and to reduce the opportunities for battles. Your child is used to approaching life like a fight; you need to refuse to play your part. If you do not fight back, over time your child may feel safe enough to experiment with new behaviours.

Some children need this very low-pressure environment for longer than others. Some need it even though they have never been to school. It seems like some children are born temperamentally sensitive to control and pressure, and they have a sixth sense for the hidden pressure in seemingly innocuous statements like 'The rain has stopped' (to which their answer is 'No, I don't want to go to the park and you can't make me.'). These children are a challenge. They are also a gift, because they sniff out control that other children miss, and which adults pretend isn't there.

For them, pressure is always counter-productive. Their resistance is fuelled by anxiety, and pressure increases anxiety. They require super-flexible adults, who become aware of their own controlling tendencies and learn to keep their mouths shut. For them, a gentle reminder feels like a telling-off.

Even for these children, it's not for ever. They will grow and develop the ability to reflect on their behaviour. One child I know started at the age of eight to talk about his 'automatic no', which was the 'no' which came out in response to any suggestion. Once he'd identified it, it could be talked about and discussed. Now when he said, 'NO . . . you can't force me . . .' it was the start of a conversation rather than the end of one.

For children who refuse to go out, it can help to have a schedule so that they know what is coming in advance. A system which seems logical and fair may also help. If you can plan things in advance, before the moment, then you stand more of a chance of it working.

Meet Josie.

By the time she was seven, she'd been at school for two years and it had not gone well. She had been facing exclusion for throwing a table at a teacher when her parents withdrew her from school.

Josie was constantly angry. Her mother bought workbooks and set up a school corner, but Josie refused to go anywhere near it. She would throw chairs and ripped up a reading book. She responded to any request with shouting, and any suggested activity was met with a loud 'NO WAY!' and often a kick for the person who suggested it. Josie refused to leave the house, barring the door when her mother suggested they go to the playground.

Her sister was four. After six months of this, the whole family was frazzled and her sister was bored and wanted to go to school. Josie's mother was starting to think that might be a good idea, except that then she would have to get everyone, including Josie, out of the house twice a day for drop-off and pick-up.

Josie's mother introduced a system of turn-taking: each person would get to choose what happened on alternate days and the time-table was put up on the wall. First Josie chose, then her sister, then her mother, then Josie and then her sister again. At the weekends, they split up, one parent to each child, so both children could get a choice of activity. The agreement was that on Josie's days, no one else would even suggest going out, so Josie could relax. On the other days, Josie needed to come out for at least an hour and then they could go home again. They also might invite visitors on those days, but Josie could go into a different room when visitors were there if she wanted.

Josie was immediately calmer when she knew on which days outings would be suggested. At first, she did continue to protest but, as she got more used to going out, they died down a bit. The exercise of getting out calmed her down and she was less angry. She started to enjoy going out and then, one day, suggested her own outing.

Josie's story illustrates the importance of considering everyone in the family when supporting a child's autonomy. It might have seemed like the least controlling response would have been to accept Josie's refusal to go out at all, but this would have meant that her sister and mother had no autonomy at all. Josie would have held all the power.

So her mother set up a structure in which Josie could make choices, but so could she and her sister. Her mother also knew that Josie's refusal to go out wasn't because she really wanted to stay in but was due to the intense fear and anxiety she had experienced at school. She needed to learn that it was safe to go out, and that she wouldn't be returned to school. As Josie became less anxious, she was able to make real choices about what to do. The whole family was happier.

When Choice Makes Things Worse

Sometimes parents try to give their children lots of choice, and that in itself contributes to their anxiety. For some children, being given two options for outings is just too much. They'd be able to cope with a choice between the park or staying at home, but a choice between the park, soft play and staying at home? Overload. Going into a shop to buy a snack with so many options? Overload. This makes them anxious, which triggers resistance, and they can't do anything.

If it seems like your child can't handle choices, reduce the options for now. Instead of taking them into the shop to choose, say, 'Would you like a banana?' before you go in and, if they say yes, buy one. Or if even that is too much, say, 'I'm going to buy a banana . . .' and do so. Say, 'We could go to the park . . .' and leave it at that. Don't mention the other option. Don't dither. None of this is for ever. They will develop their capacity to cope with choices, but they need to reduce their anxiety first, and they can't do that if they are constantly in overload.

I've met children who become very anxious when they are warned of things which will happen in advance, and others who are very anxious when they have no warning. You are the person who will know your child best. Watch for what happens and learn from your mistakes. See if you can identify what it was that pushed them over the edge and try something different the next time.

Anxious Children, Anxious Parents

Anxiety leads to many children being withdrawn from school. Separation anxiety, school refusal, generalised anxiety – they're all ways of saying that this child gets very upset about the demands of school. Sometimes, this anxiety resolves once school is out of the picture, but anxiety sometimes has a way of sticking around, particularly if everyone responds with avoidance.

Emotions can be contagious. Mood and worrying spread from person to person like an infectious disease. When parents are more anxious, children feel less safe. And if children think that parents are anxious about their anxieties, then they may start to believe that they are right to feel the way they do.

Pippa had always been anxious, getting very worried about things like changing her clothes or her parents going to work, so her parents decided to educate her at home instead of sending her to school. They thought she would grow in confidence with the one-to-one attention and would gradually become more outgoing.

In fact, the opposite happened. Pippa developed a terror of supermarket trolleys and squirrels. No one knew quite why. Pippa's parents were very child-led and had always tried to follow Pippa's needs. So they helped her avoid her fears. They mostly stayed at home and, when they did go out, they took the long way round so they didn't walk past Morrison's and see any trolleys. They had shopping delivered so they never had to go to the supermarket. They also went the long way round to avoid the park, just in case of encountering any squirrels. They had hoped this would calm Pippa down, but actually it seemed to make her more anxious. She was looking around the whole time they walked along the road in case a squirrel jumped out, and she started to get anxious about scooters as well as supermarket trolleys, further restricting what they could do and when they could go out.

Pippa's parents have acted entirely naturally in trying to help Pippa avoid her fears. Unfortunately, what Pippa has learnt from her parents' behaviour is that she's right to have those fears, because she thinks that her parents think they are so realistic that they, too, will try to avoid supermarket trolleys and squirrels. Because Pippa isn't seeing any trolleys or squirrels, she's never getting the chance to learn that actually these things are safe and won't harm her. Her world is narrowing rather than expanding, and it's likely that that will continue if Pippa's parents carry on avoiding the objects of her fears.

Pippa's parents had to change their approach. They told Pippa that they were sorry, but things needed to change. They said that they weren't scared of trolleys, and they knew that they were nothing to be scared of, and so they weren't going to help Pippa avoid them any more.

The Worry Gremlin

They used the analogy of a 'worry gremlin' sitting on Pippa's shoulder, telling her that things were dangerous when they weren't (this terminology comes from a workbook by Kate Collins-Donnelly, which is worth reading if this is something your child struggles with). Pippa liked this idea and drew her worry gremlin, with all the things that she said in speech bubbles. She even drew a little supermarket trolley. Pippa's parents started walking past the supermarket and, when Pippa got upset, they would say, 'Oh, it's that worry gremlin again, making up stories, those trolleys can't hurt us . . .' and keep going. They started to act as if there was nothing to be scared of and, over time, Pippa saw that and learnt to do the same, even when she felt anxious. They bought a toy trolley with a squirrel to go in it at home and kept it somewhere where it could be easily seen. Pippa's world started to expand again.

When Do We Need Outside Help?

In some cases, a child's life can become dominated by fears or they are very low in mood. Then, you might want to find a therapist who could work with them to help them feel calmer and reconnect with the world.

Finding a therapist who doesn't see a return to conventional school as the aim for therapy may be a challenge. You will want to have met the therapist first to explain your philosophy of education and parenting. If they aren't open to listening, find someone else. You and your child should be setting the goals collaboratively with the therapist, not struggling against them.

It's normal for a child to change once they leave school, and sometimes there is a period of readjustment. Even when a child wanted to leave school, losing that structure and regular social contact can be a shock. It's fairly common for a child to have a period after leaving school during which they are exhausted. This, in itself, isn't cause for alarm; it's when it goes on for months with no change that you might need to start thinking about looking for help.

Further Reading

Ciarrochi, Joseph – *Get Out of Your Mind and into Your Life for Teens: A Guide to Living an Extraordinary Life*, New Harbinger (2012)

Collins-Donnelly, Kate – *Starving the Anxiety Gremlin: A Cognitive Behavioural Therapy Workbook on Anxiety Management for Young People*, Jessica Kingsley Publishers (2013)

Ernman, Malena – Malena Ernman on daughter Greta Thunberg: 'She was slowly disappearing into some sort of darkness', the *Guardian* (23 February 2020)

Faber, Adele & Mazlish, Elaine – *How to Talk So Kids Will Listen and Listen So Kids Will Talk*, Third Edition, Piccadilly Press (2013)

Greene, Ross – *Raising Human Beings: Creating a Collaborative Partnership with Your Child*, Scribner (2017)

Huebner, Dawn & Matthews, Bonnie – *What to Do When You Worry Too Much: A Kid's Guide to Overcoming Anxiety*, Magination Press (2005)

Ironside, Virginia & Rodgers, Frank – *The Huge Bag of Worries*, Hodder Children's Books (2011)

McCurry, Christopher – *Parenting Your Anxious Child with Mindfulness and Acceptance*, New Harbinger (2009)

Sedley, Ben – *Stuff That Sucks: Accepting What You Can't Change and Committing to What You Can*, Robinson (2015)

Siegal, Daniel & Bryson, Tina – *The Whole-Brain Child: 12 Proven Strategies to Nurture Your Child's Developing Mind*, Robinson (2012)

Wilson, Reid & Lyons, Lynn – *Anxious Kids; Anxious Parents: 7 Ways to Stop the Worry Cycle and Raise Courageous and Independent Children*, Health Communications (2013)

12

HELP! The Self-Directed Education Problem Corner

These questions aren't from individuals – they are composites, the result of years spent moderating forums about self-directed education online, talking to other parents and seeing the questions that come up again and again. I've also worked professionally with parents and children. All of the problems are ones that real parents have had.

Q: I'd like to give my teenager more control over their education, but I can't give up work and there is no other adult able to be at home full-time. I don't want them to be at home all day alone. How can I give them more control over their education while they are at school?

You can increase their autonomy while they are in school. For a start, you can make it clear that you are not focused on grades and that they don't need to report to you. You could give them responsibility for their homework and avoid being the person who makes sure that everything is ready in the mornings. You can let them choose not to do things at school; many parents pressure their children into particular choices, or into extra-curricular activities. You could change the way you relate to their choices of activity outside school, supporting them with those as much as you support them with their schoolwork. This might involve helping them find resources they need or making sure that schoolwork doesn't dominate their time.

Outside school, you could avoid the temptation to suggest lots of classes, and make sure that there is space for them genuinely to do what they want to do, without expectation of achievement. You could be autonomy-supportive at home, giving choices rather than issuing commands. You can let them know that for you, exams are not the be-all and end-all. Look for ways they can do things that make them feel competent, no matter what those things are. See if there's anything you can join them in – would they let you play a video game with them maybe? Or could you find a new joint activity which is based on their interests, rather than school priorities?

Q: My children choose to do such trivial things. My son spends his time reading Choose Your Own Adventure *books and my daughter watches* My Little Pony *on a loop. I'm worried that if I take them out of school, they will fall years behind the other children and that letting them choose what they do is educational neglect. How do I get them to do something more worthwhile?*

Who gets to decide what's trivial? You only need to read a school curriculum from another time period to see that information that was considered essential a hundred years ago is now considered irrelevant. If your children are engaged and interested in what they are doing, then they will be learning from it. Your son could be learning about choices and consequences from *Choose Your Own Adventure*, as well as narrative structure, while *My Little Pony* is a psychological drama which has many adult fans. How about, instead of trying to make them do something else, join in with them in what they are doing? Read a *Choose Your Own Adventure* yourself so you can discuss it with your son. Watch some episodes of *My Little Pony* together with your daughter. Look for what they are getting out of it, rather than how deficient you think those choices are.

The concept of 'falling behind' is a school one. It's not possible for a child to fall behind their own developmental schedule, unless their environment isn't providing them with the right conditions to learn. Learning is not linear, and it doesn't stack up in the way that schools would have you believe. Your children will develop differently outside school, and this is diversity in action.

Q: I can see how self-directed education would work well for teenagers who already have the basics in place, but how can children know what's open to them if someone hasn't taught them basic skills first?

This is such an interesting question. Lots of people feel that they're fine with teenagers who might choose to read lots of books, or spend their time drawing, or designing science experiments, but they can't see how a young child spending their whole time playing is going to result in a teenager who has the skills that they need.

Play is an amazing vehicle for learning. Through play, children learn many skills including complicated social reasoning, perspective-taking, emotion regulation and problem-solving. These are all 'basic skills' which, if you lack them, no amount of academic knowledge will make up for. Play is also a very wide category, and it's important that children have the opportunity for many types of play. Playing with Lego, for example, develops different skills to playing 'shops', and playing outside is different again. As children get older, if they aren't dissuaded from playing, their play naturally becomes more sophisticated and even more complex. Part of self-directed education is valuing all those types of learning, rather than focusing just on academic subjects, particularly when children are younger. Some young children are interested in reading, others aren't, and perhaps the time and effort spent trying to motivate those who aren't might be better spent providing opportunities for them to play and develop other skills, until they want to learn to read.

Self-directed education is not about a child learning in a vacuum. They need an environment of opportunities. At home, this often means parents being one step ahead, thinking about what might interest them and acquiring resources. It can be more work than following a curriculum, because it has to be individualised. It also sometimes involves acquiring resources 'just in case', which a child then does not find interesting. Libraries, charity shops and free samples of ebooks can be helpful here. Meeting up with other people is essential because, through social connections, learning is shared and therefore multiplies. At a self-directed school, the environment itself is full of opportunities due to the presence of other children and adults, but parents of children at self-directed schools are still often thinking about opportunities at weekends.

If a skill is fundamental in our society (as are basic literacy and numeracy), then children will at some point want to acquire them. Some will do that without formal tuition, in a similar way to how they learnt to talk. Others will benefit from following a reading scheme or structured programme. Self-directed education doesn't rule any of those things out, but they rule out forcing children to do them, or telling children it's time to start learning something because of their age. Self-determination theory would also suggest that it would be good to avoid external motivators for skills such as reading and maths, as this is likely to damage children's internal drive in the longer term, even if in the short-term it keeps them going.

Q: My son has autism, ADHD, OCD and sensory processing disorder. He is at school, but he is totally miserable. However, I'm worried that he has such severe and complex special needs that I can't provide what he needs at home. The school tells me that he needs specialists and I don't have the training. I don't know what to do.

Your son sounds like he really isn't a good fit with school. Schools are always going to tell you that what they are doing is important and that you should keep sending your child there. They really believe it. Very few teachers have any experience at all of self-directed education. They know what children are like in school, but they don't know how different it can be. They also don't know just how distressed children can sometimes be after school as a result of their school experiences. You know your son better than they do.

You don't know what your son would be like without the pressures of school, but if he's miserable at the moment, you haven't got a lot to lose. All of the diagnoses he has are about how he responds in particular situations. Change the situation, and you may well change how he feels and what he is capable of. Your son isn't broken, but the environment he's in isn't allowing him to thrive.

School won't go away. If you take him out of school and feel out of your depth after about a year, he could always go back. You can also look for different sorts of support once it's clearer what his needs are when he's not at school. You are also likely to find lots of children with similar needs to him in the community of children outside school.

Recovery from school will take a long time for someone who has struggled this much. It will be a bumpy road. You might want to make connections with other parents who have had similar experiences to help you through the hard times. If he has any sorts of therapy that he finds useful and wants to continue, you'll need to make sure that they understand your choices and don't see a return to school as a goal.

Q: My eleven-year-old spends hours and hours each day on her tablet. It's the first thing she reaches for each morning, and the last thing she does at night. I worry that she is not developing any other skills, and that she is addicted. How can I encourage her to do something else?

Fear of screens is so prevalent in our society and, when we start to panic about something, we rarely think straight. Take a step back a moment and think about what's going on here.

What is she doing on her tablet? Tablets are tools, not activities in their own right. With the concept of 'screen time,' we behave as if everything that a child does on a screen can be lumped together, but actually a child could be reading a book, drawing a picture, playing a game, coding a programme, listening to a podcast, chatting to a friend, making a stop-motion animation, doing research, writing a story – all on their tablet. It's not surprising that someone might spend a large proportion of their day on a device which does such a variety of things.

Could you join her while playing on her tablet? If you have your own tablet, or phone, you might be able to join her virtually in her games. Alternatively, you could sit with her and see what she's doing. If she's only doing quite a limited range of things, then it might be worth exploring whether she has access to other things she might want to do on the tablet. When my children were young, I spent time in the evenings searching for new games for them, to give them more options. We discovered some wonderful apps which are still popular with them today. You can start by searching for things like 'apps like X' where X is one they really enjoy. Or 'great apps for eleven-year-olds' or whatever age your child is.

If you have a tablet, you could explore its potential near her, so she can get a chance to see what you are doing. It's also worth considering whether you have some counter-productive rules, such as not paying for games on the tablet. This often results in children only playing free games, which are very frustrating, because they are designed to get you to spend money on in-app purchases. These games keep children playing them for hours in a state of semi-boredom, because they have to wait for everything to happen rather than paying to speed them up. If you can find some high-quality games which you pay for up front, then the playing will be a lot more rewarding.

Q: I worry about maths. I always found maths difficult and I think my son might be the same way. I just can't see how he's ever going to learn maths if he doesn't follow a curriculum.

Maths is the first thing that many people worry about. The strange thing is, the people who worry most are usually those who have spent twelve years at school being taught maths, and yet they still find it difficult and frightening. They're worried that unless they do the same to their children, their children will also find it difficult and frightening. That doesn't make sense to me – why would you repeat a process that didn't work for you, in case your children have the same outcome without going through that process? Even if your children become teenagers with only a rudimentary understanding of maths, they will have not had the experience of struggling with maths at school for years, and so it will be easier for them to learn when it becomes necessary.

Maths is all around us – numbers and patterns wallpaper our lives. At school, the focus for maths is on getting the right answer. This makes it a scary experience for many children, particularly if they are being asked to understand maths concepts which are beyond their developmental level. Out of school, children can explore maths without fear of getting it wrong. It's just another part of life. My children have learnt fractions through cutting cakes and dividing boxes of ice creams. They have learnt about percentages from watching the battery charge drop on their tablets and from Monopoly. They have learnt about decimals from money. They have learnt about volume and area from building houses in Minecraft. These things are around in our life. If they decide they need to memorise their times tables, then they can do that, but they may decide, as I have for myself, that it's not worth the effort. You can get maths programmes for tablet computers which they might find interesting, but don't force it. The easiest way to make them dislike maths is to put the pressure on. Instead, why don't you use their education as a chance for you to change your mind about maths? You could learn how to do maths again, but this time without the worry. There are books for adults who want to learn maths to keep up with their children – you could start there.

Q: My fourteen-year-old came out of school last year after years of bullying. She is so sad. At first, she was happy and relieved to be away from school but now she says that her life is over, and she'll be a failure for ever. How can I help her see that she can take control of her life?

What's her life like now? What can she do each day? Is she alone at home, while her schoolfriends carry on without her?

It's hard for children who were bullied when they leave school, because they have often been told to keep going as otherwise the bullies will win, and so when they leave it feels like they have lost. For teenagers used to school, the lack of structure can be particularly difficult to adapt to. You might need to be quite proactive at this stage, looking for other families with teenagers around her age who are out of school and inviting them round for pizza, or finding places to meet others like theatre groups or choirs. There might be volunteering jobs that you and she could do together, or that she could do alone. Some teenagers work in charity shops, if their insurance covers it. Advertising her services as a babysitter, mowing lawns or doing odd jobs could be a possibility if she's interested. She might be able to help other home-educating families with young children – it's often hard to find people to help out during the school day. It also might help to look for home educators' camps to go to in the summer; there are several different camps in the UK, Europe and North America, and families with teenagers will often be there. You could think about what makes her feel good and see if you can do more of that. It sounds like she's felt like a failure for a long time, and you might need to help her think about what would help her feel more competent. It could be taking on responsibility for a task in the home – for example, meal planning and cooking – or it could be learning a new skill which she and you could do together.

If she is self-harming or suicidal, then I would seek a referral to the Child and Adolescent Mental Health Services (CAMHS) and try to find a private psychologist if you can afford it. You can look on sites such as Psychfinder, the EMDR UK Association and the BABCP.

Q: My eleven-year-old can't read. She wants to join the Guides but she's too ashamed of her lack of reading ability to do so. I tell her she'll learn when she's ready, but she says that the fact that every-one else was ready before her means she's stupid. I really wanted her to learn naturally. What do I do?

Ask her what she wants to do. If she would like to use a reading pro-gramme to learn to read, then get one and help her with it. You can do that in an autonomy-supportive way – do not force her, do not use rewards or punishments, and show her that you know she'll learn to read at some point.

There are many ways to learn to read and, as the parent, you need to be flexible and respond to her. Getting fixated on 'natural learning' as the best way is just as problematic as if you were trying to force her through a phonics scheme. The idea of 'readiness' can also be tricky for older children, as they can see that most children learn to read at school much earlier than age eleven, so it raises questions for them about their capabilities. It might help to explain that school children spend years being taught to read, and she hasn't had that, so it's more that they have a skill they have learnt which she hasn't yet acquired. You could use the example of swimming or cycling, people learn at different times; some people learn through being taught and some through practising themselves. It doesn't mean anything about their abilities in the long term.

As regards the Guides, I'd see if you can talk to the Guide leader beforehand, explain that she can't read and that she's self-conscious about it, and ask if they can make sure it's not made an issue. They should be able to manage that sort of variation; there are many reasons why an eleven-year-old might not be able to read, and no reason at all to make her feel uncomfortable about it.

Q: We've decided to take the children out of school so they can take more control of their education — but they don't want to come! My son says he doesn't want to be a loser and my daughter says she'll miss her friends. What do we do?

Ah, the children who want to stay at school. Of course they do – they've been told how important it is, and they have no idea what life would be like without it. It would be against every principle of self-directed education to force them to leave school and would set you off on the wrong foot from the start. Instead of that, make sure they know it's an option, and give them more autonomy about how they do school. Give them the responsibility for doing their homework, for example, rather than you nagging them. Part of the deal with school is that you need to go every day, but you don't have to buy into their system of assessment, for example, by telling children how important their grades are. You can talk about other ways of learning and show how you are learning new things all the time without going to school.

You could perhaps suggest a trial; some families go off travelling for six months and give self-directed education a try. This is more socially acceptable than simply taking the children out of school and that would give you all a chance to see what it's like, but it's obviously quite hard to organise around work and other commitments. Then, if your children do choose school, they are doing so from an informed perspective. Remember, the autonomy of the learner is fundamental in self-directed education and, if a child chooses to go to school, that decision needs to be respected, too.

Q: We took our teenage children out of school last month. Since then, they are doing absolutely nothing at all. They lie on the sofa all day in their pyjamas and watch pointless soap operas. They resist all suggestions of activities or outings. Should I send them back to school?

This is deschooling. When children come out of school, they need time to recover. Often, this takes months, and the longer they've been in school (or the worse their experience) the longer it takes. The first month is still acute recovery time; it's not even longer than the summer holidays.

If all your suggestions are met with resistance, stop suggesting. Instead, start doing things that you find interesting. Go out, if you want to, invite them to come, too, but do something you want to do, rather than hoping that they will become enthusiastic about an idea. Take up a hobby, cook new recipes; invite people round. Let the children participate if they want but, equally, not if they don't want to. Take the pressure off the children and focus on you regaining your sense of intrinsic motivation.

It might also help if you don't refer to their TV choices as pointless, as you have no idea what they are learning through them or why they find them engaging.

Q: My son is highly anxious. Some days, he won't even come downstairs. We took him out of school because he was refusing to go, and the school said that if we didn't take him off the roll, they would send the truancy officer round. Now we don't know what to do . . . things seem to be getting worse rather than better.

This is where it can get really hard. Your son sounds very unhappy and that's why he came out of school. You've removed the stress of school, but he's still highly anxious. Anxiety can be a self-perpetuating problem. We avoid things that we are anxious about, and the more we do so, the more anxious we feel. Your son sounds like he is trapped in a cycle of avoidance and anxiety.

There are several self-help books you could try, and they are listed in the resources section of Chapter 11. Most important would be to talk honestly to your son about how he is feeling and how avoiding the world is likely to make him feel worse rather than better. You could talk about what you do when things make you anxious, and how you have dealt with anxiety in the past.

Exercise is the best thing we know for helping with anxiety, so see what you can do to introduce more activity into his life. There are exercise programmes on several consoles which can be done at home but, if you can find something which he enjoys doing outside, that's even better. Cycling, scooting, rollerblading or running can all be fun.

I wonder if he's worried about going outside because the other children might see him and ask why he's not at school? You could ask him if that's a concern and, if it is, at first you can plan trips at times when other children won't be around and so that you don't have to walk past the school at break time. In the longer term, it would be important to help him feel comfortable with the idea that he might meet other children while out, and perhaps rehearse what to say, but in the short term it might help to focus on one thing at a time.

It also might be important for him to know that if he does recover, he won't be made to go back to school. Sometimes, children are very unhappy at school, and they show us that through anxiety and depression. When they leave school, they need to know that they can recover without this meaning that they have to return to school.

If things carry on getting worse, see if you can find a sympathetic therapist who won't try to get him back into school and who might be able to help.

Q: I think my children were born without curiosity. They just don't seem interested in anything. I'm there, ready to go with whatever interests them, but they never ask questions or show any spark at all. It doesn't matter what we do: museums; theme parks; trips abroad . . . they just seem apathetic. Other people's children are so much more engaged, and they go to school. I thought self-directed education was meant to result in children who loved learning. What can I do?

Are they really lacking in curiosity at all, or just for the things that you'd like them to be interested in? Are they interested in social media, or their peers?

I wonder if it feels to them like you're poised, ready for them to show any interest. This feeling of expectation can actually inhibit children from exploring. It's pressure, a parent watching you like a hawk for signs of curiosity. They need to feel that it would be OK to be interested, but also OK to be interested today and not tomorrow.

Could you step back, stop organising the trips and instead focus on your own life? What could you learn? What really interests you? Let them see you doing interesting things without the expectation that they will join in.

Q: My three-year-old spends hours watching videos of surprise eggs being opened on YouTube. They seem so pointless and such a waste of time and that's all she wants to do. How can I move her on to something more useful for her learning?

Surprise egg videos! A phenomenon of our time. Totally boring and pointless to adults, yet endlessly fascinating for the under-fives. There's a good reason why young children love surprise egg videos (and surprise eggs). They are developmentally at the stage when they are learning about mental states, and how they can change. Very young children think that thoughts and reality are the same thing, and that what they think is the same as what everyone else thinks. Over the years between two and five, they become aware that thoughts can be different to reality, and that our perspective can change.

Surprise eggs provide repeated experiences of not knowing, and then, just through opening the egg, suddenly the truth is revealed and our mental state changes. Then if you rewind the video and watch it again, this time you do know what's inside, but it's like you can take yourself back to the time before you knew. Children love them for the same reason as they like hide and seek, even when they play it by hiding their eyes and saying, 'Come and find me!' as they stand in plain view. They are experimenting with changing mental states.

Having said that, YouTube, in particular, can be hard for young children to stop watching, because it provides an endless selection of new options on the same theme. There's no natural end, and young children are developmentally at a stage where they can find it particularly difficult to pull themselves away. They often protest very loudly when an adult says it's time to stop.

It's important for all children to have time to move around and engage in all sorts of play. You can make this easier by making sure that the tablet is not always visible; research with adults shows that just having their smartphone visible reduces the quality of conversation they have with someone. It's a distraction, and we are compelled to keep checking. So try to introduce times when all of you are not using devices or agree specific times when the tablets are available. Plan in advance when they will stop but, rather than laying down the law, have an exciting activity to move on to. Look for opportunities to meet the same developmental need as the surprise egg videos. Make your own surprise eggs with playdough, hiding small toys inside, and then you can do your own surprise egg opening. Hide things in envelopes for them to find. Play hide and seek. You might find that they also enjoy setting up hunts for you to search for things. If you have older children, maybe they can make their own surprise egg videos which the younger child can watch or star in.

13

Self-Directed Learning in Action – Personal Stories

What's it really like? You don't need to just take my word for it that this very different way of education can work. The best people to ask are those who have lived it, and who are living it now. I've collected some stories from adults who were self-directed as children, parents of self-directed learners, and educators at self-directed schools and learning communities. Some of these stories have been published already in their blogs or in online magazines, while others have been written specially for this book.

Observing Self-Directed Learning

One of the biggest concerns for parents is how children will ever learn to read without being taught. Juliet Kemp is an author of science fiction and fantasy who can be found at www.julietkemp.com. In this piece, they write about their son Leon, who learnt to read early and with no formal instruction.

> Leon learnt to read very young (seems to run in the family; I did, too), and without any direct teaching or specific directed effort on our part.
>
> We did, of course, read to him a lot – both books, and incidental words around the place. Growing up in central London, he saw a lot of the Tube map from a sling as entertainment while waiting for trains; and one of the first things

he read aloud, somewhere around the age of two, was the electronic 'PLEASE WAIT' sign in the Post Office. He was deeply interested in words and letters from very young, in the way that some children are interested in diggers or dinosaurs or stuffed animals; they were his friends, almost.

I find the boundary around 'teaching' interesting. We never set out to deliberately 'teach' him to read or walk him through resources with 'learning to read' as a goal. He did, however, watch a lot of YouTube videos aimed at teaching small children the alphabet, but under his own steam and at his own rate (with occasional adult assistance in searching). In fact, navigating through alphabet video after alphabet video, he eventually fetched up on similar videos featuring the Cyrillic and Arabic alphabets, and somewhat to our surprise learnt those, too. (Sadly, now aged eight, he's forgotten both!) He would also ask us to look for 'word' or 'letter' iPad apps, most of which were explicitly educational, but again he engaged with them at his own pace and in pursuit of his own goals, rather than as part of an externally directed process.

He was actively resistant to some traditional 'learning-to-read' activities; knowing that he could read a fair few words already, I tried suggesting that we take turns reading a line each in picture books, and got absolutely no buy-in. Reading aloud was definitely an adult job. (At a later stage, he did for a short while insist on reading some of the dialogue – only the dialogue – in his favourite Star Wars picture books.)

As far as I can tell, his approach to reading wasn't the synthetic phonics one currently used in UK schools and, of the resources available to him, he was least enthusiastic about the phonics-based ones. He learnt to recognise various whole words first, and then, at some point, seems to have worked backwards on his own to the kind of approach that a competent adult reader will use for an unfamiliar word, breaking it into recognisable chunks. It was noticeable that although he could 'read' in the sense of 'decoding any writing he encountered' by around three, this didn't automatically mean he could make sense of it! His vocabulary and story-structure skills didn't come along for the ride with the technical practice of 'reading'.

Most of the time, this was a very private process for him. We knew that he was heavily engaging with words/letters in lots of different forms (magnetic letters, puzzles, books, videos, games), but we had very little external evidence of exactly what he was learning until he chose to do something that demonstrated it . . . such as suddenly reading aloud, aged three, all the 'Rules of Behaviour' up on the wall in a museum we were in, or the 'Things Not to Send in the Post' list in the post office. It wasn't something imposed on him from outside, it was a skill he was deeply interested and invested in acquiring, and evidently for him that was the right time for it.

Another common concern is science. How do you do science without a lab? Self-directed science starts with the sense of enquiry which is nurtured through an education led by children's questions.

Laura Grace Weldon (author of *Free Range Learning*, a handbook on natural learning) writes about her children's scientific explorations:

We spread thick layers of science on everything at our house. Yes, occasionally it smells.

Sometimes our science-y obsessions are entirely nonsense, such as a typical dinner table conversation about how many citrus batteries it might take to start a car. Ideas were proposed for this never-to-occur project, including the use of lemon juice instead of whole fruit.

Sometimes, that science is pseudo-educational, such as the time we swabbed between our toes and let the bacteria grow in petri dishes. The 'winner's' dish had such virulent growth that she felt sure it deserved to live. She gave it a name and tried feeding it extra glucose and agar. It quite effectively kept her siblings out of her room. I insisted she throw it away when it began creeping past the lid. I am still blamed for the demise of this biological fright.

Sometimes, it goes on and on. My offspring seem driven to find out. They can't spot a spider without observing it, wanting to identify it, and then going on about the hydraulic features that are basic arachnid operating equipment. Then there was a certain months-long project that involved observing and sketching the decomposition of a musk-rat. They have to discuss all possible angles of a problem, often in such depth that my far more superficial mind drifts off. They tend to walk into a room announcing odd factoids which invariably leads to strange conversations about recently declassified Russian research, turbo-charged engines, or riparian ecology. Or all three. They insist I look at video clips that go on much longer than my attention span. Woe to me if I question a postulate put forth by one of my kids. They will entertain my doubts playfully, as a cat toys with a mouse, then bombard me with facts proving their points. Lots of facts. I've tried to uphold my side in science disputes but it's like using a spork to battle a lightsaber.

Other family homes probably have video game controllers. Our house has stacks of books and periodicals ('Who took the neutrino issue of New Scientist*?' someone yells); tubs overflowing with one son's beakers, tubing and flasks; culturing products in the kitchen (like the jar with a note that says 'Leave me alone . . . I am becoming sauerkraut'); and random sounds of saws, welders and air compressors as something entirely uncommon is being constructed or deconstructed. I know other families have nice normal pictures on their refrigerators. Ours tends to post odd information. The longest-running fridge feature here is a card listing the head circumference of every person in the family. By the time the youngest was eleven, my head was the smallest.*

Science shouldn't be confined to a formal study. My hus-
band and I have never worked in science fields. But we've
found that keeping scientific curiosity alive isn't hard.
It's about an attitude of 'yes'. Projects that are messy,
time-consuming and have uncertain outcomes are a form
of experimentation. They are real science in action. When a
kid wants to know, they want to find out – not later, not next
week, right away. My kids are much more science-savvy
than I'll ever be but, more importantly, they're capable of
discovering anything they want to know.

Self-directed learners learn through doing, which isn't easily divided
up into subjects. Lehla Eldridge is an illustrator and author, with her
husband, Anthony Eldridge-Rogers, of *Jump, Fall, Fly, from Schooling*
to Homeschooling to Unschooling. She describes her daughters learning as they bake a cake:

This cake represents a way in which our children learn.
Through observing unschooled children, I have noticed
that learning is rarely a linear process. One thing leads
to another and learning happens organically. All the
time.

Let's take the simple process of making a cake:

Cooking – *The girls sit at the table looking up recipes. They fix on a cake. They decide they are going to make the chocolate one. They read and they look up the ingredients. Then they scout around the kitchen for what they need. They get into action.*

Maths – *They weigh everything out, scrunching up their faces and concentrating on getting the right amounts. They try to get each ingredient exactly as it should be. Sometimes, there is chaos. Flour doesn't always move in the way that you expect it to.*

Reading – *They keep reading and reading, flicking back and forth to the recipe on their phone. They say the words out loud. The words float across the room like ribbons on the air.*

There is work going on in this kitchen.

Logic – *They follow the steps. Sometimes, things don't go so well, flour gets spilt on the floor and they pour too much water in. They make it right eventually, logically getting the ingredients right and in the correct order.*

Science – *They don't want to use eggs. They figure out that for this recipe they need to replace the egg with linseed. They look that up, follow the 'linseed egg' recipe, they blend the linseeds then add the warm water to them. They watch them swell and go slightly slimy. They see the chemical changes in the food as it is all mixed together. It goes in the oven one way, uncooked. It comes out another, cooked.*

Socialisation – *The cake is ready. They leave it to cool for a while then they declare it is cake time. They find out who is around and who would like a piece of cake. They make tea and invite people in. We all sit and chat and eat the cake. If you were here, you could have a piece.*

Heidi Steel is a qualified teacher who decided to do something very different with her children. She educates them at home and blogs about their life on www.liveplaylearn.org. She writes here about how each of her four children learn differently, even when they are all playing with the same toy – Lego:

Before having my children, I was a qualified teacher.
I studied child development and different educational
approaches. I'd spent fourteen years watching young
children play and develop. I'd never heard of unschooling
or autonomous education, or of life learning.

I had followed a traditional path through the school
system, but my training had broadened my understanding
of how children learn. Our children had never attended any
form of pre-school, yet they had learned to walk, count,
name colours and many other things without my directly
teaching them. There was also the side of education that
I felt uneasy exposing my children to: the tests; the goal
setting; being forced to sit still; being told constantly what
to do, when to do it, how to do it and for how long.

As we became part of the home-educating community
and read around the subject ourselves, we discovered
unschooling.

Moving to unschooling did not change anything in our day-
to-day lives. We simply carried on supporting the children's
autonomy and helping them do the things they enjoy. We do
the things that they love, and we do them as and when they
want to.

Each of our four children has different preferences for
learning. One of my children has learnt to read by playing
computer games, another learnt by being read to daily
for years and discovering graphic novels. Another enjoys
writing to friends and has learnt words by writing famil-
iar phrases repeatedly. My eldest prefers to sit back and
watch before trying something new; our second feels most

*comfortable when in a familiar place. One of our daugh-
ters thrives when with friends or working intently with an
expert, while our youngest enjoys the freedom to dive in
and explore on her own terms.*

*Our children's interaction with Lego is a perfect example
of their varying approaches to learning. We have had Lego
in the house since the children were small. My eldest has
always been happiest free building with our collection of
bricks. Even when he got Lego sets, he preferred to use
the pieces to build his own creations before referring to
the instructions. Our second son wasn't interested in the
instructions at all and is solely focused on his own projects.
Now both of them are able to free build anything they want
and confidently know which combination of bricks they
need to create their model. Our older daughter is set on
following the instructions while our youngest daughter will
follow the instructions and then make modifications of her
own. All of them are learning how to build with Lego but
they are also learning about how they prefer to learn.*

*Sometimes, we dip in and out of things over a long period
of time; sometimes, we immerse ourselves in an interest for
days on end. Sometimes, questions and queries are fleeting
and merely pondering (for now at least). I know they are
learning because they share with me things that they didn't
know yesterday, or they have developed skills that they
didn't have before. I notice connections that they have
made with previous events or conversations we have had. I
have confidence that they are learning all the time.*

Kezia Cantwell-Wright is a founder of East Kent Sudbury School. Her
daughters have never been to school. Here she writes about watching
her oldest daughter explore maths and literacy.

*The maths phase hit us when she was five and a half. It
started very subtly, like a hint of what is to come. From
the back seat of the car she asked me, 'What does three*

and three and three make?' I answered and explained we called that 'times or multiplying'. During the course of that conversation, we worked our way through the two and three times table and only stopped because we reached our destination.

A week later, walking through town, she explained all the number bonds to ten and how they related to each other, just something she'd been pondering. She invented a game where we would challenge each other to sums to work out. She would try really hard to catch me out with a super hard one. She was wanting more and more sums, so I asked her if I should get a book of them. Over the next few months on her request we worked our way through most of a Star Wars-themed maths book . . . until she'd had enough or satisfied her desire for maths mastery for now anyway. She still tells me sums or writes them down occasionally, but it's not the same level of intensity any more.

The interest in words has manifested itself in different ways over time. There have been periods of rhyming games, 'What else starts with B?' type games, phases of 'What does that say?' Tracing letters on road signs, tracing letters in magazines, copying labels off bottles and packaging. We have made comics and she has dictated stories to me, we've read simple books guessing the last word on the line and novels like Narnia and Harry Potter. The novels spurred conversations about punctuation and italics, as well as games like, 'Stop. I'm going to find every Aslan on this page.'

There have been times when she has been quite determined to learn to read or write. For several months, we worked diligently through some Jolly Phonics books and she invented all sorts of complicated fun games where I had to guess which word she had read by the actions she was doing. But these phases passed, and I wondered when we would progress from reading single words to actual books.

*Last summer, while out she read the word 'Please' on a
sign. I suspected then that this might be the start of a new
phase. This was a word much harder than we usually came
across in any phonics book, so came from her own deduc-
tions. A few weeks later, while on holiday, she wrote a
made-up dictionary of her own language. We were reading
the second Harry Potter book at the time,* The Chamber of
Secrets, *and she was fascinated by Tom Riddle's diary in
the book with its magical powers. Over the next few weeks,
she made several copies of the diary. Each one contained
plot spoilers and gradually the spellings within them
improved. 'I'm going to be a writer,' she declared. And yet,
still no advance on reading.*

*My daughter is seven now. A few weeks ago, she
announced, 'I just want to read . . . I want to be able to
read anything you can read, I want to do everything you
can do, I just want to be an adult already!' This pretty
much sums up her attitude since birth. 'Why don't you try
then?' I said and handed her a copy of Dr Seuss'* Hop on
Pop. *'Just see how far you can get.'*

*She took my challenge and, over the next three nights,
almost completed the story. Exhilarated and proud, she
asked for more books; she has now read several Dr Seuss
books and is spending lots of time poring over them
working out the tricky words and practising them so she
can read them fluently with dramatic flair. Her goal is to be
able to read anything and I know she'll do it.*

Some parents make the choice to unschool as part of a wider philosophy of life. Akilah Richards is the author of *Raising Free People,
Unschooling as Liberation and Healing Work.* She and her partner,
Kris, unschool their two daughters. In the following piece, published
in 2016, she writes about the reasons behind their choice.

The Mindset Behind the Unschooling Lifestyle

Kris and I help our daughters get access to information and guide them through everyday living and the life skills to navigate adulthood. We don't position ourselves as their primary teachers, nor do we see ourselves as their role models. Though we understand our position of power as their parents and default primary influencers, we believe in the old adage of it taking a village, and actively help our daughters seek out mentors and other resources for their areas of interest.

As their parents, we work toward a shared goal of raising women who are comfortable in their skin, versed in the skill of confident autonomy, and experienced in how to mine and utilise information in the digital age. We unschool because having our lives revolve around our children sitting in a building for six hours per day stopped making sense for our interests and needs as a family. We are not anti-school, we are pro-learning, and for our daughters, school put unnecessary boundaries and segmented blocks of time around their ability to explore and process the information they had gathered.

Also, school can create a dangerous reliance on external validation (teacher's approval and social acceptance), which we find particularly dangerous for Black children, as most of the teachers in our daughters' school did not look like our daughters, nor did they share our family's cultural and spiritual values. Those values are a vital part of raising a whole child who is not just savvy in their current time, but has a growing awareness of their context inside the American system, and as part of the developing world.

We believe that traditional grade school and the pursuit of a university education offer one path to professional and perhaps personal fulfilment, but there are many alternatives, especially today. And especially because Black children, in particular, are grossly underestimated and unfairly punished across American schools.

When our girls were in public school, they were both labelled as gifted children and their elementary school did a great job putting together a special curriculum to fit our daughters' appetites for information. But it was not enough, nor could it ever be, because our children — like most children — do not learn by collecting information; they learn by experience and guidance. And when you take the lid off a child's learning environment, you really get to see their incredible capacity to absorb, interpret and utilise information to affect their environments and get what they want.

Instead of trying to work within the system to lobby and hope for change, we are designing our own liberation. The four of us are learning how to seek, gather and process information using new media tools and resources instead of textbooks, teacher's interpretations and bosses. Each of us is developing relationships with people all over the world, instead of just the people who happen to be geographically close to us by means of our careers, school or social circles. We connect with people based on our interests and goals, not just happenstance, age or geography. Marley and Sage create community based on their own needs and engage in healthy competition through digital meet-up communities like DIY.org where they earn badges for everyday life skills, and Khan Academy, where they take as much time as they need to practise the math skills they'll actually use in life.

Some parents create intentional self-directed group learning settings for their children which don't bear any resemblance to school, even to the extent of not having a building that they meet in. Alexander Khost is a father and children's rights advocate; in this piece he describes his latest venture, Flying Squads:

Flying Squads started in a library in Brooklyn, New York, in the fall of 2018. But the concept behind them began years earlier.

At the time, I was reading Colin Ward's book, The Child in the City, *which discusses how, to truly be free, children must be a part of the city itself. Children need to feel comfortable on their own streets and must be welcomed in public spaces, a concept that no longer exists in today's modern culture.*

Unlike school field trips, the Flying Squad does not have a predetermined destination but, instead, the young people practise the crucial skills of deciding together where to go and how to spend their time. We meet once a week. Each day starts in a public space (typically a library) documenting and reflecting on previous time together in a communal journal. The group then sets out into the world to explore common interests together, experimenting on how to build community and deciding how to voice group concerns on the social justice issue of being a youth in a city built for adults.

This means that anything can happen.

Here's what we did one Tuesday in November, after starting off at the library to make our plans. My son James was ecstatic about introducing us to buns 'as light as clouds' at some shop he had discovered in Chinatown. He rallied enough votes to get us to start the day out there. We took the subway to Chinatown guessing at James's location of the place. 'It's near the Manhattan Bridge, over by that corner, you know, where there's a dragon . . .' I literally use James as a guide to New York City now. I had faith he would find the place.

Without one wrong turn, he took us on to a side street off Canal and into a tiny little door down a hallway that I never would have guessed led to a store. As one of the kids said to me a few minutes later, 'I feel like we've entered the Twilight Zone.' It was definitely a very different feeling of New York than the everyday life of our crew. And it was clear everyone was excited to have a hint of this new one.

James was right, the buns were as light as clouds and delicious. We each had one and then planned our next move. The intention was to make it to Pier Six (a popular playground destination on the shore of the East River) back in Brooklyn, and a kid sneakily got us all to walk the Manhattan Bridge back over. It was the most beautiful day out and the walk was perfect. I dared a little boy to 'clippity-clop' skip across the entire bridge. He exclaimed to me halfway across, 'I had no idea this bridge was so long!' I asked around, only to realise that nearly all of the kids had never walked the bridge before.

As we got off the bridge, there were many complaints that legs were going to fall off and this is as tired as a person can get! So we decided on Pirate Ship Playground instead of Pier Six. Miraculously, all of those exhausted little bodies 'resurged' for many rounds of our game, Friday the Thirteenth, before we had to head home.

On the subway ride back, one of the girls dared me to get the train car's attention and sing the My Little Pony *theme song at the top of my lungs, which she very happily videoed. By the time we got back to headquarters, the whole gang looked exhausted. The smiles on their faces reflected what a perfect day it had been.*

Developing Mastery

Many parents are fine with allowing their young children control of their education. They can see learning through play works for the under-eights or even the under-twelves, but they don't give the same value to the activities chosen by teenagers. They can't see how self-directed teenagers will become employable adults.

Judy Arnall is the bestselling author of *Unschooling to University: Relationships Matter Most in a World Crammed with Content*, in which she followed the paths of thirty unschooled young people. In this piece, she writes about how Josh, an unschooled teenager, moved from no formal education to being able to attend university:

> *How does unschooling work when a child is a teenager*
> *and is beginning to choose a career path? Many people are*
> *fine letting young children play away their day, but what*
> *about when the time comes to start thinking about their*
> *life's work? And what if that passion is a STEM [Science,*
> *Technology, Engineering, Mathematics] career?*
>
> *Let's take an example from one of the Team of Thirty*
> *profiled in my book. Josh is sixteen years old. He has had*
> *no formal schooling and loves spending his days with his*
> *cat, meeting up with other unschooling buddies for movies*
> *and lunch, reading all kinds of genre, tinkering with game*
> *modifications and playing Fortnite.*
>
> *By following his passions, Josh has decided on a career.*
> *He passionately wants to be a software engineer. He has*
> *seen what they do by talking to family friends and people*
> *he knows who work in the industry.*

The Science Behind Accelerated Learning

> *When young people choose a career path, many people*
> *think that the unschooled kids must catch up on twelve*
> *years of education. However, we forget that the brain has*
> *been working all those years processing, acquiring and*
> *synthesising information. By age sixteen, the brain is in*
> *the final stages (until age twenty-five) of maturing the*
> *prefrontal cortex. The teenager's neuro capacity to reason,*
> *think critically and abstractly, plan, make decisions and*
> *implement self-control (motivation) is ramping up to its*
> *peak performance.*
>
> *Unschooled kids are not uneducated. Josh has spent*
> *sixteen years reading, theorising, writing, learning and*
> *understanding science, history and mathematics in the*
> *real world through experiential education. He may need*
> *some practice applying it to paper, but that is what high*

school courses are for. That may take one to three years, depending on the jurisdiction he lives in. It goes by fast. Meanwhile, the love of learning and curiosity has been preserved.

I know what you are thinking: mathematics is linear and builds upon previous knowledge. How can Josh possibly do ten grades of mathematics in one year? The answer is that Josh is not starting from Grade 1; he has acquired previous knowledge. Josh has almost certainly learned sixteen years of mathematics experientially. He has baked, shopped, checked the weather, built a project, mailed a package and played Battleship. He has learned addition, subtraction, multiplication, division, measurement, fractions and decimals as well as integers and co-ordinates experientially through just living his life and going about his activities. He may need a four-month prep course to transfer his mental mathematical learning to working out calculations on paper but, when he is ready, he will learn fast. It's hard for parents to look ahead at their child and imagine what they will be like when they are older. Many parents look at their six-year-old child and can't imagine how capable and smart their child will be at sixteen years, without any formal education.

Unschooled kids are not catching up on knowledge but are synthesising that knowledge by switching to a different track – one that requires more output/demonstration of what they already have learned, combined with new learning in areas that interest them. Josh knows how to calculate the volume of a package but may not have been required to calculate it on paper with demonstrable steps. At age sixteen, his learning has never been limited by conventional education. Josh is excited to try it, when quite a lot of his school friends are burning out from thirteen years of coerced learning (possibly including three years of pre-school). If Josh is motivated and software engineering is his passion, nothing will stop him. Nothing!

Hope Wilder, living in Durham, North Carolina, describes herself as a lifelong learner and supporter of self-directed education. She is the core founder of Pathfinder Community School, a self-directed and self-governing learning community for ages five to fourteen.

She writes here about Uli, Pathfinder's first graduate, and how he honed his programming skills through informal learning:

> *The first time I met Uli, he was trying to hack into the library computers. A pre-teen kid with a ponytail, he had a sneaky smile and said something like, 'Looks like someone needs to work on their computer security.' My husband Jesse, a software engineer, was excited to talk to a young person with a kindred spirit. They spoke in languages I don't understand.*

> *'Let me know when that kid turns eighteen, and I'll hire him,' Jesse said.*

> *Uli has been self-directed all of his life. He attended the Agile Learning Centre Mosaic and then moved to Pathfinder, the self-directed school I founded in 2018.*

> *At Mosaic, Uli played, made friends and also got hooked on Minecraft. His parents struggled with his interest in computers and, eventually, they left the school. At some point, they let him self-regulate his screen time. They decided to trust that Uli would figure out this whole screen thing by himself.*

> *It wasn't much of a surprise when Uli became 'The Computer Guy' at Pathfinder. You could depend on Uli to install and re-install Linux as a dual operating system on our Chromeboxes, painstakingly, over and over again, after kids would accidentally delete the operating system. (Uli: 'Why, Chrome, do you make it so easy to delete the OS with a space bar??!!')*

> *He wrote down the instructions so I could manage to switch between operating systems when he was away.*

Uli was constantly talking to anyone who would stand still long enough about programming. At open houses, he would gravitate towards the parents who worked at tech companies, asking random strangers questions about the projects he was working on. His mom Laura said to me that, someday, when someone asks him where he learned how to code, he will say, 'Oh, just people walking by,' and be totally correct.

Having noticed Uli's extreme interest in coding, I arranged for him to try visiting one day per week at the firm where my husband Jesse works. When he first went, he was working on altering a complex program that enabled cute 'turtle' robots inside Minecraft to self-replicate like viruses, a devilishly frivolous exercise which he seemed to get a lot of enjoyment out of.

Less than six months of mentorship later, he was working on useful projects and participating in the worldwide network of collaboration in advanced programming topics.

I want to make the point clear: Uli was exactly the kind of kid that parents are most afraid of – one who is completely obsessed with computers, who spent twelve hours a day hooked to his screen, playing video games. For years.

And the result of letting him follow this obsession is that he is now a highly-skilled computer programmer, and capable of doing things with computers that most people get paid for. And he's only fifteen years old.

Here's an example to show how much the tables have turned. Many Pathfinder parents have offered programming lessons or advice to kids. Uli has taken the time to learn a bunch of different programming languages, and now he is the one offering Pathfinder parents programming advice. In addition, he has his own business with over twenty clients in his hometown, giving computer help.

To me, this is a case in point to argue that free, unlimited

*play can turn into exceedingly useful and meaningful work.
For kids, play is work. If you're lucky, as an adult, work is
play. It is not a bad time in the history of humanity to be
interested in computers.*

*I don't know if programming will be a lifelong passion for
Uli, but I trust that he will be able to dive deep into whatever he chooses, and he will be just fine.*

Changing Their Minds

Letting go of expectations can be hard and sometimes painful for
parents. Some parents find themselves on a path which they never
expected, and their children lead them towards self-directed education.

Sarah's eldest child left school in 2015 aged seven while the youngest
has never been to school. The eldest has diagnoses of ASD, ADHD,
bilateral hearing loss and sensory processing disorder. The youngest
has a diagnosis of ASD. Sarah says:

*My eldest attended mainstream primary school for three
years. It was horrendous and by far the worst years of
our family lives. In hindsight, his Reception year was the
best, but the more demands increased, the more problems
increased. The school were dismissive of my input and
feedback. They were poor to communicate and did not
acknowledge many of his needs, much less meet them. He
became verbally and physically aggressive. Despite the fact
that his behaviour was deteriorating, the school adamantly
refused to say they couldn't meet his needs. As a result,
they blocked a move to a special school. I felt I was losing
my son. I had researched home education and decided that
it had to be better than mainstream schooling. By then, I
had realised that formal schooled education was just not
designed to suit him at all.*

*I personally preferred semi-structured learning. I kept
testing the water with slightly more structure or more*

formal learning but each time it was resolutely rejected. On one occasion my eldest said to me, 'You want to do this way, but I don't . . .' and I realised he was telling me loudly and clearly that my preferred method didn't suit him. As I was also becoming increasingly aware of the impact school had left on him, I decided to wholly embrace life learning as being the ideal way to meet his needs. It was a steep learning curve for me, though.

We don't have a typical day. Some days we have definite plans – for example, trips out, visits or playdates. On days where we don't have specific plans to go out, we go through our day doing our things. I make sure I offer time and availability to both boys (they rarely like to do things together) with me one-to-one to pursue things. This could include reading together, art or science. Sometimes I have an idea I think they may like or that I fancy doing and invite them to join. We sometimes have a 'theme' that they have shown an interest in so we may develop that in some way.

One of the most satisfying things for me is seeing how their passions, interests and learning develop. A passion for a particular video game led to a huge growth in interest about world geography, world history, political figures, historical figures, historical events, landmarks, political systems and religions. This is on top of the skills of strategic and tactical thinking, planning, evaluating and resource management which they developed while playing the game.

I've gained a real trust that children are constantly learning and learn most efficiently and effectively when pursuing their own lines of interest.

Being outside the school system has allowed me to be able to tailor the environment to meet their special educational needs, one of which is to have a high degree of autonomy. But the biggest benefit has been to leave peer comparison behind. Every child's path is unique and every step on their path can be celebrated for what it is. This is a total life-saver for children like mine.

Iris Chen describes herself as a recovering Chinese-American 'Tiger Mom' who blogs at untigering.com. She writes about her own deschooling and the process of letting go of compelling her children to learn:

Exactly a year ago, I finally came to a point in my unschooling/deschooling journey where I was ready to let go of piano. If you're not a recovering Chinese tiger mom, you might not understand how difficult this was for me. I had dropped every schoolish subject (including mathe-matics!) already but had held out with piano and Chinese. Finally, after coming to terms with the fact that insisting that my kids learn piano was inconsistent with what I truly believed about self-directed education, I sat NoNo and KK down and gave them the option to continue or quit, bracing myself for their answer.

They surprised me.

'We wanna keep playing.'

I tried to keep a poker face, but inside I was breaking out into hallelujahs.

We assume that children will not want to learn unless they are compelled to; that they will not persevere and have grit when the going gets tough. We are mistaken; children are naturally motivated to learn what they find interesting and necessary. We just need to give them the freedom to discover what those things are.

In the past, I set that timer and stood over them every day during practice like the archetypal tiger mom. Nowadays, I'm learning to empower my kids to define their own learn-ing process and progress. They practise for as long (or as little) as they like, just as long as they complete the assignments by the next lesson. They can request songs they want to learn, whether it's a pop song or a sonatina. They're not required to perform for recitals, take piano exams, or test for some sort of certificate. Far from being unmotivated and undisciplined, their sense of joy and interest in piano has only increased as a result. They are empowered to learn in a way that is meaningful to them instead of doing so to simply please others or receive recognition.

Not every kid wants to become a virtuoso, a star athlete, a famed artist. Some kids enjoy playing for the sake of playing. If your child is not naturally driven or ambitious, let them be and celebrate their enjoyment without insisting that they meet some benchmark of success. If your child is a go-getter, seek out resources, opportunities and mentors to foster their growth, but also remind them their worth is not based on their performance.

When I asked the boys how to make piano a more sustainable and enjoyable practice, NoNo wanted to slow things down and learn fewer new songs each week. We asked the teacher to adjust and she obliged. This took the pressure off him and allowed him the freedom to simply play around, like making up a theme song for his comic book villain. KK, on the other hand, got bored easily and wanted more of a challenge. He was motivated to learn songs from The Greatest Showman *and the score from* Jurassic Park, *pieces that were difficult even for me. He even created a coding project that featured songs he's played, figuring out the number value that corresponded to each tone.*

Following each child's lead has allowed them to both enjoy piano in their own way. Instead of imposing cookie-cutter expectations upon them, my role is to help them follow their bliss, satisfy their curiosity, and reach their own goals.

Grown Self-Directed Learners

This isn't a new idea. There are adults whose education was self-directed, and who can now look back and reflect on the process.

Bria Bloom was unschooled as a child. She describes how she learnt and continues to learn:

> *My education can be described rather simply – if I loved something, I followed it . . . as far as I could.*
>
> *I learned through play. Each of the stories I tell describes different kinds of play that I engaged in, and continue to engage in, throughout my life. I played at the creek where we built bridges, created forts, and made up stories. I tested materials (stones, bricks, wood, mud) and physics, and I played with basic ideas of survivalism. I wrote, read and researched about aspects of nature and living off of the land, because it was interesting to me. I played games that my friends and I created, negotiated and changed based on outcomes and appeal. I played fantasy games inside and outside, created storylines and characters, and connected my fantasy worlds to those created by others. In my fantasy play, I developed, among other things, a better understanding of roles, emotions, characters and empathy for different perspectives.*
>
> *I learned through genuine conversations with people in my life. At a recent birthday party that my friend hosted, she asked each person to share a favourite memory of me. When it was my father's turn, he told the story of driving with me to the karate dojo, during which we would have lengthy discussions, playing with ideas together. This is also one of my most treasured memories and a situation in which I learned so much. Our discussion topics ranged from politics to plays, to psychology and social interaction, as well as obscure pieces of US history; our discussions were some of my first experiences using collaboration as a way to expand and challenge ideas.*

*At the heart of our conversations was a genuine relation-
ship. I learned from my father, not because he forced or
expected me to, but because he trusted and respected me.
I learned from him because I chose to. I learned about the
importance of having conversations with people whose
opinions, thoughts and information differ from mine.*

*These conversations are powerful because of the varying
knowledge and experiences that each person has, and the
way that knowledge sticks with you when you repeat it to
another person. Every day I am with self-directed young
people, and we talk about everything from culture, to fads,
to media, to memes, to politics and more, I feel intense
and deep learning about human relationships, culture and
ideas. Many believe that teaching is the best way to learn,
but I would reframe that to 'mutual sharing', instead of
'teaching'. Take a group of fifteen people, each with a
unique set of knowledge, and each one discussing ideas
with another. Not only will these people acquire knowledge,
but the knowledge that they are sharing with others is more
likely to stick with them.*

*While growing up, I also learned through freely choosing
to go deeper into the activities that I enjoyed. Spanish, as
both a learner and a teacher; martial arts; musical theatre;
various forms of dance; having different jobs from the
time I was ten; managing my own money; lots and lots of*
Dungeons and Dragons; *and plenty of computer games . . .
to name a few. Each of these activities I pursued of my own
volition. Again, each person's path will be different, but
one of the most important aspects is that they choose what
they are doing. Many unschoolers choose to take conventional classes or engage with conventional educational
programs, but the difference is that they are choosing to do
so based on their interest and desire to learn.*

*My life was fuelled by passion, curiosity and collaboration;
the same values that have stayed with me as an adult
self-directed learner.*

So how did I learn the things I needed to know?

The same way that I still learn: through play and self-direction; discussion and collaboration; direct experiences; and community and relationships. I learned exactly what I needed to know. I learned what my passion is and how to pursue it. I learned how to continuously learn and grow through conversations with people and in reciprocal relationships, and how to direct my experience to the areas that I am passionate about. I learned how to find and pursue the knowledge that I wanted and needed for my own life.

Idzie Desmarais is another grown unschooler. She blogs at 'I'm Unschooled. Yes, I Can Write.' www.yes-i-can-write.blogspot.com. With vivid, sensory descriptions, she writes about her experiences of growing up and a childhood structured by the seasons rather than the school year:

When I think of my childhood, I think of it in seasons.

Spring was peepers and fat tadpoles. It was burying peas in newly thawed ground, cold earth lodging under my fingernails. It was a carpet of white trilliums rolled out through the woods, ghostly on dusk walks, punctuated by occasional red ones, foul-smelling if you leaned too close. As spring grew into summer, we'd spend afternoons picking strawberries at the farm up the road, the sun hot on our backs.

Summer was for frog and grasshopper catching. It was fields filled with bright flowers. It was black raspberry picking, thorns sharp as they caught on purple-stained fingers, and fruit bright on my tongue. It was lying on soft-prickly grass and sunning on big, sun-heated stones like some warm-blooded lizard. For years when I was small, we'd head north-east, following the Saint Lawrence all the way to Gaspe, right as summer started to fade into fall.

I'd spend hours picking wild blueberries, running through unmown fields and bushwhacking my way through the woods to marvel at ancient, twisting crabapple trees. I'd walk along the beach, mesmerised by crashing waves, and sometimes seals would swim close to the shore, watching us with the same curiosity with which we'd watch them.

Autumn was leaves shading into yellow and orange, red and purple, and crunching most satisfyingly underfoot. It was ponds stilling and reeds browning, the scent of decomposition in chilled noses. It was carefully deliberating over the selection of decorative gourds at the farm stand, fingers tracing stripes and ridges. It was the excitement of Hallowe'en, clamouring over prickly straw bales, and trying to catch the first flakes of snow on our tongues.

Winter was chilled faces and sparkling fresh snow, cross-country skiing and snowshoeing in the strangely quiet, creaking woods under the muffling blanket of a heavy snowfall. It was the bright red flash of cardinals against a white backdrop, tottering out in ice skates on to a frozen pond or rink, or sliding carefully along in boots, arms outstretched for balance. It was winter festivals and toes too long in the cold, bright pain burning as they thawed out near a warm fire, or merely the car heating vents.

Kids who don't go to school do not have a monopoly on outdoor exploration or seasonal traditions, not by any means. But what I want to highlight is the flexibility life-learning provides in allowing families to choose where and how they spend all the hours of their days, instead of only being left with a handful of evenings and weekends to do with as they wish. I want to celebrate the way that seasons can take precedence over a school calendar in structuring life, how nature can be the primary force that shapes your days, instead of a schedule set up with the best interests of an institution in mind, not the best interests of children.

When you're not in school, you simply have time. Time to be outside, time to lie in the grass, time to organise last-minute group hikes, time to stay up late watching bats, time to go on a trip when other kids are in school. Not going to school doesn't necessarily mean you'll spend more time in nature. But it means that you have the time – boundless, limitless time – to do so.

These excerpts were originally published in the following places:

Judy Arnall – extract from 'The Unschooled Engineer', first published on Unschooling to University: https://unschoolingtouniversity. com/2018/09/10/the-unschooled-engineer/

Bria Bloom – extract from 'How I Learn(ed)', first published on Tipping Points online magazine: https://www.self-directed.org/ tp/how-i-learned/

Kezia Cantwell-Wright – extract from 'Waves of Learning', first published on East Kent Sudbury School Blog: https://eastkent sudburyschool.org.uk/learning/waves-of-learning/

Iris Chen – extract from 'How to Learn Piano (or Anything!) the Untigering Way', first published on Untigering.com: https:// untigering.com/how-to-learn-piano-or-anything-the-untigering-way/

Idzie Desmarais – extract from 'On Seasons and Cycles: Unschooling and Nature', first published on her blog 'I'm Unschooled. Yes, I Can Write': http://yes-i-can-write.blogspot.com/2019/

Lehla Eldridge – extract (including illustration) from 'Unschooling – How Does Learning Go On Outside a Classroom?' First published on Unschoolingthekids.com: https://unschoolingthekids. com/2018/11/11/unschooling-is-it-really-a-piece-of-cake/

Alexander Khost – edited extract from 'The Perfect Day', first published on Flying Squads blog: https://www.flyingsquads. org/2019/11/26/the-perfect-day/

Akilah Richards – extract from 'The Freedom of Unschooling. Raising Liberated Black Children without the Restrictions of School', first published on My Student Voices: https://mystudentvoices.

com/the-freedom-of-unschooling-raising-liberated-black-children-without-the-restrictions-of-school-58347bf5919

Laura Grace Weldon – extract from 'Getting Science on Everything', first published on Laura's personal blog: https://lauragrace weldon.com/2013/06/19/getting-science-on-everything/

Holly Wilder – extract from 'From Video Game "Addict" to Software Engineer', first published on Pathfinder Community School blog: https://pathfindercommunityschool.com/blog

Afterword

I called this book *Changing Our Minds* for many reasons – schooling literally changes our minds as we go through it, teaching us to think about ourselves, other people and the world in particular ways. No one comes through twelve years of schooling without being profoundly altered by the experience, whether for good or bad. That is, after all, the point of schooling. We carry it with us for life.

In order to choose a truly different education for our children, adults have to start with themselves. The first thing we must do is to change our minds about many of the things we were taught to take for granted – change our minds about the need for compulsory instruction, for example; about the need for learning to be forced; and for children to be motivated with rewards and punishments.

Equally important is changing our minds about what our role should be as parents and educators. We're encouraged by the culture around us to think of our role as moulding future people – parenting, disciplining and educating so as to increase our chances of an optimal outcome, whatever we consider that to be. Embracing self-directed education requires us to focus on nurturing the child who is already there, rather than shaping them into the person we think they should become. This isn't easy to do; we are so used to controlling children that, most of the time, we don't even notice what we are doing.

Parenting by control is all around us. As my children and I read together, I have been surprised to see their responses to the books I read as a child. Things which were perfectly straightforward to me seem incomprehensible to them. Parents in these books regularly wield power over their children by withdrawing meals, or confining them to their rooms. They ban them from seeing their friends; they send children to schools which make them miserable and insist they do their homework rather than play. To children who are used to being in control of their own lives, it makes no sense at all.

Even parents who consider themselves to be gentle and child-led usually have areas where they may not even be aware that they are wielding control. Many of us prefer to tell ourselves that our children freely choose the things that we would have chosen for them, rather than reflecting on our own subtle methods of using our power. Some parents happily tell all and sundry that their children freely choose not to play video games or read particular books, while apparently oblivious to the child listening carefully and learning exactly which choices gain parental approval. It's easy to think of yourself as a non-controlling and responsive parent when your children do what you want without you having to insist. It's when the child's choices differ from yours that you really discover your propensity to control.

No one said that changing your mind wouldn't be painful. You may need to give up fondly held dreams of long country walks or reading *The Lord of the Rings* together, when it turns out that your child has their own preferences, and these aren't the same as yours. It's here that the challenge of self-directed education really starts, when a child asserts their own choices, and the parent responds by giving them the power to do so.

The last meaning of 'changing our minds' has to do with children themselves. Running through this book is the idea that children are active participants in their own learning. They influence their environments, creating the best circumstances they can with whatever raw materials we provide. As they do this, their minds are changed through that interaction. Brains are incredibly plastic, and the experiences that children have growing up really do matter. But the way in which they matter will be different for each child. There is no 'one size fits all'. The more flexible and responsive the environment, the more likely it is that it will provide what a wide range of different children need in order to thrive. Self-directed education literally changes the minds of children. They will not be the same as if they had gone to school.

The evidence is all around us that pushing children to conform to our pre-determined ideals creates problems. Some of these are evident while they are still children; others only become clear when they are adults.

I've taken you on a journey in this book. I've asked you to consider how we learn, why we do things and how education interacts with the psychology of learning and motivation. I've suggested that schooling is not the only way to become educated and, for many children, it has serious disadvantages. I've shown that self-directed education is a viable alternative to schooling, and that there is evidence that it works. I've shared stories of self-directed education and discussed the research which has looked closely into the process.

Perhaps, when you started reading, you were hoping for techniques and ways to plan projects so that children learn 'without even noticing'. Or maybe you hoped for strategies which would help you persuade your children to sit at the kitchen table and read textbooks for five hours a day, through choice. Instead of that, I've invited you to focus on your own thinking, to challenge yourself to think deeply about children and education.

It's my experience that when you do this, it becomes clear that there are serious incompatibilities between the ways in which school requires children to learn, and the characteristics of the children themselves. The two things simply don't add up. Self-directed education offers an alternative which works with, rather than against, the way children actually are.

Working with Children as They Actually Are

In the final section of this book, I'm going to summarise four key ways in which the school system clashes with human psychology. These contradictions mean that schools may be working extremely hard and doing their absolute best, but much of that effort is counter-productive and, in fact, makes it harder for children to learn. It makes life difficult for the children who get caught in cycles from which there is no way out. I'll then show how self-directed education resolves these paradoxes and sets children free to learn.

1. Control

Schooling is based on the assumption that, without being controlled, a child will learn nothing of value. This belief goes beyond the mainstream. There are many alternative and progressive schools who impose a different set of values, but who impose it nonetheless. Banning computers or handheld devices is as restrictive as banning books and toys. Control of this type may look less harsh to adults, but the iron fist is still there and children know it.

Taking away control from children in order to educate them sets up a paradox. When we take away control, we diminish motivation and we strip learning of much of its joy. The way which we try to educate children makes it harder for them to learn.

This is hard for many of us to hear, because when we were children we were told that if we didn't do what we were told, we would never learn. We grew up to believe that we must be made to do things, and that we must make our children do things. Many of us carry this into adulthood, where we continue to force ourselves to do things which make us unhappy, in the belief that if we didn't do that, we'd do nothing at all.

The adult need to control children's learning sets us all up for failure, because humans dislike being controlled. Basic psychology tells us that taking away a person's autonomy has a profound effect on their wellbeing. Research shows that taking away choices about learning has a deep and lasting effect on motivation.

Self-directed education resolves this by never taking control away from the children. Just as when they were very young, they retain control over their own learning. This means that adults cannot control exactly what children will choose to learn – but the idea that they can do this is anyway largely an illusion. No matter how controlling a school system is, the children educated within it will never all learn the same thing or make the same progress.

2. Power

There is a huge disconnect in the way schooling is talked about – as empowering, essential and life-enhancing – and the way in which many children experience it. These children tell us through their words and behaviour that school is a hostile environment for them. They tell us that they feel powerless and that they need something different. Then, in many cases, the response is to call these children 'disordered'. By doing so, we avoid having to listen to what their behaviour tells us about the school. We locate the problem in the child.

Perhaps we should not be asking what the problem is with them; perhaps a more pertinent question is why so many children do not fight the system. Why do more children not refuse to go, or refuse to comply with demands once there? What happens to those feisty four-year-olds, as they learn to stand in lines and sit still in class? One thing that happens is that they learn to value the opinion of others over their own. They learn that what they think and feel is unimportant, because their role is to listen and do as they are told.

No matter how much we talk about education as empowering, the fact remains that empowerment cannot start with forced compliance. This is a contradiction in terms. It simply makes no sense to tell children that doing what they are told for twelve years will empower them at the end of it all. A system which requires unquestioning obedience can never be one where we learn to share and use power well.

Self-directed education resolves this by empowering children through meaningful choices now rather than the promise of a good job in the future (if they do as they are told). It listens to each child's interests and needs, and empowers them to take charge of their own learning. This means that the adults around them must give up some of their power – or perhaps, more accurately, their illusion of power – over the child's learning.

3. Context

School removes learning from context. It makes abstract what could be concrete, and thereby creates a problem. Context-free learning loses much of its meaning. Learning to read because you want to understand is very different to being taught to read because you are five, and the curriculum says that five-year-olds must learn to read.

Again, a psychological paradox is set up. We know learning is easier in context, and that context provides motivation for children to learn. Children want to participate in their community on their own terms, and they are driven to learn the skills to do so. Removing learning from context means that schools have to try to create motivation through systems of rewards and punishments – but these damage intrinsic motivation, making learning less enjoyable. The more schools try to motivate children, the more they come up against this problem.

Self-directed education resolves this by keeping learning in context. In this way, children can learn from the whole world around them, not just from the restricted environment of school. Large amounts of psychological research show that young children are capable of sophisticated social learning from the people around them, without direct instruction. In fact, the research finds that direct instruction has a detrimental effect on children's learning, and that exploration is more effective. There is no reason why this changes when children reach the age of five. Self-directed education therefore avoids instruction unless it is something the child wants, and makes space for exploration.

4. Anxiety

The final paradox is one which is close to my heart. In the course of my work, I regularly meet children who are anxious, and am asked if I can help them feel less anxious using psychological therapy.

Many types of psychological therapy (and in particular cognitive therapy) are based on the idea that the reason a person is anxious is because their thinking is irrational. The theory is that the reason that they are anxious is because of their interpretation of events and, if we can change that interpretation, they will feel less anxious. For lots of people this makes sense – if a person is afraid of spiders, or balloons, then therapy might well help them feel less anxious. Therapy is very effective for children who feel anxious because of things that have happened to them in the past, but which are over now.

School isn't like this. It's not just that school is an anxiety-provoking place for many children – although having no control is anxiety-provoking in itself. Being anxious about school is not the same as being anxious about spiders *because often it is not irrational.* The school system uses shame and anxiety to motivate children. From very early on, children are threatened with failure, and told that their life depends on how well they perform. Constant competition and comparison, regular grading, high-stakes testing, public humiliation or rewards – children cannot get away from public, anxiety-provoking exposure at school. Many of them learn to study to avoid the shame of failure, not because they want to learn or are interested. In addition, children become anxious because the standardised requirements of school may be out of sync with their developmental stage. They may be pushed to learn things before they are ready, particularly if they are young in their year group. Or they are bored, being taught things that they learned years before.

So children are in a situation where their anxiety is being deliberately used to make them behave in a certain way at school, but then when they actually do become anxious, we say that this means they have a psychological problem and are being irrational. It's as if schools are saying, 'You must have enough anxiety to serve our purposes and no more.' Anxiety doesn't work like this; you can't deliberately create 'just enough' of it, and then say that any more is irrational.

There's another paradox with anxiety – anxiety blocks learning. Anxiety is a fear-based response which would have kept our ancestors safe and close to the fire. It is about survival – and when survival is the priority, learning algebra really isn't the most important thing. The more rational parts of our brain shut down when we are highly anxious, leaving just the parts necessary for keeping our body alive.

The more that a child becomes anxious at school, the less effective their learning will be. And when their learning is less effective, they become even more anxious about failure. Schools bring in measures such as closer monitoring and control, or putting the child in a remedial class – and this creates more anxiety. The children get stuck in a vicious circle of anxiety and failing at school, and it appears there is no way out. Some of them express their anxiety as anger and then they will be punished for this, again increasing their anxiety.

Self-directed education resolves this by not using anxiety as a motivator. There is no age-based comparison, no testing and no public humiliation. Adults do not deliberately make children anxious by telling them that their future rests on what they do now, or that they'll never succeed if they don't pass these exams. Children learn because they want to learn and, if they want to take a test, then that is up to them. Even when they do something anxiety-provoking, it is in their control and is their choice. In addition, self-directed learning environments are generally much more informal and individualised than schools, and so provoke less anxiety.

In this way, they free children up to learn.

Conclusion

School is not the only way to become educated. Self-directed education is a real and viable option, and I've shown how and why that is in this book. Giving children control over their own learning means that adults must give it up and, for many adults, this is a terrifying prospect. Many adults cannot imagine what would happen if they did not control their children's learning, just as they cannot imagine how they themselves would have learnt without being controlled. Rather than face up to this fear, we tell ourselves that school is the only way. This comforting belief helps us to avoid the reality that this is a choice we make for our children. Yet understanding that this is a choice is vital. For if it is a choice, then we have to weigh up the downsides as well as the benefits; we have to decide that the downsides are worth bearing, because the benefits are enough to compensate.

For some, that will be the case. For other children, the downsides are so severe that understanding that other options are available is imperative. While we continue to act as if school is the only way to learn, many children are told that if they are distressed by school then they themselves are at fault, rather than the system.

Self-directed education isn't an easy option. However, it is an approach that works with, rather than against, human psychology. It works with children's natural desire to play, to socialise and to explore; it works with their need to be autonomous; and it works with their motivation, allowing them to learn about the things which matter to them when they become relevant in their lives. All of this means that, rather than needing to fit children into a pre-determined box, self-directed education allows them to blossom and grow, in whatever direction they choose.

Afterword

For many children, this is liberating. For others, it saves their self-esteem and their sense of themselves. It's something which all parents should know about – otherwise, generation after generation will choose schooling without ever knowing they had another choice.

I hope that, by reading this book, you'll be empowered to make an active choice for your children. Schooling is not the only way to become educated. We can go with the flow, rather than pushing our children upstream through the school system. We can work with their natural tendencies, rather than against them. Recognising the choice we are making is a frightening responsibility, but with this recognition comes the possibility of change.

Over to you.

Index